The Tanana Chiefs

The Tanana Chiefs

Native Rights and Western Law

William Schneider

with contributions by
Kevin Illingworth
Will Mayo
Natasha Singh
Thomas Alton

University of Alaska Press
Fairbanks, Alaska

Royalties from this book will be paid to The Chancellor's Advisory Committee on Native Education (CACHE) Native Leadership Scholarship fund in the name of Chief Peter John.

Published by
University of Alaska Press
P.O. Box 756240
Fairbanks, AK 99775-6240

Cover and interior design by Paula Elmes

Cover image: *Tanana Chiefs*, 1915 was painted by prominent Alaska artist Karen Austen. The large-scale oil painting, in the collection of Tanana Chiefs Conference, is displayed at the Chief Andrew Isaac Health Center, Fairbanks, Alaska.

The cover painting is based on the photograph that appears on page xvi of this book. Not all meeting delegates are represented here.

Library of Congress Cataloging in Publication Data

Names: Schneider, William, author.
Title: The Tanana chiefs : native rights and western law / by William Schneider ; with
    contributions by Kevin Illingworth, Will Mayo, Natasha Singh, Thomas Alton.
Description: Fairbanks : University of Alaska Press, [2018] | Includes bibliographical
    references and index. |
Identifiers: LCCN 2017028636 (print) | LCCN 2017034834 (ebook) | ISBN
    9781602233454 (ebook) | ISBN 9781602233447 (pbk. : alk. paper)
Subjects: LCSH: Tanana Indians—Government relations. | Tanana Indians—Legal
    status, laws, etc.—Alaska. | Wickersham, James, 18571939—Relations with
    Indians. | Tanana Indians—History.
Classification: LCC E99.T187 (ebook) | LCC E99.T187 S36 2018 (print) | DDC
    979.8/02dc23
LC record available at https://lccn.loc.gov/2017028636

To the men and women who work in libraries, archives, and museums. Without your documentation and preservation and without support for your efforts, scholarship would be impossible.

Contents

Preface   *ix*
Acknowledgments   *xi*
Introduction   *xiii*

1   From Fur to Gold   1
by William Schneider

2   From Native to White Man's Country   21
by William Schneider

3   July 1915: Wickersham Meets the
Tanana Chiefs   37
by Thomas Alton

4   Alaska Native Leader Will Mayo Shares His
Perspective on the 1915 Tanana Chiefs Meeting   49
by Will Mayo

5   The Fester   57
by William Schneider

Postscript   67
by William Schneider

Appendix 1   Introduction to the Transcript of the
1915 Tanana Chiefs Meeting in Fairbanks   73
by Thomas Alton

Appendix 2   The Original Transcript of the
1915 Tanana Chiefs Meeting in Fairbanks   77

Appendix 3   The Alaska Purchase and Alaska Natives   113

Appendix 4   Timeline of Important Laws and Events
Impacting Tribal Governments in Alaska   133
by Kevin Illingworth

Notes   *141*
References   *157*
Index   *169*

Preface

In 2017, Alaskans celebrated the 150th anniversary of the Treaty of Cession, the Alaska Purchase. This treaty was important for Alaska Natives because it established their status as "tribes." In legal terms this meant that they had government-to-government relationships with the federal government that was responsible for ensuring their well-being. This included protecting their rights and interests, particularly as this applied to the land they occupied and used, and medical, educational, and legal services. The 1915 Tanana Chiefs meeting with Judge Wickersham is the subject of this book, and it is important because when the meeting took place, forty-eight years had passed since the treaty had been enacted and this was the Interior Natives' first opportunity to publicly ask the government officials what they might reasonably expect from the United States government. They expressed their concern about encroachment on the land they used and on the fish and game they depended upon, and they asked about their rights under Western law and how they could have better access to wage labor, education, and medical services. Wickersham, in holding this meeting, publicly recognized their concerns and their legal status. The transcript of their meeting provides a unique window into Native life at that time and is a yardstick for measuring the efforts of Alaska Natives to gain recognition and control over key aspects of their relationship with the federal government.

Acknowledgments

This work began with the prodding of my friend Ron Inouye, whose good deeds and civic consciousness are well known. The team of collaborators, Tom Alton, Kevin Illingworth, Natasha Singh, and Will Mayo, brought historical, legal, and cultural knowledge that shaped this story and gave voice to perspectives greater than what any of us alone could provide.

I am ever more conscious of how important the collections and staff at the Rasmuson Library have been in helping with this study. That is why I have dedicated this work to professionals in the fields of librarianship, archives, and museums. Colleagues Paul Adasiak, Rose Speranza, Charles Hilton, Lisa Norris, Karen Brewster, Leslie McCartney, Robyn Russell, and Joanna Henzie, I appreciate your help and interest in my work. A note of appreciation to the Rasmuson Inter-Library Loan staff who brought me the world's documents not available at Rasmuson Library. To Dixon Jones, graphic artist extraordinaire, thank you for lending your skills and patience in the production of the Tanana Chiefs Map. My friend Karen Austen graciously shared her commemorative painting of the Tanana Chiefs so we could use it on our cover. Karen researched Athabascan chiefs' clothing at the Museum of the North. Assisted by Angela Linn, collection manager of the ethnology and history collection, they examined dentalium necklaces, knife sheaths, and other examples of beadwork and skin sewing from the early twentieth century. Their work brought the image of the chiefs a step closer to how they appeared at the time they were photographed. Thanks to James Simard and Zach Jones at the Alaska State Library and Archives for your close attention to my requests and questions, particularly as we pursued the original copy of the 1915 meeting. My appreciation to Karen Spicher, Archivist at the Beinecke Rare Book and Manuscript Library at Yale University, for help with my long-distance requests about

Lt. George Thornton Emmons who played such a key role addressing the plight of Copper River Natives. To the National Archives for copying the Berrigan files and thereby providing valuable keys to the ruling in this seminal law case.

Thanks also to Sue Beck for transcription of the Alaska Purchase interview.

Over the course of research for this book, Lee Saylor generously shared his knowledge of the Healy Lake band and their life in the transition years before, during, and after the gold rush. Thank you, Lee, for your interest and assistance.

A note to the reviewers of the manuscript, thank you to the anonymous reviewer, to William Simeone, Natasha Singh, and Ross Coen. I hope that you will see how I have benefited from your suggestions and that I have not disappointed in the final product. Your thoughtful comments and time spent on the work are appreciated.

To Garnet, thank you for suggesting that there should be a fund established at the university in support of Native students in the name of Chief Peter John. The royalties from this book will contribute to that goal.

I appreciate the support and understanding shown by the staff of the University of Alaska Press. I particularly appreciate Krista West's willingness to shepherd this work with patience and persistence.

As always, thank you to my wife for understanding how important this work is to me, and to my daughter, Willa, who often asked, "How is it going?" and then, because she too understood my love of the research, she would often follow up with more questions. Thank you both.

Introduction

In the summer of 1915, Athabascan chiefs on the lower Tanana River met with James Wickersham, Alaska's delegate to Congress at a historic meeting of Native leaders in Fairbanks. The leaders came from small settlements scattered up and down the valley. At least one of the Indian leaders, Chief Ivan of Cosjacket (Crossjacket), could remember back to the purchase of Alaska. All could recall the years before the prospectors entered the country, a time when one could truly say Interior Alaska was Indian country. The leaders and their followers had lived through the military expeditions of the 1890s undertaken to find an "All-American route" to the Upper Yukon goldfields. Stories of these expeditions depict how Native people guided, fed, and in some cases saved the men's lives. How quickly life had changed. By the turn of the century, the prospectors had finally penetrated the Tanana and Copper Rivers, bringing with them a way of life based on Western law, a set of values rooted in an agrarian way of life, and new attitudes about how to live a productive life. In the new era, Natives were no longer needed and ironically, they had to fight for recognition of their place in the country. The 1915 Tanana Chiefs meeting was a clarion call for a place in the new order. The meeting was their first chance to explain their way of life in their own words to the public and the government officials. For Native leaders and students of Native history, the record of this meeting is a baseline for measuring progress in areas such as governmental relations, recognition of legal rights, land claims, health care, social services, and education. The meeting is also important because it demonstrated the leadership of the Native chiefs, who stated their concerns and expressed their desire to work with the federal government, even though they couldn't agree with all that was asked of them.

Wickersham knew how important this meeting would be and he pub-
licized the leaders and their concerns. A professional photographer was
summoned and produced a formal photographic record of the meeting;
a newspaper report covered the proceedings; a stenographer prepared a
formal transcript (today preserved in Wickersham's archival collection,
Alaska State Library, ASL-MS-107); and Wickersham sent a report of the
meeting to the secretary of the interior, Franklin Lane. Wickersham didn't
have to do all of this; in fact, it would have been easier for him to ignore
the Natives' concerns, but when we look at the history leading up to this
meeting, we see how instrumental he was in adjudicating the government's
responsibilities and the Natives' rights and interests. We also see that his
legal hands were tied by a legacy of rulings and treaties that defined Natives
as less qualified for the full benefits of American society.

As district court judge, James Wickersham arrived in Fairbanks in 1903,
having traveled over the trail from Circle where news of gold strikes was
bringing a wave of prospectors to the Tanana Valley, all eager to find their
fortune. Wickersham's first look at the log cabin settlement held little to
recommend it: "Across the river we saw a half-dozen new log cabins, a few
tents, and a rough log structure with spread-eagle wings that looked like
a disreputable pigsty, but was in fact, Barnette's trading post. That was
Fairbanks as I first saw it at five o'clock in the afternoon on April 9, 1903"
(Wickersham 2009:144).

Besides the dog team trail from Circle, another trail, bound to become
the Richardson Highway, led from Valdez to Fairbanks and connected the
Tanana Valley with a year-round ice-free port. In summer, steamboats on
the Tanana River provided access to the Yukon River and its tributaries.
Fairbanks was a gold-mining camp poised for development, but big development would depend on infrastructure, a railroad, and financial backing.
By 1915, the rush of prospectors that Wickersham had met on his way to
Fairbanks had left; the gold prospects had been claimed and the profitable ones were destined to big mining companies. In 1915, Fairbanks was
caught between a brief past of prosperity, present realities of hard times,
and hopes—*but no guarantees*—for a brighter future: "The era of profitable
pick and shovel placer mining in the Fairbanks district ended by the time
of the First World War. Costs rose sharply due to war time inflation and
furthermore many of the richest gold deposits had been exhausted, causing

a collapse of the economy in Fairbanks and throughout Interior Alaska"
(Cole 1989:11).

Between 1910 and 1920, the population of Fairbanks dropped by 67
percent. President Wilson signed the Alaska Railroad bill in 1914, and
plans were underway for construction of track from Seward north. The
railroad held promise in many ways—employment, the transporting of
large-scale mining equipment and coal to fuel industrialization—but the
next stage of economic development for Fairbanks wouldn't begin until the
1920s (ibid.:11–12; Williams and Bowers 2004:13).

Pictures of Fairbanks from this period depict the struggling settlement
poised to shift from transitory gold camp to established supply center. In
1905, Danish-born photographer Albert Johnson chose to make his home
and business in Fairbanks. Hired as the official photographer for the Alaska
Engineering Commission, over the years Johnson amassed a huge collection of high-quality images. The corpus of his work documents life during
the period from 1905 until his early death in 1926. Many of the images
are from Fairbanks and the Tanana Valley. Three photos are noteworthy
because they provide a visual glimpse of the people and places significant
to the 1915 Tanana Chiefs meeting.

The most famous of the three photographs features the delegates to the
1915 meeting. The image is the most recognizable symbol of the roots of
the modern Tanana Chiefs organization. The image has become a symbol,
a monument to Native organizational strength and commitment to the
issues raised by the Native delegates at the meeting. The image is important because their descendants fondly remember these leaders today. The
professional photograph was prepared to preserve a record of the meeting,
a statement of the meeting's significance.

The photograph reflects the attention and respect accorded the Native
leaders by Wickersham. Johnson's photograph was recently the subject of
Karen Austen's beautifully rendered painting of the leaders. Austen's painting, reproduced on the cover of this book, shows the leaders' ceremonial
regalia in color, adding a new dimension to the black-and-white image
originally captured and preserved by Johnson. She prepared her painting
to commemorate the 100th anniversary of the meeting, to recognize the
leaders and the issues they raised. The painting is now hung in the new
Chief Andrew Isaac Health Center in Fairbanks. This is a fitting site since

one of the issues raised by the Native leaders in 1915 was the need for medical care.

The second photo is of Judge Wickersham and his first wife, Deborah, on the porch of their home in Fairbanks. When Wickersham arrived in Fairbanks in 1903 to take up his legal duties, one of his first priorities was to build a modern home. This was the first frame structure in the young settlement. The image that Johnson captured of the couple at their home (sometime between 1905 and 1919) reflects the realization of Wickersham's

Tanana Chiefs, Fairbanks, Alaska, July 1915.
UAF 1989-166-371 print. Albert Johnson Photographic Collection, 1905–1917.

vision of what Fairbanks could and should become: settled, permanent, modern, and comfortable. The white picket fence and the flowers planted in the yard depict this vision.[1]

While Wickersham embraced the outdoor life and was sympathetic to the Natives and their needs and concerns, his image of the good life for himself—and for them—pointed to development and the domestic model of white society of that time.[2] It is not surprising that these same social attitudes were also reflected in the laws he was sworn to uphold.

A third image that Johnson captured is of the George C. Thomas Memorial Library. This "Queen Anne" or "Cottage" style structure was

Mr. and Mrs. James Wickersham.
UAF-1989-166-463. Albert Johnson Photographic Collection, 1905–1917.

built with funding from George Thomas, a wealthy Philadelphia man who provided the money to the Episcopal Church to build the structure in 1909. It was a place for people to come and read from an array of donated magazines and books (Galblum 1980:59–60; Bonnell 2013:80–81; Griese and Bigelow 1980:22–26; Coen 2011:117–120).

The log structure is still standing at the corner of First and Cowles Street, one of the last vestiges of early-days Fairbanks architecture. For most of its life it served as a library, but it is also where the Native leaders held the historic 1915 meeting. A step removed from the bustle of town, the reading room represented respite and added an air of responsibility, respectability, and seriousness to their work.

Together, the three images take us back and situate us in a time of transition. For instance, we see the Indian chiefs wearing ties and in some cases, suits. Their ceremonial and titled regalia includes beaded jackets and sashes indicating their status, but also, to Western eyes, we see the more

Public Library, Fairbanks, Alaska.
UAF-1989-166-548. Albert Johnson Photographic Collection, 1905–1917.

casual and comfortable and accessible traditional moccasin footwear. In the second image, Judge Wickersham is on his front porch in suit and tie looking out across a lawn. A well-tended flowerbed surrounds the front of the house. There were certainly other modern structures and a sawmill that provided lumber by this time, but Fairbanks was still just a frontier town with a few residents working hard to make it look as modern as any small town in the states. Fairbanks was hardly settled nor was its future. In the third photo, there is the stately library built in the architectural style of the South, but constructed mostly of logs and situated just a short distance from the less tasteful elements of frontier life, an island of respite, with construction that reflected a step toward modernity.

The Native leaders at the 1915 meeting represented groups of families from the Tanana Valley. Chief Alexander from Tolovana provided the names of leaders from the mouth of the river to Fairbanks, and these men were invited to the meeting. There were representatives from Tanana, Cosjacket, Tolovana, Minto, Nenana/Wood River, Chena, and Salchaket (Salchakat) The representative from Salchaket was added to the list, perhaps at the urging of Reverend Madara, a representative of the Episcopal Church whose duties included ministering to the community.

Tanana, where the Tanana River joins the Yukon River, was really several settlements: the Army post, Fort Gibbon; the white settlement; and the Native settlement, with many Native families living around the Episcopal mission. (The U.S. census for 1910 registered 114 people at the mission site.) Cosjacket, located at the mouth of the Cosna River, is on the travel route to the Kantishna country, and links the Upper Kuskokwim Native population with the lower Tanana River people. It was also the site of a telegraph station. Farther upriver is Tolovana, located at the mouth of the Tolovana River where it joins the Tanana River. By 1915 it was serving as a telegraph station. It was on the trail from Nenana and Fairbanks to Tanana and the Yukon villages. Farther upstream and also on the trail is Minto, what is now referred to as Old Minto. Nenana, located at the confluence of the Nenana River and the Tanana River, had a large Native population (159 recorded in the 1910 census). This was also the location of an Episcopal mission station. (Thirty-one people were recorded in the 1910 census. A dormitory for children was built in 1908, and the church noted thirty children in residence. In 1910 the church built an infirmary that was quickly expanded to a hospital (Griese and Bigelow 1980:30). Chena

Delegates Attending the 1915 Meeting of the Tanana Chiefs

Chief William
of Tanana

Chief Alexander William
of Tanana

Paul Williams
of Tanana

Johnnie Folger
of Tanana

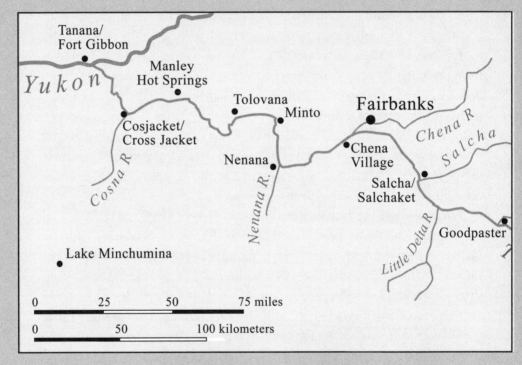

Chief Evan
of Cosjacket

Titus Alexander
of Manley Hot Springs

Chief Charlie
of Minto

Jacob Starr
of Tanana

Chief Thomas
of Nenana

Julius Pilot
of Nenana

Chief Alexander
of Tolovana

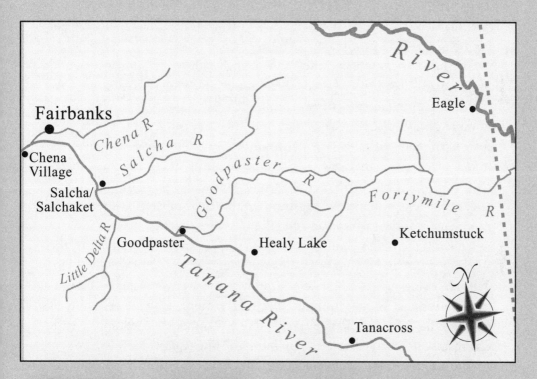

Chief John
of Chena Village

Chief Joe
of Salchaket

Albert*
of Tanana
*Possible delegation member

Map by Dixon Jones. Photos of identified delegates are taken from images referenced in this book.
Photo of Albert is UAF-1997-122-37, from the Alaska Digital Archives, Richard Frank Photograph Collection, 1913–1939.

Village, across the Tanana River downstream from the mouth of the Chena River, was a small Native settlement. (Forty-seven people were recorded in the 1910 census.) Upriver from Chena and Fairbanks was Salchaket, where the Salcha River enters the Tanana. At that time it was the home of another Episcopal mission and near a telegraph station. Unlike the other villages, Salchaket was located on the trail that would become the Richardson Highway from Valdez to Fairbanks. In 1911 it was reported to have a population of forty Native people at the mission (Bonnell 2011:E2). At the 1915 meeting, when Delegate Wickersham asked Reverend Madara how many Natives were living between Tanana and Salchaket, inclusive of both places, Madara estimated seven to eight hundred.[3]

The locations just mentioned varied in their level of permanence and importance to the Native families because the yearly cycle of hunting, fishing, and trapping took them away from the trading post or church mission to more distant places, such as their traplines and fish camps, which were their livelihood. In 1915, few if any families could afford to stay full-time in one place, a fact that was poorly understood by the government representatives at the 1915 meeting. The settlement was a place to get supplies and, in the case of the church missions, a source of medical assistance and rudimentary formal education and religious instruction.

One thing striking about this settlement pattern is the presence of the Washington–Alaska Military Cable and Telegraph System (WAMCATS). Telegraph stations stretched across the Interior and were staffed by military personnel. They were built every forty miles, with relief cabins at twenty-mile intervals. The telegraph line personnel were equipped with dog teams and charged with maintaining the line (Quirk 1974:7).

The other obvious influence was the Episcopal Church. Beginning with the establishment of the mission at Tanana in 1887 and then in the early years of the twentieth century, with the Tanana Valley missions just described, the church made a concerted effort to provide religious, medical, and educational assistance to Native people in the Interior. In many areas, they were the only source for medical care and Western education. Of all the representatives of white society, the church workers were in the most direct contact with the Natives. At the 1915 meeting, Reverend Madara served in what might be called a cultural broker capacity, attempting to reinforce and explain comments by the Native leaders. In the most fundamental way, he knew the importance of their seasonal rounds and their need for unfettered access to the fish and game. He struggled with the land solutions offered by Wickersham and the other government representatives because he knew firsthand how poorly they fit. Surprisingly, Madara's superiors, Archdeacon Stuck and Bishop Rowe, did not play a part in the 1915 meeting, although they too struggled with the conflicts over the impact of white settlement on Indian life. Stuck's solution was to establish the missions as refuges from the worst aspects of white society. He also knew firsthand the value of their lifeways and he respected their survival skills. His yearly circuit of dog team trips to the Native camps gave him a very personal view of the impacts of white settlers on Native life. The missions at Tanacross and at Allakaket were his idea to buffer some of the people from the negative influences (Dean 1988:186–187). There is no question that he too had a vision for the Natives' future, an alternative to the white man's town, but nonetheless, one of his making within the church, and not necessarily one that individual Natives imagined and created for themselves. For all their good intentions, the Church, like the other white institutions of that day, assumed they knew what was ultimately best for the people. This pattern, so typical of the time, is another reason why the 1915 meeting is unique and significant. Finally the Natives' voices are part of the record.

The forces that took hold of Native life in the aftermath of the gold rush had their roots in a nation convinced of its superiority, responsibility, and duty to shape the lives of "lesser" folks. By 1905, the United States military force was equaled by none, and there was little reluctance to exert its might. American missionaries representing Christian denominations were scattered to distant lands to save the souls of the less fortunate. Across the entire reach of the American continent, the Native tribes had been driven from their land to reservations, subdued in battles, and subjugated to the white man's customs and laws. A photo from President Theodore Roosevelt's 1905 inauguration parade captures this sentiment (Library of Congress cph.3b03887).

A line of six Indian chiefs on horseback, including the famous war chief Geronimo, are in procession. Behind them are the Carlisle Indian School students. The school was designed to assimilate Indian students to white society. Its founder, Captain Richard Henry Pratt advocated the slogan: "To civilize the Indian, get him into civilization. To keep him civilized, let him stay" (Pratt 1964:283).

The image is haunting in its message: Natives must learn to be like white men, a theme symbolized by the students in military uniform. Yet, there are also the chiefs, symbolic of the past, riding on horseback in full regalia. It was safe to begin to see the Native in a new light, that is, as long as it

Indian Chiefs headed by Geronimo, passing in review before President Roosevelt, Inauguration Day, 1905, Washington, D.C., U.S.A.
Library of Congress Prints and Photographs. Digital ID https://www.loc.gov/resource/cph.3b03887/.

was clear that they had to give up their tribal ways.[4] It was almost as if old Native culture was to be collected and displayed but its meaning had to be divorced from any current social significance.

Nostalgia with the past was one thing, but federal Indian policy was clearly wedded to assimilation. It would be many years before the country was ready to listen to the concerns and views of Natives. White society found it hard to find room for agendas other than their own, and they made sure that the law reflected abolishment of tribal ways.[5] It was no different in Alaska, and yet, here, in 1915 was Wickersham inviting Native leaders to speak their minds and express their concerns to the secretary of the interior.

Besides Madara and Wickersham, Thomas Riggs and H. J. Atwell were also participants at the 1915 meeting in Fairbanks. And like the others, they had their agendas as well. Riggs was charged with building a railroad, and he wanted the Natives to know that this would happen and it would bring more people and more pressure on the land. Atwell, the government's land office representative, was there to assure the Natives that he would help them apply for allotments or establish reservations, what he and Wickersham could do under the laws they were bound to uphold. Reading the transcript of the meeting, it is easy to be left with the impression these representatives of the church and the government were concerned and respectful. They listened but, with the exception of Madara, they were inextricably bound to their jobs and vision for how things could or couldn't work for the Natives. They, like the Natives, were products of their culture. However, there was one big difference between them. On certain topics, the Natives were open to and actually wanted change. This was particularly true in the area of wage labor, education, and health services, as well as representation in the new order. In these areas they clamored for opportunities. The meeting is a testament to both their clear resolve on issues such as protecting their use of the land and the game they depended upon, as well as their open desire for learning new skills, finding opportunities for wage labor, and their wish to be informed of the government's plans. They wanted to have a say and be part of the new society, and they saw education as a way to become informed and involved.

Unfortunately, the 1915 meeting has often been portrayed solely about conflicts over land,[6] but we see from the full transcript of the meeting that when the delegates could not resolve this question they went on to discuss and explain their other concerns, areas where there was room for assistance from the government. The land issue would take many more years to resolve, but the working relationships that made that possible have their roots in events like the 1915 Tanana Chiefs meeting, where the Natives' voices are on record. Almost lost to Western written history and relegated to archival status, the meeting and the words of the delegates have not been forgotten by Native leaders who trace their heritage to these men. This is made abundantly clear by Will Mayo who began his address to the Tanana-Yukon Historical Society by pointing to members of the audience and indicating which Native leaders at the 1915 meetings are their relatives.

The 100th anniversary of the meeting should have been an important time to pause and reflect on the historic experiences and current realities of life in what we now recognize and respect as the Natives' place in this country. Unfortunately, the anniversary passed without the serious public reflection that it deserves. It is hoped that this volume of essays will help fuel more discussion of the issues the early Native leaders raised with the government. It is also hoped that the 150th Anniversary of the Alaska Purchase in 2017 provided opportunity for public reflection on the rights of Alaska Natives under Western law.

This volume was written as we straddled the two anniversaries and as signs are emerging that Native tribes in Alaska will find new ways through cooperative agreements with the government to gain jurisdictional authority over their communities' affairs. The delegates who met with Wickersham in 1915 were eager to clarify these questions under United States law. They were eager to begin to improve opportunities for their people. This was a historic moment for Natives in interior Alaska with continuing significance today.

We turn now to the events leading up to the meeting, the meeting, and the events that followed. There are five essays in this collection. The first two are by William Schneider, an anthropologist with a particular interest in Native history. He describes the history leading to the 1915 meeting and the evolution of relations between Natives and the whites. Thomas Alton, a historian who is a scholar of the Progressive Era in Alaska, then describes the 1915 meeting, the participants, and the issues that were raised. The fourth essay is by Will Mayo, a past president of the Tanana Chiefs Conference and a National Native leader. Mayo provides his personal thoughts on the meeting, and on the issues that were raised and how they are important today, in light of his experiences working for the Tanana Chiefs and Native communities.[7] The fifth essay is by Schneider. He places the 1915 meeting in the historical perspective of events after the meeting and leading up to the land claims settlement for all Alaska Natives. Kevin Illingworth has provided a legal timeline and commentary in the form of footnotes reproduced in italics throughout the text to mark his contribution. He is a lawyer and professor of tribal law at the University of Alaska Fairbanks. It will become evident that his contributions go much further since so much of the story that is told is about the legal struggle to establish Native rights in a legal system deeply rooted in white societal norms and Western jurisprudence. Finally, there are four appendixes: an introduction to the transcript of the 1915 meeting by Alton, a reproduction of the transcript from the meeting, an edited discussion by Schneider, Illingworth, Natasha Singh, and Mayo on the implications of the Alaska Purchase to Native history, and the timeline of important events in Native history by Illingworth. Singh is the Legal Counsel for Tanana Chiefs. Dixon Jones made the map of the Tanana Valley in consultation with Singh and Schneider.

With respect to the chiefs' names, there are some discrepancies in spelling between photograph labels and the original transcript of the 1915 meeting. This is particularly true for Chief Ivan, whose name is also spelled Evan. There are also numerous photographs of the delegates; not all delegates are represented in each image.

1

From Fur to Gold

by William Schneider

At the 1915 meeting of Native leaders, both Chief Ivan (Evan) and Chief Thomas recalled the time that had passed since the purchase of Alaska and they wanted to learn what they could expect from the government. There was little evidence of government in the forty-eight years between the signing of the treaty and the Chiefs meeting, but then, with the gold rush, their way of life was threatened and they needed to determine a relationship with the new government. Government officials, caught off guard by the new urgency, looked to the language embedded in the Treaty of Cession and this guided their policy toward Natives in Alaska.[8] Under Article III of the Treaty of Cession with Russia, the population of Alaska was divided into the "inhabitants" and the "uncivilized tribes." Most Natives were classified as "uncivilized"; they were not citizens. Instead, they had tribal status, which meant that the government had to recognize their "aboriginal title" to land, but, in the language of the treaty, they were to be "subject to such laws and regulations as the United States may, from time to time, adopt in regard to aboriginal tribes of the country" (Case and Voluck 2012:62–63).[9] The full implications of this classification and its impact on land claims became ever more evident as pressure built on land and resources. In this chapter we describe those changes.

William Seward, the secretary of state who had negotiated the treaty would not live to see the full richness of his investment, the gold rush that would transform life in even the most remote places. But there is some evidence that he thought Alaska was destined to be a "white man's land" and the fate of Natives was inevitable in the onrush of Western civilization.

Addressing the citizens of Sitka in 1869, Seward summed up the fate of Alaska Natives: "[They] can neither be preserved as a distinct social community, nor incorporated into our society. The Indian tribes will do here as they seem to have done in Washington Territory and British Columbia: they will merely serve the turn until civilized white men come" (Seward 1869:13–14).

Early Traders

After the purchase, independent and corporate traders set up operations on the Yukon River. They introduced a greater volume of trade goods, particularly after steamboats were introduced to the Yukon River.[10] They competed for the Natives' fur and their total livelihood depended on the trade. They had no interest in the Natives' land, just the fur that was brought to trade. In Interior Alaska, for many years, there was no sign of government and the Natives were beholden to no one but themselves, but that didn't last.

During the latter years of the nineteenth century, three of the most noteworthy early traders were Leroy Jack McQuesten, Arthur Harper, and Al Mayo. These three came into the country in 1873 following the old Hudson's Bay Company route from the Mackenzie drainage and down the Porcupine River. All three men married Native women (Satejdenalno Kate McQuesten, Seentahna Jennie Bosco Harper Alexander, and Neehunilthonoh Margaret Mayo), and they made long-term investments in the country (Haigh 1996:41–45). Their families are still prominent in Alaska today.

While these traders depended on fur for their livelihood, they were also interested in the mineral wealth of the country and they played a role in opening up the country to prospecting. Harper was an active prospector on the White and Tanana Rivers, and McQuesten grubstaked other men to look for gold, such as Sergai Cherosky and Pitka Pavaloff who discovered gold on Birch Creek in 1892 (Webb 1985:324). They were unable to hold their claims. In one account this was because they did not know the legal steps to stake claims (Callahan 1975:127). In another account, white prospectors claimed they couldn't legitimately hold title to land because they were Natives and therefore not citizens. McQuesten tried unsuccessfully to intervene (Haigh 1996:50). Of course, both interpretations may have been the case.[11] In 1898, United States Geological Survey (USGS) geologist, Harold Goodrich reported similar sentiments in the Rampart area. The miners considered the Natives unreliable, claiming that they lacked "the perseverance and steadfastness of purpose which sustain the white man under difficulties and reverses" (Goodrich 1898:161–162).

John Minook (Mynook, Manook), a Native miner in the Rampart district where Goodrich had made his report, fought for his right to hold a mining claim and his case, adjudicated by Judge Wickersham, stands out as an early example of how the legal process was entangled with common attitudes about what it meant to be "civilized."

In an irony of history, Minook was related to both Pitka Pavaloff and Sergai Cherosky. Pitka was his brother and Sergai his brother-in-law (Callahan 1975:127; Haigh 1996:49).

John Minook family and home.
UAF-0897-002A. Mr. and Mrs. Gregory Kokrine Collection, Vertical File Photograph Collections – People.

Two Pivotal Law Cases

Minook would, in time (1904), win his case and his right to citizenship, in part because of his Russian blood[12] but also because he had "voluntarily taken up his residence separate from any tribe of Natives and had adopted the habits of civilized life" (Cohen 1986:404; Wickersham 1906:224). In essence, this meant evaluation and approval of the way he was living: his housing, clothing, and conduct, his knowledge of white ways, and his abstaining from Native ceremonial or social life.[13] The description in the legal report of the decision is instructive:

> John Minook, whose true name is Ivan Pavlof, is the son of a Russian trader at St. Michael and an Eskimo mother. Both parents were members of the Russian Church, were married in and according to the rites and observances of the church, and their son, the applicant herein, was born in 1849 at St. Michael in the Russian possessions in North America. Both parents resided in Alaska at the time of the cession to the United States on March 30, 1867, and continued to reside there until their death. The applicant was married subsequent to 1867 to a native woman. They have reared a family of children whom they have attempted to educate and teach the principles of the Christian religion. The largest mining stream in the Rampart mining district was named "Minook Creek" in recognition of his worth as a man and miner. He has adopted the habits of civilized life, in dress, manners and habitation, has considerable knowledge of and renders obedience to the laws of the United States and speaks the English language. His witnesses and neighbors testify that he is a fit and proper person to be made an American citizen. (Wickersham 1906:201)

The judgment reached on *Minook* is significant to our unfolding story because it stands in contrast to the legal opinion reached one year later in the *Berrigan* case, a Native land dispute on the Tanana River. In the *Berrigan* case, white prospectors on the Little Delta River, a tributary of the Tanana River, were eager to purchase the rights to land occupied by Chief Jarvis and another Indian named Henry. They are the men who appear on the legal documents, but the group of Natives consisted of a small number

Fishing in clear water, spearing salmon going over the riffles.
UAF-1985-0072-00073. Walter and Lillian Phillips Photograph Collection.

of families. John Jesson, a witness who gave testimony at the inquiry said there were six or seven men and five women and several children and three houses.[14] The prospectors wanted to use the land where the Natives lived as a staging site for the mining prospects up the Little Delta River that they expected to become very important. The legal proceedings did not include Chief Jarvis or Henry; the questions were addressed to white men from the area with some knowledge of the Natives. The questioning itself followed a familiar pattern with inquiry about how well the Natives understood white culture, business practices, the value of fur, sale price for a cord of wood, and how well their living standard approximated that of white society. There was a question raised about whether this was their permanent village. To this question, the respondent said it was their permanent village, "winter quarters,"[15] but earlier in the questioning it was noted that they sometimes went on hunting trips to Salchaket, Shaw Creek, Goodpasture (Goodpaster), and sometimes the Big Delta.[16]

This line of questioning was designed to determine if they lived in one place—a basis for evaluating how civilized they were and therefore how qualified they were to function in white society and apply for citizenship, the prerequisite to owning and selling land.[17] Permanent residence was a persistent theme in the evaluation of whether an individual was worthy of the rights of citizenship.

Wickersham ruled on the case, finding that the prospectors could not legally purchase land from Chief Jarvis and Henry, nor could these Natives hold a legal claim to land because they were not citizens. The prospectors were to stop cutting the timber on the land in question and to vacate the site.[18] In making this judgment, Wickersham legally established the government's responsibility for the Natives and the land they depended on for survival.[19] How much the questioning of the witnesses had influenced his decision is not known. We do know from his journal entries that Wickersham was familiar with the Native village, having stopped there on March 5, 1905, and reported: "[G]ood log houses and the Natives seem well and to have plenty."[20] There is no question that Wickersham's action protected the Natives from immediate exploitation and raised awareness that there was need to find other legal ways to protect their land-use rights.

In both cases (*Minook* and *Berrigan*), the social yardstick of evaluation imposed on Natives and their lifeways at this time in history is clearly evident, if not the determining factor in determining their rights. Natives were not entitled to legally hold land until and unless they became like white men. This was the case, even though it was legally recognized that they had claims to land that had to be settled at some point. The *Minook* case stands out as the first legal ruling on Native rights to ownership of land in Interior Alaska, and the *Berrigan* case established the federal government's responsibility to protect Native interests in the land, even though those interests were unspecified. This meant that Natives would remain subject to the decisions and care of the United States government until the relationship was resolved.[21] There were legal and circumstantial differences between the two cases and there were practical considerations, but there were two common threads: competition for land and questions about ownership and use. These considerations hadn't been issues until the Cherosky and Pavaloff discoveries on Birch Creek in 1893; up until then, there hadn't been land disputes between Natives and whites, that is, in Interior Alaska.

When the prospectors arrived they wanted to claim and patent land, to get legal title. This brought into stark relief the question of who qualified for land rights and the differences between a Western legal system based on individual ownership of land, with boundaries and legal rights of acquisition, disposal, and trespass, and the Interior Native concepts of land-use rights. The Native system was based on groups of related kin, dependent on each other and operating as loosely defined (because of changing conditions) groups, dependent on hunting and fishing free-ranging game.

Native Land-Use Patterns at the Turn of the Century

Descriptions of Athabascan society at the turn of the twentieth century (Callaway and Friend 2007: McKennan 1959:121, 1965:102, 1981:566) depict small isolated groups of related families, referred to in the anthropological literature as "bands," but what in legal parlance might be termed "tribes." Each band occupied a particular region where they could benefit from a variety of seasonally available resources.[22] The Middle Tanana region is of particular interest in our reconstruction of band life at the end of the nineteenth century because it remained relatively isolated from Western influences until the gold rushes spilled over into the Tanana Valley and then it felt the full force of the prospectors. We are fortunate that there are detailed genealogical, photographic, and archival documents that help depict life at this time, just before the advent of prospectors streaming into the Tanana Valley.[23]

The Healy Lake band plays a prominent role in this story. This band occupied the territory from Healy Lake on the Middle Tanana north up into the Forty Mile country. They relied on the whitefish that spawned in the Healy River and on the caribou that migrated through the Forty Mile country (Callaway and Friend 2007:148; Brewster 2013:5). They traded for Western goods at trading posts on the Yukon River at Eagle, Forty Mile, and Dawson. The band size was determined by the resources available to support the group of several related families. Group size was determined by the impact of disease and by allegiance to the leadership of a headman or chief. The chief's primary role at this time (before the movement of white people into the country) was to provide for the band members. The chief ruled by virtue of his skills as a hunter and his ability to provide for people (for Upper Tanana, McKennan 1959:131–132; for Ahtna, de Laguna 1975:91). As an indication of their ability to provide, chiefs might have more than one wife, a sign of wealth, competence, and ability to support an extended family. For instance, Chief Healy's father,

Chit'ai Theeg, (Callaway and Friend 2007:145) was reported to have had two wives (genealogical information provided by Lee Saylor).

Marriage partners were recruited from other bands and often came from a considerable distance. Traditionally, marriages were arranged and followed a matrilineal pattern; children were members of their mother's clan and when they grew up, they married a person from a different clan, often from a different band. For instance, intermarriage between the Healy Lake and the Ketchumstuck bands was common, but it was not uncommon for people to seek marriage partners from even more distant groups. The marriage pattern assured that the ties between different bands were continually reinforced. Potlatches were another way ties were built between groups, and they were a way for an important person to demonstrate his wealth and influence as well as strengthen relations with neighboring groups.

Band structure was flexible, with movement between groups based on personal circumstance,[24] including death of a spouse or the search for marriage partners. Bands had recognized territories based on protection of hunting and fishing rights, but this was less a concern over trespass and more about protecting one's own access to resources. Sometimes

People at Healy River, Alaska, circa 1905. Left to right: Kataba (Old Sam's brother), Kataba's wife (Belle Sam's mother), Kataba's son, Old Chief Healy, another of Kataba's sons, Chief Joe, Chief Joe's first wife Lucy, and Belle Sam.
UAF 2000-0181-00001. Jeany Healy Photograph Collection.

groups came together for communal hunts. This was the case at the caribou fences in the Forty Mile where Healy Lake and Ketchumstuck people were known on occasion to participate together in the hunt (Callaway and Friend 2007:x).

Before 1900, traders and settlers knew little about the Natives inhabiting the vast country stretching between the Tanana River north to the Yukon River. Native bands of the Middle and Upper Tanana came to the Yukon River trading posts but then returned to their homelands. It is fair to say that, at this time in history, these Natives knew more about the traders than the traders knew about them or their homelands. Natives of the Middle and Upper Tanana could selectively trade and learn about Western culture and then return to a way of life undisturbed by newcomers. Trips to the trading posts and the missions provided opportunities to learn rudimentary English and to gain familiarity with the customs of the traders and missionaries. This knowledge became important when the gold rush awakened the government to the need for exploration and development of routes into the Interior. In several cases, Native knowledge and assistance proved invaluable to the exploration parties. We turn to that record now because it depicts life on the brink of rapid change and stands in such contrast to Native–white relations after the turn of the century. Considered in this way, this record gives us a basis to see the changes chronicled in the next chapter.

Gold and the Military Explorations

In the years after the purchase up until a few years before the turn of the century, the United States government showed little interest in Interior Alaska. Alaska historian Morgan Sherwood argues this is because the United States had little need to pay attention to Alaska, given "more pressing matters nearer home" (1992:5). There is one exception that stands out because of the magnitude of the feat and because of what we learn about the Natives and their role in assisting the explorers. This is the expedition of Lieutenant Henry Allen, who in 1885 ascended the Copper River, descended the Tanana, and ventured up the Koyukuk River before making his way to St. Michael on the coast (Allen 1900:411–487). As he traveled through the Copper River country, the band leaders shared both knowledge of the route and their food with him.[25] On the hundredth anniversary of Allen's trip, a gathering was held with Ahtna elders and at that gathering, Katie John related the history of Lieutenant Allen's trip from the perspective of her mother, who was a young girl at the time. Her account tells how they trusted Allen and his men, fed them, and ensured that they were guided through the country, from one camp to the next: "Some time before, the one called Lt. Allen came up here from down the Copper River. He went among the Ahtnas as he came up the river and some Ahtnas went along with him. He did not know the Ahtna trails. From Chitina, he came upriver with some Chitina people" (Kari 1985:115–116; full account is 115–121).

In the last quarter of the nineteenth century, Alaska and the Yukon gained attention for its mineral prospects. Gold strikes at Forty Mile in 1886 (Brooks 1973:328); Birch Creek in 1893, with Circle emerging as a supply point (ibid.:332); Rampart in 1893, with earlier signs of gold found in 1888 (ibid.:332); and then the big Klondike strike in 1896 (ibid.:334) brought a large number of people seeking wealth. It was just a matter of a few years before the miners made their way farther into the Interior up the tributaries of the Yukon River and up the Copper River Valley. For the Upper Copper River country, historian Michael Brown reports that in 1898 there were several thousand people on the trail between Copper Center and Mentasta Pass (Brown 1984:15).

Twelve years after Allen's expedition and in response to reports of hardship among prospectors, in August 1897, Captain Patrick Henry Ray was dispatched to investigate conditions on the Yukon River. That summer, the Yukon River was running particularly low water and Ray was held up in making his way through the Yukon Flats upriver to Fort Yukon, Circle, Eagle, and Dawson. This fact and the mobs of restless miners eager for supplies prompted him to report on the need for better routes into Interior Alaska and for Army posts where soldiers could help to maintain law and order.[26]

As the number of prospectors increased and reports of low supplies reached Washington, the government finally became alarmed. In the summer of 1897, Ray sent his report out via the North American Trading and Transportation Company in Dawson. The agent in Dawson was Captain Johnny Healy. With insufficient supplies arriving in Dawson for the winter, Healy was in difficult straits himself. He was unable to meet the needs of his customers (Hunt 1993:184–185). Healy turned to E. Hazard Wells, a prospector, miner, adventurer, and most important to our story, a well-traveled journalist connected with major publications. Wells left Dawson with Ray's dispatches on December 20, 1897, and reached Skagway on the coast on January 24. He sailed the next day and successfully delivered Ray's calls for action to General Merriam at Vancouver Barracks. From there the messages were transmitted to Washington, D.C. (Wells 1900:511–512), and this led to major military exploration for routes into the Interior.

Wells was no stranger to Alaska. His first expedition was in 1880 when he traveled the length of the Yukon to St. Michael, but most important is Wells's 1890 expedition to Alaska when he traveled up the Fortymile River and overland to the Tanana River. This stands out as one of the earliest accounts, and certainly the most detailed account, of the Forty Mile country and people living between the Yukon and the Tanana Rivers. This trip was supported by the Coast and Geodetic Survey and *Leslie's Illustrated Weekly*, where Wells published detailed installments (*Leslie's Illustrated Weekly*: 1891, vol. 72:339 and vol. 73; see also Wells 1900:513).

Leaving Franklin Gulch on the Fortymile River, Wells's expedition proceeded overland toward their destination, the Tanana River. They had hoped to secure Native guides, but the report from miners at the gulch was that the Natives had left to fish on the Tanana River (*Leslie's Illustrated Weekly*: 1891, vol. 72:412).

In a pattern that began with Allen and would become all too familiar to the military exploration parties that followed, Wells's party found themselves in need of Native assistance.

> In the afternoon we began the descent of the divide toward the Tanana. Short rations were beginning to tell upon us, and we longed for fresh meats. So far, our rifles had been useless. Fortunately we obtained a few dried ducks from an Indian chief named Adam, whose house we found in the woods, and also secured two of his boys as packers and guides as far as the Tanana, for which we started the next morning. (ibid.:431)

Near Mansfield Lake, the party came upon Chief John's camp and was fed whitefish in exchange for tobacco and tea (ibid.:432). Returning later to this camp and in need, they were again fed.

> We pointed energetically into our mouths with our fore-fingers, and then with pantomimic gestures sought to convey

the idea to her mind that we were famished. She appeared to comprehend, for reaching up she took down from the rafters an old deerskin package which we had not investigated and revealed to our eyes some dried moose meat. This she handed over in entirety. Leaving us at work on this new supply she hurried out of doors, and after an absence of some fifteen minutes returned bearing oil and a fish-skin bale of dried whitefish." (ibid.: circa August 1, 1891)

The old woman's generosity did not end there; she fished that night and produced a dozen whitefish for their breakfast. Not satisfied with her kindness, they found Chief John's cache and helped themselves to more fish and oil, leaving money and articles, presumably of clothing, as payment.

Leslie's Illustrated articles are a window into Indian–white relations before the turn of the century. The Natives and the miners were familiar enough with each other for Wells to think he might be able to get assistance in his travels and for the miners at Franklin Gulch to know that the Ketchumstuck Natives would be down on the Tanana River fishing. Salmon only migrate as far up the Tanana as the Goodpaster River, but the Upper Tanana Natives had a very reliable whitefish population that they could depend upon year-round (Randy Brown, personal communication).[27]

Besides providing one of the earliest views of Native life in the Upper Tanana region, Wells's 1890 expedition laid the groundwork for his claims about the mineral values of the Tanana Valley. This was not emphasized in *Leslie's Illustrated* articles (Wells 1891), but he lost no time going on about the mineral wealth of the Tanana in his report to the *New York Times*, February 11, 1898. The *New York Times* article began by announcing his role in bringing out Ray's dispatches, but then turned to an accounting of the mineral wealth of the Tanana Valley. This is a theme he reiterated and developed even further in his official report to the military when he wrote: "There is a well-defined movement in Dawson among pioneer miners looking to a stampede across the hills to the Tanana in Alaska, 200 miles distant. . . . I feel certain that before next summer has passed away, hundreds of men, if not thousands, will be upon the Tanana" (Wells 1900:514–515).

Lost to the public in the *New York Times* article (February 11, 1898), was Ray's descriptions of the lack of supplies on the Yukon, the need for military bases, and his call for exploration that could lead to overland routes to the Yukon goldfields. Fortunately, these messages were heard and acted upon by the government; they led to the extensive search for an "all-American" overland route to the Interior and these expeditions provide further examples of how the Interior Natives assisted exploration parties.

Before the twentieth century, there were three recognized ways to get into the Interior of Alaska; one was via the old Hudson's Bay route from the Mackenzie River to the Rat and Porcupine Rivers and down to the Yukon at Fort Yukon. Another route was up the Yukon River from the Bering Sea, an easier way to travel after the advent of steamboats on the river. A third route became available in 1880 when Captain Beardslee of the U.S. Navy negotiated safe passage for prospectors seeking to use the Chilkoot Pass into the Interior (Brooks 1973:323–324). All these routes were rather circuitous if one's goal was the Middle and Upper Yukon.

In response to Captain Ray's request, the government mounted expeditions from Cook Inlet and from Prince William Sound to establish an overland and year-round route to Interior Alaska. Lieutenant Joseph Herron's expedition from Cook Inlet to the Upper Kuskokwim is noteworthy because of the aid he received from Chief Sesui who rescued and guided him to the newly established military base at Fort Gibbon (Tanana) (Schneider 1985). Chief Sesui had been to Tanana to trade the summer before and recognized the tracks of the horses from Herron's party and tracked down Herron and his men. Clothing, feeding, and guiding them to Tanana, Chief Sesui was offered paper money as payment but requested hard currency. The account of how Sesui rescued Herron is also preserved in the oral record. Charlene LeFebre, an anthologist, heard the story from Chief Sesui's son, Carl.

> My father went down with a canoe and he took me down below my place. We see on other bank some kind of track there. He says, "horse." That summer he been to Tanana and he see white man and horse. That what he know. And he talk me that is white man and I don't believe it because I don't see that kind of track. . . . Go down 4-5 mile and see horse and my father told me we see horse. Still alive. And few miles further father find men.[28]

In an even more dramatic rescue, Lieutenant Joseph Castner and his party in 1898 were swept off their raft on the Goodpaster River and barely made their way to the Native village at the mouth of the river. There, they were fed and guided down the Tanana River to the Chena River.

> The first to discover our approach was a squaw repairing a birch bark canoe on the bank of the Volkmar (Goodpaster). Never having seen white men before, it is not to be wondered at that she was surprised at the sudden and dilapidated appearance of those she beheld, and that she ran screaming toward home. In a few moments five bucks came running toward us armed with Winchester rifles. They were evidently prepared to fight, but when they saw me wave the Indian's peace sign, they greeted us in the most friendly manner. The only one who could speak a little English approached me, and placing his hand on my shoulder and looking me squarely in the eyes, said, White man plenty hungry." (Mitchell 1988:51–52)

These Natives received no compensation for their efforts, despite the extent they went out of their way to help Castner.

The Goodpaster village was visited that same summer by the geologist Alfred Hulse Brooks (August 20, 1898). According to his journal entry, no one was present. He spent time photographing the cabins, caches, and graves and, in hard to decipher penmanship, he wrote a rich description of the site.

> "[Houses] are of hewn timber and have —— glass windows."
> —— the windows showed evidence of comfort [?] and cleanliness, mirrors, pictures from [Police Gazette?] and other —— of civilization were visible. Three [Bibles?] —— of civilization were —— to rafters . . .
> . . . repeating rifles —— —— —— —— evidence of the wealth of the owner . . .
> The graves were small cribs built over the graves in the graveyard with a —— [fork?] at the top and covered with some —— of cloth ——. Each had a flagpole with a piece of colored calico attached to it. (Brooks, August 20, 1898)

Brooks also made note of markings on one of the caches (Brooks, August 19, 1898) that he photographed and then described as ownership marks.[29]

Indian house and cache at the mouth of the Volkmar River,
Donnelly district, Yukon region, Alaska, August 20, 1898.
bah00126.Tif. Brooks, A.H. United States Geological Survey, Denver, Colorado.

Telegraphic Communication and More Trails

Following up on Ray's recommendations for establishment of forts on the Yukon River, a military post was built at Tanana (Fort Gibbon), and at Eagle (Fort Egbert). Captain Charles Farnsworth was put in charge of these posts, and it is from his letters and his son's narrative of life in the country (1899–1901) that we get another glimpse of Native life in the Forty Mile country before the onslaught of prospectors spilled over from the Klondike. The Farnsworth collection at the University of Alaska Fairbanks Archive contains letters that the captain wrote reporting on the progress of his work on the telegraph and the Natives he encountered in the Forty Mile country.

Charles Farnsworth was a photographer and the collection contains his extensive images from the period and, of particular interest, images of the Natives from the Forty Mile. His son Robert Farnsworth's manuscript is based on his father's letters and his own observations. Farnsworth and his men worked on surveying and the initial brushing out of the route for the Washington–Alaska Military Cable and Telegraph System (WAMCATS), a telegraph line down through the Forty Mile country to the Tanana. It also connected to Dawson, providing service through Canada to the continental United States. The line would eventually provide rudimentary communication from Nome to Valdez and eventually by underwater cable to Seattle (Mitchell 1988:x; Cole 1981:46). The line connected the string of military bases that were erected in response to Ray's recommendation.

One photograph from the Farnsworth collection that particularly stands out is of Old Sam, his wife, Belle, and their daughter, Jeany.[30] The

Family at winter camp, date and location unknown.
UAF 2000-181-245. Jeany Healy Photographic Collection F.

photograph is taken at what appears to be their caribou hunting camp in the Forty Mile country, replete with a meat rack and skin or canvas tent.

A personal link to this photo comes from genealogical reconstruction provided by Lee Saylor. Jeany Healy was the young girl in the picture, and as noted, this was Lee's mother-in-law. The image of Old Sam and his family is also in the Jeany Healy Collection at the University of Alaska Archives.[31] The image was used in a publication by the anthropologist, Robert McKennan. He identified Old Sam and placed the location at his winter hunting camp on the Middle Fork of the Fortymile River, near the village of Joseph. He further stated that the image was taken during March, 1901, during Farnsworth's preliminary survey work on the telegraph route from Eagle to Valdez (McKennan 1981:573).[32] What is significant about the reconstruction for this story is the personal connection through genealogy and photograph collection with a particular family and the depiction of how they were living at the transition point just before the influx of prospectors.

A few years after Farnsworth, Billy Mitchell was put in charge of finishing the telegraph line. Mitchell was posted at Fort Egbert. In the cold winter of 1903, he surveyed a route down the Goodpaster River to the Tanana River to connect with the line work coming from the lower Tanana. By this time, prospecting in the Fairbanks area had shown enough promise to necessitate overland access and communication, hence the attention to road building and telegraphic communication through the Tanana Valley. On that trip Mitchell was accompanied by Chief Joe.[33]

Mitchell had met Chief Joe in 1902 on his way back to Fort Egbert at Eagle: "On this trip I fell in with the Middlefork [*Middle Fork*] Indians on the Fortymile River, whose chief, Joseph became one of my great friends and companions later on" (Mitchell 1988:46).

Later when Mitchell encountered another Native from the band, he asked him to summon Chief Joseph to see him in two months' time (ibid.:57). Mitchell consulted with Joseph several times and finally convinced him to make the 1903 trip down the Goodpaster River to the Tanana. Joseph was reluctant: "These Indians were very bad, he explained. If they looked at you intently, they made you sick" (ibid.:66).

Joseph's fears centered on a strong medicine man at the Goodpaster village. This was probably Chief Jarvis's brother, Luke, who bore that reputation.[34] Despite the fear, Mitchell convinced Joe to make the trip. The

Goodpaster Natives were startled to see them but were quite familiar with white men and their activities.

> The Indians seemed tremendously astonished to see us, and examining our equipment, eyeing my indian, Joe, curiously. He spoke an entirely different language from their own, but he made himself understood by signs and a few words common to all Indians. Several of the Good Pasture Indians spoke quite a few words of English, having been down to the mouth of the Tanana River with their furs to trade. (Mitchell 1988:73)

On the question of the telegraph line, the Natives voiced concern: "One asked me if it would bring more white men into the country, and I told him it probably would not, because the 'talk string' would do the work of many mail carriers who otherwise would have to go through that country" (ibid.:73).

Unfortunately, this did not prove to be the case. The trail actually attracted prospectors, who saw it as a shortcut to reach the gold diggings on the Tanana (Cole 1981:46–48). Mitchell wrote:

> I met a couple of Indians from the Good Pasture tribe, who said they had heard that many White men were going to stampede over my trail to Fairbanks. It was evident now that we were in for it. The stories that had gone out from Fairbanks, added to by traders who were taking goods in there to sell, had spread not only all over Alaska, but also to the United States. With the memory of Dawson and Nome before them, men were making a frantic rush to get to Fairbanks before it was too late.[35]

The movement of prospectors into the Tanana Valley had begun at least five years earlier. Brooks estimated that there were about a hundred prospectors in the Tanana basin in the summer of 1898 when he made his reconnaissance (Brown 1984:17; Brooks 1900:193), but after the turn of the century the movement increased dramatically.

The other concern of the Goodpaster Natives was the impact of the telegraph on caribou: "One Indian said he had heard that game would not cross the 'talk string,' and that therefore the migration of the caribou would be changed, much to their disadvantage" (Mitchell 1988:73).

Chief Joe and Billy Mitchell's trip is remembered and mentioned often in interviews (Callaway and Friend 2007). There is also an account recorded by Craig Mishler with Eva Moffit in which she recalls how she heard about the expedition: "And then [C]hief Joe say, 'I think they want somebody to lead them [d]own the river.' 'Yeah. Son, go with them'" (Mishler 1986:82).[36]

By the time of Mitchell's expedition down the Goodpaster River with Chief Joe, prospectors had made their way over the hills and up the Copper River; the Valdez Trail linked the port of Valdez with the new mining center at Fairbanks. The military explorations, spurred on by Ray's plea for an overland route to Interior Alaska, met Natives witnessing the rapid changes. Many spoke a few words of English and probably understood a great deal more. They bore English names; many from baptism by Anglican or Episcopal clergy. Some like Chief Healy and Chief Jarvis probably took their names from prominent white men. Chief Healy may have been named after Johnny Healy, the trader at Dawson.[37] Chief Jarvis may have adopted his name from David Jarvis, the customs agent at Eagle.[38]

Portrait of Chief Joe of Salchaket with his wife Agnes and possibly their children Alex and Walter. *UAF-1991-46-494. Drane Family Collection.*

A New Era for Interior Natives

In a window of five short years (1898–1903), we have our last glimpse of a way of life in the Middle and Upper Tanana River and Upper Copper River, a homeland remote enough to insulate for many years most of the

Natives from white competition for their land, but for the Tanana Natives, close enough to the traders and missionaries on the Yukon who offered Western goods, English language, and religion. Then, in the aftermath of the military expeditions that had depended on Native help, life changed drastically for the inhabitants of this land. Pavaloff and Cherosky's experiences with the prospectors foreshadowed increased competition for the land, but it is unlikely that this received much attention at the time.

In many of their accounts, the explorers and scientists were surprised at the Natives' imported clothing, amount of trade goods, and rudimentary knowledge of English. They appreciated the help they got from the Natives, but their understanding of Native life was limited and colored by their own, often desperate, needs. They had very little to say about the Natives' needs and the impending changes that would come to them. The Goodpaster Natives' concern about whether the telegraph line would bring more people to the country is prophetic. Soon it would no longer be Native country under Native terms. Chief Jarvis and Chief Joe would face new challenges from the influx of miners and their personal lives would become entangled in new ways as well. Chief Healy would attempt with some success to keep his band members away from the negative influences brought by the prospectors (Saylor 2000), but he would also develop a strong relationship with the trader John Hadjukovich, and that would allow him to sponsor his elaborate and well-publicized 1927 potlatch (Endicott 1928).[39] In the coming years, with the increasing importance of village-centered services, bands would consolidate into village areas for part of the year and the role of chief would expand to include meetings and negotiations with the government officials in support and defense of their way of life.

From Native to White Man's Country

by William Schneider

By 1900, the prospectors had made their way from the Yukon and its tributaries to the Tanana and Copper River Valleys. Many were still searching for their bonanza, others had left disillusioned. In all cases, their impact was evident. In a matter of a few years, Interior Alaska went from the province of the Natives, a few traders, and missionaries, to a world fashioned to the expectations of the newcomers. Now thousands of gold seekers had made their way down the Yukon River, over the hills into the Tanana drainage, and up the Copper River Valley from the coast. Where once the Natives had lived their lives their way, now there was a new order that demanded their accommodation. In 1903, U.S. Senator William P. Dillingham from Vermont chaired a committee of congressmen who visited Alaska to report on conditions and make recommendations regarding what government action might be needed in light of the gold rush. The Klondike gold rush had attracted international attention and the discovery of profitable gold in Alaska brought prospectors and merchants. Alaska Natives were just a minor part of the inquiry, but the sentiment expressed by David Jarvis, whom they interviewed in Eagle, captured the essence of the impacts of the prospectors on Native life. Jarvis, the customs agent in Eagle, had been in Alaska long enough to know Alaska Native life before the gold rush. He could clearly see the negative impact on Native life (U.S. Congress 1904:83). William P. Dillingham echoed his sentiments in his report of findings to Congress: "The business of Alaska is carried on by citizens of the United States. It is claimed by them to now be a 'white man's country.' To all intents and purposes such is the fact. In every contest for gain the white man has been the gainer" (ibid.:29).

The changes had come fast and were poorly understood, merely accepted by the settlers as the price for development. Only a few others bothered to consider the impact on Native life. An exception was Lieutenant W. R. Abercrombie who, as early as 1884 predicted that conflicts would be inevitable. He wrote then: "The conflicting interests between the white people and the Indians of the Territory were likely in the near future to result in serious disturbance, hence it was deemed important that all possible information as to the facts should be obtained for the guidance of the military branch of the Government" (Abercrombie 1900:383).

Abercrombie was back in Alaska in 1898 to lead a military reconnaissance of the Copper River Valley. In his report on this work, he commented on how the large number of newcomers was depleting the supply of game available to the Natives (ibid.:579). Two areas that were particularly impacted by the influx of prospectors were the Tanana and the Copper River Valleys. These were considered remote before the gold rush but in time, they became a major route to the Interior and the Natives living in the region felt the brunt of development. In hindsight, it was inevitable with the spillover from the gold rushes on the Yukon River and the new transportation and communication systems that linked the coast to the Interior.

Gold and Its Impact on the Interior

Gold strikes in the Fairbanks area in 1902 (Cole 1981:36) led to the diversion of the Valdez trail to the new town of Fairbanks. Construction of the WAMCATS line, completed by 1905 (Mitchell 1988:x) ran through the Tanana Valley and down the Copper River Valley to Valdez. By 1903, cannery operations at the mouth of the Yukon and the Copper Rivers were seriously depleting the amount of fish available to Interior Athabascans, who depended on the fish migrating upriver each year.[40] Steamboats linked the town of Fairbanks with the Yukon River villages and tributaries such as the Koyukuk River. Native village camps along the lower Tanana such as Nenana, Old Minto, Tolovana, and Cosjacket (Crossjacket) also saw increased traffic and some opportunities to sell cordwood to the steamboats.

There was little thought given to the impacts of development on Natives until the inquiry by Senator Dillingham in 1903. The government's first response was to assess access to the goldfields, establish communication, and ensure law and order. The government sent military men to establish routes (Ray 1900a:495–504), to build the telegraph system (Mitchell 1988; Farnsworth Papers), and geologists to map the country's mineral wealth (Brooks 1973).

Land ownership, rights of purchase and sale, the Western legal meaning of boundary markers, and the legal claims that are the backbone of American land law were foreign concepts to most Interior Athabascan Natives and incompatible with their way of life. It must have been a huge cultural leap for the Native groups to even consider that Alaska could be sold by Russians to the United States. The Russians had never had more than limited presence in the Interior, and the United States, at the time of the purchase, had even less presence (Coen, personal communication, 2016). Then came the prospectors, who wanted to establish claims that would ensure, in a Western legal way, their hold on particular lands.

By the turn of the century, Interior Natives felt the impact of white prospectors and settlers. They turned to the government for help. One of the earliest examples of this is a letter written by Chief Ivan of Cosjacket and Chief William of Fort Gibbon and Tanana. The letter was addressed to the secretary of war. The letter concludes with a plea for help to stop the white people from cutting wood around their grounds: "We are self-supporting Indians and all we want to ask of you is to stop the whites to cut wood around our grounds."[41]

The Western legal system came equipped with precedent and prejudice and little room to accommodate different ways of life. The newcomers viewed land as either owned or available to be staked. The notion of a group of people sharing and agreeing on land-use rights, so basic to Native notions, was foreign to the prospectors and settlers.

Ironically, as we have seen, in the years leading up to the twentieth century, in case after case, it was the Natives who assisted the military exploration parties, in some cases, saving them from starvation (Castner 1984; Herron 1909; Allen 1900). Now, the Natives had to defend themselves against competition for the fish and game resources that were vital to their lives. In addition, they found themselves subject to a new legal system that saw them at best as "dependent subjects" (Richards 1906:3). They were legally in limbo until the United States government determined how to move from protecting their rights to use and occupy the land without interference to granting them ownership. As we have also seen, the basis for this classification goes back to the Treaty of Cession with Russia in 1867 when the people of Alaska were classified as "inhabitants," and "the uncivilized tribes" (Case and Voluck 2002:45). The uncivilized tribes were to be administered and cared for by the government, which meant they had little recognized rights beyond the assurance that the government would look out for their interests.[42]

Tribal Ties and the "Civilized" Life

Tribal law experts David Case and David Voluck write that "[c]ivilization, abandonment of tribal relations, and citizenship were often synonymous under U.S. naturalization statutes common to the period of the Russian–American Treaty" (2002:47). The implication is that there might be a path out of the dependent legal status of "uncivilized" and it is based on giving up one's "tribal affiliations." In practice this meant living separately from other Natives as a nuclear family and deriving your livelihood from a specific location. By 1901, the opinion expressed by the Board of Indian Affairs was "to make all Indians self-supporting, self-respecting, and useful citizens of the United States" (Prucha 1984, vol. 2:779). Achievement was measured in how well one, as an individual, understood, emulated, and took up white ways. An early legal opinion on how to define civilization was offered by Lyman Knapp:

> The habits of civilized life for the purposes of good citizenship ought to at least include living in permanent homes; conforming in dress and outward habits to the customs of civilized peoples to such an extent as not to shock their sense of decency and propriety; using cooked food; recognizing the family relation and manifesting reasonable respect for it; giving some attention to the education of their children; and acting generally, in the ordinary transactions of life, upon the theory that right, justice, and law have claims superior to those of physical power and brute force. (Knapp 1891:338)

The legal and social distinctions, established at the time of the treaty and explored in the above quote had little direct meaning for most Interior Natives until competition for land and resources became an issue. Then, the questions of Native legal rights were tested in the *Minook* and *Berrigan* cases discussed in the last chapter.[43]

In terms of land rights, the only legal protection for most Alaska Natives was the weak language in a provision of the 1884 Mining Act that provided that their rights to the land were to be respected and not disturbed: "That the Indians or other persons in said district shall not be disturbed in the possession of any lands actually in their occupation or now claimed by them but the terms under which such persons may acquire title to such lands is reserved for future legislation by Congress."[44]

The years of indirect contact with traders and missionaries introduced the Natives of the Tanana and the Copper Rivers to Western goods, the English language, and the rudiments of Christianity but did little to prepare them for the changes brought by the prospectors and government officials.

What Constitutes a Productive Life?

The prospectors not only brought a demand for land; they came with the whole Western legal system and its societal norms. They came with a different perspective on what constituted a productive life and a different view of man's place in the world. For most Athabascans of Interior Alaska, prospecting and gold mining held little interest. Farming, the backbone of American rural life in much of the United States, made little sense in the Alaska Interior. The growing season was short and unpredictable. The crops that could be grown and preserved did not sustain a well-rounded diet high in protein and fat necessary for an active life in the Interior. The Native seasonal rounds consisted of summer fishing and berry picking and fall moose and caribou hunting. In winter they trapped for furbearers and cut wood for personal use and for sale to the steamboats. In spring they harvested waterfowl. The yearly cycle was linked to the migration patterns of the fish and game and to the seasonal changes in the animals they hunted and trapped, with a strong emphasis on taking the animals when they were available and in the best condition to be hunted, trapped, or fished.

Hunters felt fortunate that the game provided itself to them. Their responsibility was to maintain their part of the relationship by showing respect and properly treating the animals taken in the hunt. The success of a hunter depended on the hunter's relationship with the game animals.

This was in contrast to the Christian concept of man as superior to other animals and holding dominion and power over them, as in the Biblical reference: "Then God said, 'let us make human beings in our image, to be like us. They will reign over the fish in the sea, the birds in the sky. The livestock, all the wild animals that scurry along the ground" (Genesis 1:26, New Living Translation).

For much of the United States and despite the growing industrialization at the end of the nineteenth century, farming remained the backbone of American prosperity and identity.[45] Bruce Gardner, on the first page of his book *American Agriculture in the Twentieth Century* quotes the *New York Times*'s economic review for 1899: "The farmer, the miller, the stockman and all classes engaged in like industries are reaping the benefits that flow from bounteous harvests and good prices."[46]

Despite the poor fit, federal Indian laws were predicated on this agrarian model of small and segregated plots of individually owned land. Most white Americans believed that given reasonable acreage and good stewardship of the land, a hard-working family would have a chance to make a living. Westward expansion and the call for settling the West were based on this premise. The Homestead Act of 1862 gave promise to those who were willing to accept the often-dangerous trip west. In Alaska, the Alaska Homestead Act of 1898 and the Alaska Townsite Act of 1891 gave further promise to perspective settlers.

In contrast to these new legal ways for small segments of land to be secured, the Athabascan subsistence life demanded extensive access for each of the seasonal activities that sustained them and free movement to hunting, fishing, and trapping areas. Throughout the historic period and even further back in prehistory, hunting, fishing, and trapping depended upon access to large and specific tracts of land. For instance, traplines stretched for many miles and the rights to use the traplines, as well as specific fishing sites, were based on who established the trapline or fishing site, who maintained it, and who inherited the rights of use. Cabins, traplines, and equipment were not usually sold but were instead the subject of temporary and longer-term agreements. Traditionally, in the Native system rights to use a fishing site or a trapline were agreed on within the band, the group of related families that lived in an area and worked together on subsistence pursuits. Later, when there was competition from the prospectors and settlers, the rights to use sites became the purview of nuclear and extended

Native families, whose pattern of use often extended back through generations. Under this system, the land itself was not "owned" but rights were extended to "use." The system depended on recognition and respect.[47] The Native practice of passing on rights to use stands in contrast to the pattern of white settlers, who tended to favor economic exchange for actual ownership of property and possessions, such as traps and cabins. With the exception of woodcutting for steamboats, sale of dry fish for dog teams, and money earned from trapping, cash played a minor role in the Interior Native economy, although this would change as goods from the trading posts became more available and desirable.

The Government's Investigations and Response

The cultural differences between whites and Natives were poorly understood, but the practical implications were clear. The United States government was caught off guard and was unsure how to respond to the impact of the prospectors and settlers on the Natives and their way of life. For instance, in addition to Senator Dillingham's report, the secretary of the interior included in his report for 1903 a submission by Brigadier General Frederick Funston based, it appears, on his yearly inspection of Army bases in Alaska. Funston's firsthand observations were limited to his travel on the Yukon River and to Nome and Valdez where the Army posts were located, distant from the Middle and Upper Tanana and the Upper Copper River country that were, at this time, experiencing the latest impacts of the gold rush. His report in 1903 was largely based on accounts gathered from prospectors, missionaries, and traders.[48] Funston acknowledges that his knowledge of the Copper River Natives was based on the words of prospectors he met while traveling on the steamer *Excelsior* from Valdez to Juneau (Funston 1903:271). They had little respect for the Natives and felt they were not deserving of aid in any form since it would make them dependent on the government (ibid.:271).

Also attached in Exhibit H of the Funston report is a document prepared by Jas Witten, special inspector for the Land Office. His comments are based on reports received from the field. One of his sources was Judge James Wickersham, who noted the negative impact of canneries on the amount of fish available for Interior Natives (Witten 1903:278). Another of his sources was R. Blix, who was with the Copper River Mining, Trading, and Development Company. He noted direct impacts of canneries on Copper

River salmon runs and the availability of salmon for Interior Natives. He also noted depletion of game.[49]

There is no doubt that the person who had the largest impact on bringing the plight of Alaska Natives to the government was Lieutenant George Thornton Emmons. In his years as a naval officer along the coast of Southeast Alaska, Emmons had many opportunities to acquire Native artifacts and he was an active collector. He sold the collections to museums across the country. He saw the objects as valuable commodities in a world with growing interest in Natives. Beyond collecting material culture, Emmons was a student of Northwest Coast cultures and he documented the social and ceremonial life of the Tlingit people (Emmons 1991). He was also personally concerned about the well-being of Native people, particularly the plight of the Copper River Natives.

Nowhere is this last point more evident than in his letter to President Theodore Roosevelt sent from Valdez, July 31, 1904.

> Mr. President,
>
> I feel it my duty to call your attention to the deplorable condition of the Copper River Indians of Alaska. They are little removed from starvation and unless government aid is given to them immediately, many will succumb during the coming winter.[50]

Emmons's efforts led to relief for the Natives and were a prelude to a larger report that he submitted on conditions of all Alaska Natives.

Emmons full study on the conditions of Natives in Alaska was sent to the president and the president submitted it to Congress January 19, 1905. It was published in the Congressional record under the title *Conditions and Needs of the Natives of Alaska* (Emmons 1905). The report was based on a brief trip from Wrangell to the Seward Peninsula and on testimonies he collected on conditions. He may also have taken advantage of an offer from the Bureau of Education to send questions that they would then distribute to teachers and missionaries for response.[51] Emmons's report, *Conditions and Needs of the Natives of Alaska* (January 19, 1905), spoke in very general terms about all the Native groups but brought particular attention to the plight of Copper River Natives, who were impacted by the onslaught of prospectors into the country and by the canneries at the mouth of the river that reduced the amount of fish available to the Natives in the Interior.

The report also called for an industrial training school, material assistance to the Natives, and a doctor to be stationed in the region. Emmons's observations on the plight of Copper River Natives was reported in the *Valdez News* (October 8, 1904) and in the *Seattle Post* (September 10, 1904), as well as in the letter to the president dated July 31, 1904.[52] The president acknowledged the report and conditions in a newspaper article, February 16, 1905,[53] and when there was a problem getting supplies to the Copper River Natives, Emmons's note to the president was also acknowledged June 30, 1905, with the president directing the Commissioner of Indian Affairs to the problem and then ordering the War Department to correct problems of providing supplies, which he reported in a letter to Emmons dated August 3,

George Thornton Emmons.
Image number 328741, American Museum of Natural History Library.

1906.[54] In representing the plight of the Copper River Natives, Emmons was persistent and effective, and President Roosevelt was responsive.

The Upper Tanana Natives did not receive such favored treatment. Historian Michael Brown notes that Oscar Fish, a mail carrier, wrote to the secretary of the interior in 1900 describing the destitute condition of the Natives at Mentasta, Tetlin, Mansfield, and Ketchumstuck. Fish reported on the extinction of furbearers and on the large number of moose and caribou that had been killed. He didn't directly attribute this decline to the increased number of prospectors in the country, although it is fair to presume they had a negative impact on the game population.[55]

It is unfortunate that Emmons did not have access to Fish's observations since his efforts for the Copper River Natives were so effective. In terms of the general report and his recommendations to the president, and writing for all of the Native people, Emmons spoke out against reservations for Alaska Natives, pointing out that Alaska Natives have always been "independent and self-sustaining" (Emmons 1905:14). Ahead of his time, Emmons proposed granting of property rights to Natives (Emmons 1905:15). In part, this was probably to ensure they had some land to use against the onslaught of white settlers. One year after Emmons's report was received, the 1906 Alaska Native Allotment Act (U.S. Congress 1906) provided the possibility for individuals to acquire 160 acres of land if they agreed to the terms of "substantially continuous use and occupancy."[56] It was commonly believed by government policymakers that "[c]ivilization was impossible without the incentive to work that comes only from individual ownership of a piece of property" (Prucha 1984, vol. 2, 639).

Reservations in the West had proven unsatisfactory; settlers demanded more land and the restrictions of reservation life did not suit the subsistence needs of many Native groups. A change in federal Indian policy favored allotments, individual plots to heads of households. In its best light, the General Allotment Act of 1887 gave opportunity to Natives in the continental United States who were willing to till the land and make a living on 160 acres. In its worst light, it represented an attempt to destroy tribal identity and make Natives work the land just like white men.

In his first address to Congress in 1901, President Theodore Roosevelt made his now famous statement about the General Allotment Act. He said: "In my judgment the time has arrived when we should definitely make up our minds to recognize the Indian as an individual and not as a member of a tribe. The General Allotment Act is a mighty pulverizing engine to break up the tribal mass" (Roosevelt 1901).[57]

Roosevelt's pronouncement sends shivers down the spines of Native scholars today because it was intended to extinguish tribal identity and the Natives' collective power to negotiate terms with the government over tribal land.

The Alaska Native Allotment Act of 1906 provided similar conditions and opportunities for Alaska Natives (Case and Voluck 2002:102–104). One of the key provisions of the act was the call for "substantially continuous use and occupancy" (Illingworth n.d.; "Timeline of Important Laws and Events"). This was open to interpretation, but its intent was to limit land where the allottee could make a living and to segregate individuals from other members of their group. In the early years after its enactment, few Natives took advantage of the Native Allotment Act, but this new way of thinking, embedded in the law, would eventually impact Native settlement.

In his report, Emmons also advocated in favor of citizenship for Natives if they passed the education test and "relinquish tribal ties"(1905:16). The Alaska Native Citizenship Act would follow in 1915 with similar and additional provisions (Alaska Territorial Legislature 1915).[58] In these respects, we can see how Emmons's recommendations influenced the course of how Alaska Natives would be treated.

With Emmons's knowledge and respect for Native culture, it is hard to understand why he would call for "relinquishing tribal ties" (Emmons 1905:16). Did he separate his intellectual interest in Native social life from a perceived greater value of conformity to a Western model and standard of social, ceremonial, and religious life? In short, did he follow the thinking of most people of his time that Western civilization was the pinnacle that others should strive to attain if they wanted to enjoy the privileges and legal rights it provided?[59] An embedded principle of Western legal philosophy was the need for Natives to give up their tribal ties. In essence this meant living separately from other Natives as a nuclear or extended family. Even more important, giving up tribal ways meant, to the government and the Western legal system, giving up tribal status—the Natives' special relationship to the federal government.

Despite the positive impact of Emmons's work, he, like the others—Funston, Dillingham, and Witten—never got to the Upper Copper and Middle to Upper Tanana Rivers, to witness firsthand the most acute impacts. Instead, they all relied on the nineteenth-century travel routes, down the Yukon and along the coast. Little firsthand information was forthcoming about the actual conditions on the ground. The testimonies that were collected were of mixed quality and dubious value. However, there were some key people whose testimonies were the exception because of their travel and experience in the country. For instance, Judge Wickersham's comments to Witten were based on his travels through the country. His most important observation concerned the impact of canneries on interior fisheries (Witten 1903:278). There was also First Lieutenant William L. ("Billy") Mitchell, whose extensive experience was in the Forty Mile and the Tanana, building the telegraph line. Surprisingly, Mitchell's most important observations to Senator Dillingham's committee concerned the poverty of the Copper River Natives and the depletion of their fish (U.S. Congress, 1904 *Conditions in Alaska*, Senate Report 282, part 2). In terms of the Copper

River Natives, Emmons's informant, Reverend Clevenger, was probably the most important. He lived at Copper Center where he ran a mission, and he commented firsthand about the hardships the Copper River people were facing. Emmons forwarded his concerns to President Roosevelt.[60] Finally, in the list of key observers, there is Abercrombie, whose direct experience over many years in the Copper River region allowed a long view of changes and impacts that made him sympathetic to the plight of the Natives as he watched events unfold. Writing in 1898, he tempered his 1884 prediction of disturbance between the prospectors and the Natives to emphasize the kindly nature of these people. He wrote:

> It will be found to be the universal verdict of all who have come in contact with the Copper River Indians that they are honest, inclined to be friendly, and temperate. During the last season it was no uncommon sight to see these Indians wading out into the river and rescuing the supplies of some miner whose boat had been wrecked further upstream. Piling them up on shore they would go 3 or 4 miles out of their way to notify the owner where he could find them. (Abercrombie 1900:579)

With these few exceptions and taken as a whole, the government wasn't prepared to understand the Natives' way of life and evaluate them on their own terms. The Natives had very few advocates. The government was far better prepared to address the prospector and settler's needs. The newcomers came with expectations of services, a familiar legal system, and access to the land and resources to make a living. They were representatives of a nation that saw itself as the world's greatest power. That power was understood to have been gained through achievements and the destiny of a privileged class of people. "Cultural relativism" and general understanding and acceptance of different ways of life would come many years later.

Long-Term Changes in the Tanana Valley

The movement of prospectors into the Tanana Valley and up the Copper River Valley precipitated a number of changes that included the establishment of trading posts on the Tanana River that shifted Indian trading opportunities from the Yukon to the more accessible Tanana posts at

Fairbanks, Nenana, Healy River, and Copper Center. Similarly, the estab-lishment of Episcopal missions at Salcha in 1909, Chena in 1908, and Tanacross in 1912 attracted a semi-permanent coalescing of some Natives around the missions (McKennan 1981:567). At that time, the missions offered the only schooling and dedicated medical care available to Interior Natives. The missions also offered an alternative to the hard-drinking and seamier sides of Western civilization that characterized some of the larger settlements. The military telegraph line (WAMCATS) also had stations and men posted at regular intervals, including Goodpaster, Salcha, Fairbanks, and Nenana and farther down river.

By 1915, Fairbanks had become a major supply center for mining activ-ity in the surrounding hills and as a terminus for steamboats. Supplies came on steamboats from the Yukon up the Tanana River, and they came over-land up the Valdez trail to Fairbanks and then on to the steamboats headed back downriver to supply camps and villages on the Yukon River and its tributaries. Some opportunities became available for Natives to work as pilots[61] and deckhands, and as woodcutters to supply wood that fueled the boats. However, the leaders at the 1915 Tanana Chiefs Conference pointed out that their people were often overlooked when it came to woodcutting contracts and opportunities to sell dry fish to the Army posts. The dele-gates to the 1915 meeting voiced interest in this work and stated that they wanted to be notified and considered for employment.[62] Development of the country was happening without them and they wanted to be a part. This was the setting in 1915 when the leaders met in Fairbanks.

Just a few years before (turn of the century), the small band of related families had been the economic unit. Then, with the establishment of villages in proximity to missions and trading posts, the extended family became the unit of production, tending the traplines, hunting, and fishing (McKennan 1981:567; Hosley 1981:549). Earlier in the American period, the repeating rifle had replaced the need for large communal hunts and the maintenance of caribou fences became unnecessary. The introduction at the turn of the century of fish wheels on the Yukon River and then on the Lower and Middle Tanana and Copper Rivers[63] made it easier for nuclear and extended families to put up a supply of fish, even though there was still no relief from the impact of the canneries at the mouth of the rivers.

Fur trapping had always been a solitary endeavor, and it became more important as availability, interest, and demand for imported goods gradually increased the Natives' desire for cash or credit from the store (McKennan 1981:567). Family-based traplines further reinforced the role of the nuclear family in subsistence activities.

These factors influenced group organization for subsistence activities, but this didn't mean that hunting, fishing, and trapping were less important. The leaders who spoke at the 1915 meeting were very clear that their way of life was not sedentary, that they needed wide-ranging access to fish and game and their old sites, as well as new opportunities to participate in the cash economy. It was hard for Wickersham and the other government officials to reconcile this complicated new reality of Native subsistence life—a combination of living off the land, seeking ways to protect their rights of access to and use of the old sites and resources while securing financial, educational, and medical opportunities that they saw as critical to their survival in what was for them, a new economic reality. Chiefs continued to be dedicated to ensuring the welfare of their followers, but their role now also included dealing with the government and negotiating for the new opportunities. The Tanana Chiefs meeting is an early example of the chiefs' efforts to protect the traditional life on the land while also seeking new educational, medical, economic, and legal opportunities for their members. The Natives' situation was made difficult because most of the white population couldn't see any future opportunities for the Natives unless they learned to live like white men. This was evident in derogatory attitudes they expressed about the Natives' way of life. Unfortunately, this same attitude was mirrored in the legal realm. Nowhere is this clearer than in Wickersham's own response in the closing remarks to the 1915 conference. He promised to pass on their concerns to the secretary of the interior; the Natives reiterated their demands and Wickersham then responded with the social yardstick of white society as the key to citizenship and the fruits of equality under the law:

> Paul Williams: The Indians say that next time you run for a Delegate you want to be sure and notify us and be sure you accomplish this before you run again for Delegate.

> Mr. Madara: If they ever get to vote there will be enough of them to settle the delegate question all right.

Wickersham then responded, "You tell them that as soon as they have established homes and live like the white men and assume the habits of civilization, they can have a vote."[64]

The 1915 Meeting as an Important Benchmark

What is striking about the record described here is that up until the 1915 meeting, the Natives were rarely consulted; instead, it was always people describing their condition or making recommendations for and about them. It is not until the 1915 meeting that Natives in the Interior were invited to speak in public with government officials about their concerns and needs.[65] This is a further example of how sweeping the impact of this period was on life in Alaska. It was as if before this meeting, the authorities felt the Natives' concerns were not important and further, that they couldn't speak for themselves because they wouldn't know how to make their concerns known to the authorities in ways that could be accommodated. All considerations had been filtered through white social and legal understandings, and it was assumed that this was in the Natives' best interests. The price of conforming to the new order and becoming like white men was rarely, if ever, calculated in terms of impact on the Natives. Fortunately, Alaska is no longer just a white man's country. We can trace that change, at least in part, to the leaders gathered in 1915 to explain their concerns and way of life.

3

July 1915: Wickersham
Meets the Tanana Chiefs

by Thomas Alton

For two days in July, 1915, the George C. Thomas Memorial Library in Fairbanks was the scene of a remarkable meeting of fourteen Tanana River Athabascan tribal leaders with federal government officials, including Alaska's delegate to Congress, James Wickersham. It was the first discussion of its kind ever held in Interior Alaska, and it produced results that none but the chiefs themselves would have predicted. The Athabascans spoke as representatives of their respective villages, but together they presented a strong unified voice. They articulated not only a respect for their own customs and traditions, but also an understanding of current threats brought by the growing white population and a plan for directing their own future.

The chiefs "proved to be unusually intelligent" and "diplomatic," one newspaper reported in a somewhat surprised tone following the meeting. "The Indians knew what they wanted and how to get it."[66]

The meeting had come together over a period of less than two months. The chiefs were alarmed at rumors of a new railroad coming to the Interior, and they were concerned about its impact on their traditional hunting areas. They aimed to get the facts directly from Alaska's Congressional delegate.

Wickersham, at fifty-seven, was in his fourth consecutive term as Alaska's nonvoting representative in Congress. He had arrived in Fairbanks on April 25 to spend the summer following the long session in Washington, and almost immediately he set out to explore the countryside surrounding his adopted hometown. His travels took him to Minto Flats, where he visited Chief Charley's camp on May 19, and later he entered a small Native village on a point of land at the mouth of the Tolovana. There, Wickersham met Chief Alexander and, with most of the village out hunting and fishing, the two engaged in lengthy discussions over the next two days. Wickersham spoke frankly and earnestly to the chief about the government railroad that soon would be built from Seward through to Fairbanks and the impact this would have on Native life in the Tanana Valley. He told him about a variety of issues, including the demands of land-hungry miners, farmers, and settlers.

"Chief Sta-tad-tuna [Alexander] called on me today bravely arrayed in his paint, feathers, beadwork, and moose skin coat," Wickersham noted in his diary on May 22. "We had a long 'talk' about game laws, reservations, schools, etc."[67]

The talk included Wickersham's grim prediction about the future of Indian lands and his assessment of the choices then open to tribal leaders. To him the issue narrowed down to two options: either the Natives establish a reservation where all would live in a large community, or they take individual allotments of 160 acres each.

Wickersham did not record Chief Alexander's response, but his message clearly had struck a nerve. He told the chief to discuss these issues with as many people as he could. The word spread quickly from one village and fish camp to the next as far upriver as Salchaket and down to Tanana village near the Army's Fort Gibbon on the Yukon. By July 5, when the groups gathered for the opening day of the meeting in Fairbanks, the Athabascan leaders were ready with questions and prepared to state their case.

Jacob Starr of Tanana was one of the first to address the reasons for the Natives' concerns.[68] "We came up here today to talk to Delegate Wickersham because he talked to Chief Alexander at Tolovana, and we want to understand what he meant by that talk. What you told Alexander the Natives did not believe and came here to find out. After we learn that, we will talk."

Alexander then asked the congressman to repeat what he had said at Tolovana so the Natives could hear it directly for themselves.

"Oh, Alexander told you the truth," Wickersham responded. "I talked to him and told him about homesteads and reservations just as he told you I did. He told you the truth."

The testimony at the meeting was translated by Paul Williams, a thirty-three-year-old native of Tanana who had served as lay worker and reader for the Episcopal Church in Nenana and Tanana for fourteen years. As the Natives spoke no English and the white participants spoke no Athabascan, Williams was required to interpret both ways and to make certain that the English was given accurately to the stenographer employed to record the proceedings. His job was made even more difficult by the varieties of Athabascan languages and dialects present. The men from Tanana and Cosjacket spoke Koyukon, while the rest spoke one of three dialects of Lower Tanana. It is likely that the Natives all understood one another, as there was a long tradition of multilingual speech among northern Athabascans. Only Chief Joe of Salchaket spoke a dialect that was so different from the rest of Lower Tanana that Williams had to interpret for him separately.

Continuing his opening comments, Wickersham stressed the advantages of an Indian reservation. It could be made anywhere the people chose, he promised, "at Salchaket, or at Nenana, or at Tolovana, or at Kantishna, or at Cosjacket, or at Fort Gibbon. You and your people could build an Indian town there. You could have a church there, a school, and an Indian agent, an official agent of the President, who would show you how to plow land and raise potatoes and other crops."

Again, he left the Natives with a warning: "The white men are going to take all this good land, and when all the good land is gone, the white men are going to keep on taking more land. After a while the Indian will have no land at all. He cannot live in the water, and he will have nothing to do."

Wickersham's embracement of the reservation plan was in fact a reversal of a policy he had adhered to from the earliest days of his first term in Congress beginning in 1908. In response to pleas from Episcopal Alaska Bishop Peter Trimble Rowe for a reservation plan, the delegate had dismissed Indian reservations as unworkable in Alaska. Rowe's extensive travels throughout the territory since 1894 had left him appalled at the poor medical and sanitary conditions in many Native villages and at the "vicious class of white men" that profited by the liquor trade with Natives. The solution he proposed to Wickersham was to confine the Natives to their villages under the authority of the Army, and he asked the delegate to work for Congressional action to accomplish it.

Wickersham's answer to Rowe was cool and deliberate. "I have often considered the question of the reservation system in Alaska and frankly I do not like it," he wrote. "It has never worked satisfactorily outside and it would work less so here, I am afraid."

He recognized the needs Rowe had outlined for medical care and relief from famine in lean times of the year, but concluded, "If the Indians were let alone nine-tenths and protected one-tenth they would be much better off than if it were reversed." He suggested a policy of giving individual Natives a homestead in addition to issuing patents for village sites and "thus give them some hold on the great country which they once owned."[69]

Rowe, however, was not deterred. He described "conditions of widespread drinking, fornication, etc. among the Natives which fairly make my heart sink," adding, "they are simply going to destruction in the face of civilization."[70] In January 1912, Rowe took his argument to Washington, where he appeared before the House Committee on the Territories, of which Wickersham was a member. The "deplorable and shameful" condition of Alaska Natives, Rowe testified, was owing entirely to easy access to liquor and the lack of any effective law enforcement. He urged Congress to set up reservations where the scattered tribes could be gathered, where the government could provide health and education services, and where there would be no access to liquor.

"If you can only get them on the reservation," he told the committee. "Once you get them there, they would be very submissive."[71]

Wickersham said little during that 1912 committee meeting, agreeing only to confer with Rowe to develop a plan for assisting the Natives. Privately, however, he resolved to oppose any system of reservations. "I think there is but little to expect from his [Rowe's] plan," he noted, "for it has long been the policy of the government not to establish reservations in Alaska." Instead, Wickersham repeated his ideas for offering individual home sites along with tracts of about two square miles for each village. "But no more," he added.[72]

In fact, by this time, U.S. federal Indian policy had largely turned away from establishment of new reservations in favor of general allotments for individual use. The Dawes Act of 1887 created a system under which Native Americans could receive title to 160-acre parcels of land in an effort to orient them away from tribal hunting and gathering customs toward an individual agricultural lifestyle. The allotment act had been extended to

Alaska, but its emphasis on agriculture made it, like the traditional reservation system, largely unfeasible there. Assimilation of Natives into the modern American economy and society remained the goal of federal policy, but now the leading agents of government, rather than working to eradicate all elements of tribal life, had begun to recognize the worth of traditional customs and family attachments. They began to see that full assimilation into white America was an unrealistic expectation and that government should recognize the value of preserving what was best in Native culture. The focus shifted to self-reliance through education and vocational training while allowing the Natives to hold onto the heritage and customs that made them Natives.[73]

Wickersham fully endorsed such goals and values, but, as the July 1915 meeting convened and railroad construction threatened Athabascan homelands, circumstances limited his options. The best he was able to offer to the Tanana chiefs was a return to the reservation system, which he himself had rejected three years before.

Bishop Rowe and the Episcopal Church were represented at the meeting by Guy Madara, a young missionary who four years before took residency in the town of Chena as a lay worker for the church. Since then, Madara had traveled tirelessly between camps and villages along the Tanana ministering to the spiritual needs of the Natives and earning a reputation as an extremely fast and durable musher. But also, as fellow missionary Frederick Drane observed, he was "keenly sympathetic, keenly interested in the welfare of these Indians." Indeed, Drane continued, "He is perhaps the most influential man in the Valley with the Natives, and for the 600 miles of this parish he is loved by all."[74]

By 1915, the town of Chena was in serious decline. Once a thriving transportation hub at the confluence of the Chena and Tanana Rivers, it shriveled as Fairbanks grew, and now had nothing going for it except a steamboat dock and the head of the Tanana Valley Railroad. Still, the town's location served Madara's purposes well. From there he could access the Tanana River corridor upriver to St. Luke's Mission at Salchaket, down three miles to St. Barnabas at the Indian village of Chena, or fifty miles farther downriver to St. Mark's at Nenana.

On May 22, 1915, just six weeks before the chiefs' meeting with Wickersham, Madara had been ordained as an Episcopal deacon. At the forefront of his concerns on July 5 and 6 was the need to prepare the

Natives for the coming of the railroad. Since 1907, St. Mark's Mission at Nenana had developed into the Episcopalians' proudest venture in the Interior. With a church, boarding school, hospital, and seven workers to serve the Native population, it had become the "model mission" that Bishop Rowe had hoped to build.[75] And the missionaries knew that its success was due for the most part to its isolation. As Archdeacon Hudson Stuck explained, Nenana suffered none of the influences of the "low-down white population" that had caused the deplorable conditions among Natives at many other locations. Stuck cited Tanana at the confluence of the Tanana and Yukon Rivers as the example of the worst of these conditions. The white community had grown up quickly adjacent to the Army's Fort Gibbon, and the Native village at St. James Mission was only three miles away. "Toughs and bad characters," Stuck complained, are thrown out of Dawson and Fairbanks and spend their summers at Tanana "hanging about the nine saloons that the town boasts," and the result was disastrous for the Natives.[76]

Madara was well aware that Nenana was destined to become a major construction center for the railroad, and that the advantage of isolation that the missionaries had enjoyed there would soon be lost. His comments during the opening session of the conference were brief. He made only a short statement in which he cited two problems with the idea of individual homesteads. First, the system required Natives to abandon tribal relations and live alone, and, second, it demanded proof of permanent improvement and continuous occupancy. For people who lived a hunting-and-gathering lifestyle outside the cash economy, such proof was impossible to provide.

Madara then said that he wished to hear the opinions of the Natives themselves. Immediately, Paul Williams expanded on the missionary's points. "They do not have the money to build a cabin on a homestead," he insisted, "and they cannot stay there continually for they depend for a living upon their fishing, hunting and trapping and they have to travel far to do this." Williams rejected the homestead plan for the same reason he opposed reservations. "It would take them away from the old homes and habits where they have been used to living."

Already by late in the morning, it had become apparent that both the homestead allotment and the reservation plans would be hard to sell to the Natives. C. W. Richie of the federal land office in Fairbanks attempted to reassure them that the homestead program could work for them, explaining that every head of a family could file for 160 acres. "He need not live on it all the time," Richie said, "but it should be his home the same as a white man makes a homestead his home."

Finally, just before a break at 2:00 p.m., Thomas Riggs of the Alaskan Engineering Commission, the agency established to oversee construction of the Alaska Railroad, made a last pitch. In the face of what must have already appeared to be unyielding opposition, Riggs urged the Natives to take action soon. "After the railroad which we are building comes into this country, it will be overrun with white people," he said. "They will kill off your game, your moose, your caribou, and your sheep." Riggs warned the Natives that they must protect themselves through one of the methods available to them under existing law. "When you have land either in a reservation or homestead you will have something of value, something that you can live on, something on which you can always make a living by work, which need not be too hard."

The presence of Riggs and his assistant G. Fenton Cramer at the meeting was an indicator of the dominance that railroad construction held over nearly all aspects of life in Interior Alaska at that time. The gold rush had fueled the growth of Fairbanks beginning in 1903 and had sustained it during several peak production years on the outlying creeks. However, by 1915, signs of decline were evident, and the future of the city was not at all certain. Though the town boasted a modern municipal power plant, electric street lighting, and telephone service, transportation of passengers and freight was still conducted by steamboat or over the primitive trail from Valdez or Chitina. Residents and merchants were counting on the railroad to bring cheaper, faster service and a boom that would change Fairbanks from a mining camp to a city of stability and permanence. A local newspaper declared that "the new government railroad is the magic wand that is promising to change it all and make of this neglected land a country of almost unlimited opportunities."[77] In short, a group known as the Fairbanks Commercial Club proclaimed, "[It] will undoubtedly result in Fairbanks becoming the Chicago of Alaska."[78]

The bill authorizing construction of the government railroad was passed by Congress on March 12, 1914. It allocated $35 million for the project and directed the president to designate a route from a Pacific Ocean harbor to the Interior. By executive order on April 10, 1915, Woodrow Wilson directed that the line would run from Seward to Fairbanks, and he ordered the secretary of the interior to oversee construction.

For Wickersham, this authorization marked the end of a hard-fought battle. First elected to Congress as a Republican, Wickersham had drifted toward the Progressive wing of the party. The Progressive philosophy of responsible resource development and unbending resistance to corporate monopoly fit perfectly with his vision for Alaska. While Wickersham fought bitterly with Republican president William Howard Taft because of Taft's lenient stand toward the interests of large corporate trusts, he saw opportunity for the territory with the election of the Democrat Wilson in 1912. Wilson and his Interior Department secretary Franklin K. Lane immediately advanced a plan to unlock the resources of Alaska, and to do so with a railroad built and operated by the federal government. Wickersham had sponsored the legislation in 1914 to build the railroad.

"That is progressive democracy," Wickersham stated on the floor of the House of Representatives, "and I shall give it my approval and support."[79]

Key to Wickersham's enthusiasm was the administration's commitment to government, rather than corporate, control of the railroad. As delegate to Congress, he had sworn to resist any measure of corporate monopoly, and in the fight for the Alaska Railway Bill, he attacked the trust known as the Alaska Syndicate with a vengeance. Owned by financier J. P. Morgan and the Guggenheim family, the syndicate already dominated much of the territory's shipping, mining, and railroad infrastructure, and Wickersham was determined to stand in the way of further control. To him the syndicate, particularly the Guggenheims, represented nothing less than the "overshadowing evil" that darkened all of Alaska's economic future. He saw the railway bill as a struggle between federal power and the interests of the syndicate.

"Which shall it be," he challenged in debate on the House floor, "Government or Guggenheim?"[80]

Immediately following Congressional authorization, Wilson appointed a three-man Alaskan Engineering Commission, which included Thomas Riggs as head of the northern section. Beginning in the summer of 1914, Riggs landed crews of men and horses at Nenana and began survey work south to Broad Pass and north to Fairbanks. Though Riggs had impeccable credentials as a surveyor, Wickersham, for political reasons, was not enthused about his appointment as a commissioner. In 1913, Riggs's name had come up as a possible appointment as territorial governor. Wickersham opposed the appointment on grounds of Riggs's close association with Wilford Hoggatt, a former Alaska governor whom Wickersham branded as a paid Guggenheim lobbyist. "The Big Interests," according to Wickersham, "all want Riggs, who is a miniature Hoggatt."[81] In the end, Wickersham's preferred candidate, John F. S. Strong, received the appointment.

Despite their political differences, however, Wickersham and Riggs found themselves together in the log library building in Fairbanks that July day, 1915, trying to persuade fourteen Athabascan tribal leaders that they should, for their own good, confine themselves to a plot of land prescribed by a government seated four thousand miles away. When all had taken their seats after the two-hour break, it became clear that the Natives had considered the options and found their position. Chief Ivan of Cosjacket was the first to address the group. "We don't want to go on a reservation," he said bluntly, "but wish to stay perfectly free just as we are now."

The Natives took this opportunity to speak in turn. Chief Thomas of Wood River reiterated the general opposition to reservations, then charged, "You people of the government, Delegate Wickersham, Mr. Riggs, and Mr. Richie, you people don't go around enough to learn the way the Indians are living." Yet in the end he expressed confidence that the government officials would do the right thing for his people. "I wish to show you that you are touching my heart and at the same time I wish to touch your heart. We want to feel that you are going to allow us to have just what we are asking for."

Chief Charley of Minto expressed similar expectations. "If the white people are coming in here like slush ice to cover all the villages, we expect your people to protect us from them."

Chief Alexander, the man whom Wickersham met in Tolovana, summed things up in starker terms. "I tell you that we are people that are always on the go, and I believe that if we were put in one place we would die off like rabbits."

A song written by Paul Williams's brother Silas Williams and sung at a potlatch in Tanana that year implored, "Uncle Sam, please now, do not put us on the reservation." Frederick Drane recalled later that the song "had a very pretty tune and . . . was the hit of the potlatch."[82]

But while the Natives rejected the reservation system out of hand,[83] some, such as Paul Williams, were interested in leaving open the homestead allotment option. Episcopal Missionary Guy Madara, after Williams prodded him to speak, said that allotments could work in some cases, but he worried that people living separately on these parcels would kill the sense of community that was so much a part of Native life. "There is in Indian life one very sweet feature, their mutual helpfulness. There is no such thing in an Indian village of one person having plenty and others being hungry. If one man kills a moose, this moose belongs to the whole village. That is what we call a community life. It would be too bad if that were taken away."

At the end of the first day, as the Natives unanimously rejected the government's best offers, Wickersham held firm to his message. "I don't agree with the people here," he concluded. "I think that a reservation is excellent and the best thing that can be done for the Indians." He then added one final word of warning. "Mr. Riggs is going to build a railroad, and when Mr. Riggs' railroad is built, the people are going to come in here in great numbers and push and push until the Indians are clear off the best land. You must do something."

The Natives did indeed have a plan to do something, and it came clear as the meeting reconvened at 4:00 p.m. on the next day, July 6. With the reservation plan either concluded, stalled, or part of a larger discussion needing more time and discussion, Paul Williams outlined the need for government-sponsored industrial schools to teach job skills for the modern economy.

"You want to learn trades?" Wickersham asked.

"Yes," Williams replied, and he went on to ask for government assistance to build industrial boarding schools at key locations in the Tanana River region.

Lastly, the Natives wanted equal access to railroad construction jobs and contracts to cut wood and supply fish to government telegraph stations and Army posts. Williams complained that the Natives had been overlooked for such work but were fully as capable as white men to perform it. "That is why we want the schools, to learn these things," Williams said, adding in summary that the three things the Natives wanted were "school, a doctor, and some labor."

In closing the meeting, Wickersham promised to send to the secretary of the interior a full report of what the Natives said. The transcript was prepared and mailed to Franklin K. Lane on July 22 along with a cover letter in which Wickersham implored the secretary, "Will you not kindly read this record and consider what ought to be done for these people before all the good land and fishing sites are taken up by the white men?"[84]

Clearly, the delegate was at a loss for answers. Having spent most of his political career opposing establishment of Indian reservations in Alaska, he reversed himself when the reality of railroad construction presented the greatest threat ever to Native life. Yet he should not have been surprised when the Natives rejected his proposal to take title to a tiny piece of reserved land and give up their rights to the expanses of rivers and forests that their people had freely occupied forever.

In Wickersham's progressive view of American democracy, it was the job of government to open the doors to the frontier and allow miners and farmers to develop its resources and settle new regions. Similarly, Interior Secretary Lane, in throwing the full weight of his office behind the Alaska Railway Bill in 1913, envisioned Alaska as "a land not only of mines and fisheries, but of towns, farms, mills, and factories supporting millions of people of the hardiest and most wholesome of the race," and he called on Congress to make this dream a reality.[85]

It was a future that Wickersham took to heart. On the day before the opening of his meeting with the Athabascan chiefs, he delivered a speech at the laying of the cornerstone at the site where the Alaska Agricultural College and School of Mines, now the University of Alaska Fairbanks, would be built. The federal government had designated 2,560 acres for the new institution and, in addition, a land grant amounting to possibly 200,000 acres of what Wickersham termed "the most valuable lands in the Tanana valley." On that Independence Day, 1915, it was natural to view such progress in terms of the nation's history and its destiny. "Our people have spread from Bunker Hill and Saratoga," Wickersham said, "from Trenton and Yorktown to the distant shores of the Pacific and thence northward to the Arctic."[86]

Still, he lamented the loss of the traditional Athabascan way of life. Two months earlier, on a warm, cloudless spring morning, Wickersham sat on a low ridge somewhere in Minto Flats and wrote of the stunning view as he gazed across the Tanana Valley all the way to Mount Hayes in the south. "It is the most beautiful view in the Interior. An Indian's paradise. If I were an Indian I would wish to be buried on this spot." Later that day, after traveling down the Tolovana to Chief Alexander's village on the Tanana, he continued, "It has been a day to remember, a hunter's—Indian's—paradise. . . . The Indians protest against the entrance of the white man into their hunting grounds. But in vain."[87]

4

Alaska Native Leader Will
Mayo Shares His Perspective
on the 1915 Tanana Chiefs
Meeting

Mayo, Will. "Tom Alton, Will Mayo, and Bill Schneider on April 22, 2015, in Fairbanks, Alaska, about the historic Tanana Chiefs Meeting with James Wickersham in 1915." Recording 2015-10, Parts 1 and 2. Oral History Collection, Alaska and Polar Regions Collections and Archives.

This is a transcript of the 2015 recording, with further comments and editing.

My name is Will Mayo and I am the son of Arthur Mayo Sr. from Rampart and Agnes Mathew Mayo Moore. She's from Tanana and was born at Mission Creek, which is about four miles above Tanana. And I am in the direct bloodline of the delegate that is in the center row, second from the left in this photograph. He is Chief William, *Setseye*. He is actually my grandfather's brother. So that would make him my great uncle. In our Indian way I call him grandfather or *Setseye*. He was the representative from Tanana. We have in the audience Chief Victor Joseph. He is the current chief of the Tanana Chiefs Conference and he is in the direct line of Chief Jacob Starr, shown in the middle section of the photograph on the far left. We also have Guy Peters who is also in the direct line of the Tanana delegate, Chief William. Annette Freiburger is also here and her mother, Effie Kokrine, is the daughter of John Folger from Tanana. He is seated in the bottom row in the middle.

I was asked to talk about what has happened since the 1915 meeting, and I can share a perspective on that having been an elected leader of the villages in this region for several terms and I wrestle with the very issues raised at that meeting. The key thing to remember here is that the issues voiced by the Indian chiefs are still current to one degree or another. This

JULIUS PILOT.   TITUS ALEXANDER.   CRAMER.   THOMAS RIGGS, Jr.   RICHIE.   CHIEF ALEXANDER WILLIAM.
        NENANA.   HOTSPRINGS.   TANANA.
    JACOB STARR.   CHIEF WILLIAM.   CHIEF ALEXANDER.   CHIEF THOMAS.   HON. JAMES WICKERSHAM.   CHIEF EVAN.   CHIEF CHARLIE.
          TANANA.   TANANA.   TOLOVANA.   NENANA.   KOSCHAKAT.   MINTO.
      CHIEF JOE.   CHIEF JOHN.   JOHNNIE FOLGER.   REV. GUY H. MADARA.   PAUL WILLIAMS.
          SALCHAKAT.   CHENA.   TANANA.   CHENA.   TANANA.

Council held at Fairbanks, Alaska, July 5 and 6, 1915.
ASL-P277-011-072. Collection name: Wickersham State Historic Site, Photographs, 1882–1930s. ASL-PCA-277.

is true even of land claims. The land claims act was signed December 18, 1971, but ever since then, there have been land disputes and you can be assured land claims is an on-going issue. Congress has amended the Alaska Native Claims Settlement Act on a number of occasions to address land claims issues that were not adequately addressed or that were discovered later. I think it will continue from time to time and there will continue to be amendments to the Act.[88]

Alton mentioned in his talk the business of Delegate Wickersham with Chief Alexander of Tolovana. I want to add to that a bit. After he met with Delegate Wickersham earlier in the summer of 1915, Chief Alexander went to the other chiefs and began talking about that meeting. So, he was sharing with them what Wickersham had told him and, as is very clear in the record, none of the other chiefs believed him. And I imagine he was rather put out being a man of integrity. I think the Tanana Chiefs meeting was quite a big day for Chief Alexander because it is recorded in the transcript of the meeting, that he said, I told them and they didn't believe me. Immediately after Chief Alexander spoke, Delegate Wickersham rose to speak and he said, everything that Chief Alexander said is true. So, I can imagine Chief Alexander looking around at the guys and saying, see, see. He had been vindicated that day, and that's a big thing in the Native culture, to be called out as a liar or to be questioned in your leadership.

As you know, when the written language developed mankind lost their ability to memorize and that loss has been tremendous because we learned to depend on the written word. People who know about how important, how powerful human memory and memorization is, they will realize that we lost entire stories that were told verbatim. Anyone who misspoke, even one word from the old stories that were used in higher education, in the Athabascan culture, were told to step down, get back, go learn it, then maybe we'll give you another chance to tell those stories. In the Athabascan culture the time of education from elementary to higher education was in fall and winter and the ancient stories were called, *Kk'edonts'ednee*. The time of the year for storytelling began with the darkness of fall and the coming of colder weather and continued until the winter solstice. After that, the sun would show itself more and they would get back busy to the business of life. But, until that time, they would usually be ready for a long cold spell, stay indoors, and eat the food they had prepared for the winter. So, I just say that I think it was a big day for Chief Alexander and I really felt good for him as I read the transcript.

Delegate Wickersham came to the meeting with an agenda. He told the chiefs, you need a reservation to protect yourselves and you also have the opportunity of homesteads (allotments). Mr. Madara from the Episcopal Church pointed out rightfully that the Native community takes care of each other. If you are proposing that you are going to put them on a little dot of land, then you are going to change their entire way of living which is to move seasonally to fish and hunt. Wickersham really pushed the reservation as a means of protecting their land base.

I think that the reading of the transcript is a little bittersweet for me. I can't ever read that transcript without interjecting myself in the conversation and saying, "Guys, listen up, this is really amazing, an amazing opportunity." But of course, the chiefs could not understand the experience of tribes in the rest of the country. They could not understand what was coming, even though Wickersham and Riggs, and others were very clear that the impacts would be severe. They were saying, you need to address the question of land now. As I read the transcript, here is where I go in my thinking. We have villages all over Alaska that received a land settlement for land around their communities and that list of communities or villages did not include Cosjacket; it did not include Tolovana; it did not include Salchaket. All those people who are alive today, who are descendants of those communities, they were left out of receiving a land claim. Minchumina and the Minchumina settlement was also left out, even though there is clear history of their settlement and use of the area. The Bearpaw mountain settlement section should have been included as well. Representatives of these groups weren't of course at the 1915 meeting but Cosjacket, Salchaket, and Tolovana were there and they, to this day, do not have a land settlement. Also, Chena does not have a settlement. And that's a community right here in the basin. I think today, and my mind begins to imagine the descendants of Chena having a reservation adjacent to Fairbanks. I think about the success stories all across the United States of tribes that have reservation land settlements in proximity to population centers. I think about the benefits they have for economic development and community partnerships. If Chena could have secured a land base, they could have benefited from development in the Fairbanks area. If that village had been able to survive and not been overrun and if they had not, for whatever reasons, dissipated into history, in the foggy history, how could they have benefited?

In my youth, I was partially raised by an elder from Salchaket, a descendant of the Salchaket people, Eva Moffit. And I think about her descendants and the families that could have had a reservation, a land settlement in the Salcha area, and what that could have meant for them and the survival of their community. This is where my mind goes, Tolovana, same thing; Cosjacket same thing. I'm still active in the National Native American Forums and I hear all the stories, and I hear about the opportunities that they have developed. But, of course, these opportunities weren't recognized in 1915 by the leaders.

Another issue that was raised was federal consultations. The chiefs called for explanations of congressional acts in writing. This was a specific request. They said, we need consultations with the government. As leaders, we will impart to our people the information. So, they wanted to establish a government-to-government relationship whereby the information could be exchanged about fish and game regulations, legislation, and budgetary matters. That was very ably stated in the opening comments by Chief William of Tanana, and we are still working to build the relationships.

For instance, in the area of fishing regulations, we are attempting to forge new relationships, new partnerships with the government, the federal, state, and other fishing interest groups to meet these challenges. Tribal and federal consultations with our tribal leadership in the Interior is a very high priority and we will challenge both the federal government and the state government at every opportunity just as Chief William and Chief Thomas challenged the federal delegate to Congress in their day. Our chiefs are meeting and sitting across the table from congressional representatives, federal administrative representatives, anyone that they can get to the table. And the message is absolutely the same—we need consultation. And Chief William further elucidated his statement by saying we need it in writing. He said, "I don't know how to write or read writing but we have young people who are in school and they will read it to us." So, the call for meaningful consultations is verbatim what is being stated right now today in meetings across the Nation.

The leaders even called for Native representation in Congress. This was brought up in the transcript by Chief Jacob Strarr who said, "We have been discussing how we need a representative. We need a representative to speak for us." So, they were already discussing representation in the Nation's governing body. That was very striking, amazing when you think back to a time when many people thought, "ok, dumb Natives; they don't know what they don't have." But that wasn't true. As the transcript reveals in a number of places, they were very forward thinking and way ahead of their time. I was very pleased to see the issue of representation was brought up by Chief Jacob Starr.

When Riggs was giving his warnings to the chiefs about the coming impacts, he was prophetic. He talked about the fish. Now, we may have strong runs of chums and silvers, but the king salmon, the primary source of fish protein for the Interior people, has crashed and we cannot get adequate escapement to sustain the population. This is an incredible challenge. Once again, Riggs was right and we are facing that challenge right this day and we are doing our best to try to address enhancement of the fishery. Our tribes in the Interior along with tribes in the Yukon/Kuskokwim Delta last year decided to self-impose a moratorium on the fishing of Chinook stocks because of this situation. They did this even though we still had high seas interception of the fish.

Hunting threats from the influx of newcomers was a concern of the chiefs and the government representatives. In community after community, the challenges of hunting and fishing are still an issue. This last year, we had a community where only eight families successfully got a moose. Part of that was because the season was late and the weather was not cooperating in the usual way that it triggers the rut and movement of the bull moose. That was part of the problem, but the other part of the problem was tremendous pressure on the moose population in that area. I remember thirty years ago the game populations in that area were thirteen moose per square mile, absolutely the highest density of moose in the state of Alaska. That information was not widely known for many years. And when it became known, the influx of hunters from all over the nation severely depleted the population of moose and today they are tightly regulated in that area. Whether it is the Minto Flats or the Fish Creek/Fish Lake area near Tanana or the Novi (Nowitna River), or down near the Koyukuk River and up to Three Day Slough, and all those places—through the deepest parts of the Interior—there's pressure from a large number of hunters. It is just as Riggs predicted; it is exactly what is being experienced today. The management challenges of these issues are tremendous and the Native leadership is working very hard for a place at the table where we can wield real power as equal decision makers in co-management, and not just be an advisory voice among many.

As you know, the Native community in Alaska cannot hunt whenever they need meat; they can't just go get caribou or moose whenever they want. There are seasons and bag limits and gear restrictions and all kinds of things. We are made to hunt during a particular time period. That was a tremendous change from the cultural way our ancestors hunted. When I was in Canada and parts of the lower 48, I visited reserves and reservations where the Native people there have power to regulate their own take. They have their own management system for fish and game. I think about the Mistassini, the Cree of Northern Quebec, where my tribal friend there invites me all the time to come over for moose. They manage their stocks and their supplies very well. And down in the lower 48 some of the reservations there successfully manage their stocks and their fish and game. In fact, they're turning it into an economic development engine. I think about the Apache tribes that I visit. They have guided elk hunts and they have more clients than they can handle. And they use the means from those hunts to provide jobs for their tribal members as well as to provide revenues for governmental functions. I have often mourned the fact that we are not permitted to manage the fish and game anymore.

The chiefs also brought up labor contracts and jobs. This issue had considerable discussion in the meeting and they were very frank. They said, we can't get contracts. The army lets out contracts for wood and they let out contracts for other commodities. We can't get them; they give them to the white members of the community. So, they were very forthcoming in their challenge. It was interesting that Delegate Wickersham responded by asking them why they didn't get the contracts and Paul Williams, the interpreter from Tanana said it was because they couldn't read the notices and the white men would find out about the work before them. The chiefs knew how important education was and the need for schools was voiced very early in the meeting by Chief Thomas of Nenana. They saw education as a way to participate and keep informed of new developments and economic opportunities in their region.

Access to economic opportunities continues to be a challenge, so much so that Congress passed specific acts to try to ensure availability for Native Americans under the Federal Trust relationship. It is still an issue, but it's improving. There has been a lot of progress and there are a lot of Native people in the workforce who are contributing tremendously to the economy today. Our Native corporations are tremendous engines of economic opportunity and development in the state of Alaska. If you look at the top forty-nine businesses, there will always be Native American corporations. One of them broke a billion dollars in revenues. Really, there's a lot of good news, but economic opportunity is still an issue in some circles.

Health care was another issue that was raised. It's an issue in our Nation; it's an issue in our Native community. We have made tremendous strides in that area. Congress funds health care for Native Americans. Tribes in Alaska organized to assume full management of their health care system throughout the state replacing the federal management structure with a Native controlled structure. This has been an example of Native management success that has brought a tremendous improvement to our health care system. This is an unprecedented move by tribes. Alaska is the only example of this level of inter-tribal cooperation.

These are the issues that were raised. I will close by just saying, whenever I read the transcript, and I read it fairly regularly every couple of years, I just seem to glean something new, and I have become very appreciative of the intelligence and foresight of the leaders and the challenges they faced. When I take their comments and bring them forward to this day, I see we have made lots and lots of progress, but we still have a lot of challenges as well. We have a land settlement and it is working and we have made huge strides in education. I like to say, in some ways, we've been a victim of our own success. And I want to explain that. A few years ago we began to push education for our young people very hard. In fact, we produced whole crops of teachers, whole crops, and we're producing whole crops of business majors, and biologists. We're proud of every one of them and we have more coming along. There's a wave of young people with education under their belt. The victim part is that success has created an out flow from our villages. Our success in getting them into higher education created a desire for good jobs and for a different way of life or some place where there is more opportunity. And we are now looking at how we can bring that skill set back into our villages.

5

The Fester

by William Schneider

The 1915 Tanana Chiefs meeting was part of a larger long struggle that began before 1915 and would continue on afterward, and should not be viewed in a vacuum. Like a stubborn wound, the issue of land claims and Native rights is still extremely difficult to resolve. There are cultural, legal, and economic divides between Alaska's Native population and Western society, and each of these played a role in thwarting settlement. But, as I read about land claims in Southeast Alaska (Metcalfe 2014), another image comes to mind, a giant puzzle with the first pieces to the puzzle of Native land claims coming together in Southeast Alaska and as that pattern emerges, the other pieces come into place. For one thing, the Tlingit-Haida settlement in 1959 (Arnold 1976:91; Haycox 1996:357) established the precedent that Alaska Natives could sue the government for land claims (Metcalfe 2014:26). That was a big legal hurdle. Another factor leading to the larger settlement was the example and assistance the Alaska Native Brotherhood lent to the rest of the state in terms of precedent and tactical help to other Native groups. Of course, there were additional factors that added to the momentum toward recognition and settlement of Native rights. State land selections in the early 1960s and major development schemes threatened Native livelihoods. And the biggest impetus of all was the Trans-Alaska oil pipeline (Coates 1991). Taken together, these developments pushed the issue of land claims and Native rights to a head, but the fester began in Southeast Alaska and the momentum spread north.

Land Claims in the Southeast

In an 1870 Treasury Department Report, Captain Charles Bryant, special agent of the Treasury Department, stated that the Tlingit never recognized the Russians as owning their land and they held that the Russians should have at least consulted them about the Treaty of Cession.[89] In 1891, a Chilkat Tlingit leader addressing Governor Lyman Knapp stated:

> I now ask you to settle our troubles for us. We want a mark set to keep fishing boats from going above a line drawn across the inlet at Little Harbor. . . . We want to know what our rights are. Whether the whites intend to give us any fishing grounds that we can call our own. I am speaking for my people and we have a right to talk and tell the Great Father. (Price 1990:i)

In 1898, the Tlingit were on public record exclaiming their claims to Governor Brady and seeking protection of subsistence sites (Hinckley 1970). Contacted first by the Russians, then the Spanish, the English, and the Americans, the legacy of competing claims by explorers and fur traders to the land, the game, the fish, and the timber goes back to the latter half of the eighteenth century (Brooks 1973:149–163). How different this is from the Natives of the Tanana and Copper River Valleys, whose land remained uncontested until the prospectors and settlers spilled over into their homeland.

One response of southeast Native leaders to white intrusion and control was to form the Alaska Native Brotherhood (ANB). Established in 1912, the Brotherhood advocated members accept many of the requirements of white society, but in time the goal became more directly focused on advancement of Native values and rights.[90] These would eventually include citizenship and compensation for land claims (Metcalfe 2014:6–8). The Brotherhood built strength in numbers and approached the challenges of government with the parliamentary and legal tools of the Western system they were attempting to influence. This must have been attractive to James Wickersham when he joined forces in 1929 with prominent ANB member, William Paul. They teamed up to work toward a land settlement for Southeast Alaska Natives. Fourteen years after the 1915 Tanana Chiefs meeting, Wickersham had found a new way to address Native land grievances.

In 1929, James Wickersham's term as delegate to Congress was over and he was in private practice, residing in Juneau. William Paul was a Tlingit lawyer, the first to pass the bar (1921) and the first Native to serve in the Territorial legislature (Metcalfe 2014:20). Paul was educated at Sheldon Jackson, the Carlisle Indian School in Pennsylvania, Whitworth University, and LaSalle University where he studied law (*Gastineau Heritage News* 2015). Wickersham and Paul formed a team; the former brought contacts in Congress and the authority and experience of government office; the latter brought a strong passion for redress, a legal background in Western law, and a position within the Brotherhood to advance the proposal (Metcalfe 2014:104–105; Haycox 1994:508). When Wickersham came into contact with William Paul, he met a man whose cause he could embrace, and because Paul was operating in the same legal system with the same tools, they were natural partners in the effort.

The idea of taking a stand on the land issue was not new to Paul. The story is told that Paul was influenced to fight for land claims by the elder Peter Simpson, who pulled him aside at an ANB meeting in 1925 where the discussion was over fox farmers driving Natives off of the land. It is reported that Simpson whispered in Paul's ear, "This land is yours. . . . Why don't you fight for it?" (Haycox 1994:514; Metcalfe 2014:23). It is believed that Simpson's words stuck with Paul and took root in 1929 when he sought an agreement of the Brotherhood to bring suit against the United States government (Metcalfe 2014:23).

Recalling Wickersham's words to the Tanana Chiefs, "You tell them that as soon as they have established homes and live like the white men and assume the habits of civilization, they can have a vote,"[91] it is easy to see why he agreed to work with Paul and the ANB. The ANB represented the approach Wickersham was looking for in 1915 with the Interior chiefs. Members of the ANB and their families were living their lives balanced on the social scale of what was an acceptable standard in white society. William Paul's life and practice was a prime example of working within the white system to achieve extraordinary ends that benefited Native people.

Wickersham saw a legal opening as well. The Tlingit people could demonstrate clan ownership of particular sites and the history of ownership could be shown, including their mechanisms for acquisition and disposal through war, inheritance, and a complicated but specific system of reciprocity. Wickersham claimed the Natives of the Southeast were the first to make such a claim. He told them: "Nobody ever asked to be paid for their land so far."[92] Maybe this is true in a literal sense, but we are reminded of Chief Joe's comments at the 1915 meeting: "We are suggesting to you just one thing, that we want to be left alone. As the whole Continent was made for you, God made Alaska for the Indian people, and all we hope is to be able to live here all the time. And we wish to ask you to give us written instructions on our matters."[93]

Giving Wickersham the benefit of the doubt, we might suppose the Interior Natives were not directly asking for resolution of their unsettled claim to land but merely wishing to be left alone in their pursuit of hunting and fishing and to have some measure of protection against the incursion of outsiders. More likely, Wickersham was influenced by the specifics of the Southeast claims against the United States government for not protecting Native holdings on federal land in the Tongass National Forest and Glacier Bay National Monument. He may have seen this as different from the more generalized plight of Interior Natives trying to address the wave of prospectors and settlers in the Tanana Valley. Perhaps he just recognized an opportunity.

The jurisdictional act for Tlingit-Haida redress was prepared by Wickersham and introduced to Congress in 1931 but was not passed (Metcalfe 2014:26). Despite this setback, the effort toward land settlement had been formally broached and would fester. Finally, in 1935, Congress passed a jurisdictional land act that allowed the Tlingit-Haida to seek redress (ibid:27-28). Then, in 1959, Congress agreed that these Natives had a claim (ibid:8, see also *Tlingit and Haida Indians of Alaska v. United States*). Despite the setback the effort toward land settlement had been formally broached and would fester. Finally, in 1959, it was agreed that the Natives had a claim (Metcalfe 2014:8). However, the actual award of $7.5 million was not made until 1968 when the federal government issued a "determination of liability" (Jones 1981:v; Haycox and McClanahan 2007:181). The settlement recognized the existence of uncompensated land claims in the Tongass National Forest and Glacier Bay National Monument (Metcalfe 2014:39). This was both recognition of Native possessory rights and the United States government's responsibility to protect those "indigenous possessory rights" (Case and Voluck 2012:61–62). Passage of the Tlingit-Haida settlement represented a solid legal step toward a wider settlement for other Alaska Natives, but it took many more years for the rest to be achieved, for there to be a settlement for all Alaska Natives.[94]

Statehood, Development Schemes, and the Native Response

In the 1950s, Alaska statehood occupied the minds of most Alaskans and Native land claims often got ignored. The argument frequently given was that this was a federal issue and shouldn't hold up Alaska becoming a state and selecting land (Fischer 1975:137–139). However, Native land claims became a big problem when the new state began selecting land in the 1960s. Natives in the Interior took notice.[95] In 1962, at a meeting in Nenana, Al Ketzler put it this way: "If we don't act soon, the state will have taken up all the good hunting and fishing land and we won't be able to get it back."[96]

Al Ketzler was a Native leader from Nenana. He organized the meeting of chiefs to address the government's dismissal of land claims put forward by several villages in the Interior: Minto, Northway, and Tanacross. Their claims were under appeal and Ketzler wanted to get the villages of the region to act together to make a stand on land claims before the new state made further selections.[97] At that meeting there were representatives from Copper Center, Nenana, Beaver, Tanana, and Minto. In addition, there were representatives from the Alaska Native Brotherhood and the Alaska Native Rights Association. At the time, Ketzler was president of the Nenana camp of the Alaska Native Brotherhood.

The March meeting brought up some old issues and some new threats. One of the old issues was the impact of the railroad on Native settlement in Nenana. When the railroad was under construction, Nenana was a major construction center. Supplies were shipped by steamer to the mouth of the Yukon River and then transported by steamboat up the Yukon and Tanana Rivers to Nenana where a railroad town was built. Supplies also came up from Skagway via the White Pass Railroad and then by steamboat down the Yukon River and up the Tanana River (Fitch 1967:53–59). The Native housing and graveyard in Nenana were disturbed and in some cases destroyed in the course of construction, and Native people were dislocated from their homes without compensation.[98] The issue was an old but persistent sore that had not been resolved, despite Chief Thomas who demonstrated the antiquity of their claim to this site. His statement came one year after his participation at the 1915 Tanana Chiefs meeting. Chief Thomas told Mr. Riggs[99] who was also at the 1915 meeting: "The Indians have lived in Nenana for always. My mother has lived there, and her mother, and her mother, for five generations" (Toghotthele 1983:71).

The participants at the March meeting in 1962 had the question of aboriginal rights on their minds. The legal rights of Native people in the Interior had never been clear. There was the Organic Act of 1884 that provided a level of protection;[100] Natives were not to be disturbed on land they occupied. This provision didn't stop settlement and legal claims by outsiders; those continued to accrue over the years, and it didn't stop the government from removing the Natives from Nenana and destroying homes and the graveyard. At the Nenana meeting in 1962, Markle Ewan of Gulkana called for a resolution to Congress to define aboriginal rights. When the resolution passed, Chairman Al Ketzler promised to send it to the Alaska delegation in Washington and a copy to the Grand Camp secretary of the ANB.[101] If any of the 1915 Tanana Chiefs delegates were still alive at this time, they might have been shaking their heads in disbelief that their call for clear direction on Native rights had still not been acted upon in the forty-seven years since they met in Fairbanks.

At the March meeting, Ketzler also reported on the problems that Eskimos were facing: Project Chariot, the plan to detonate an atomic explosion at Cape Thompson in Northwest Alaska (O'Neill 2007) and regulations restricting hunting of waterfowl in the spring on the North Slope (Blackman 1989:180–184). Then there was the Rampart Dam proposal. In 1954, the Army Corps of Engineers proposed the damming of the Yukon River below the community of Rampart (Coates 1991:134–161). The dam would produce a massive quantity of electricity. It would also have flooded seven villages in the Yukon Flats, forcing 1,200 Native residents to move out of their homeland.[102] The dam proposal continued to be a possible threat well into the 1960s (Arnold 1976:102–103).[103]

In 1962, it was clear to the representatives gathered in Nenana that it was time to take action. One immediate result of the March meeting was the plan to hold a larger meeting that summer at Tanana to discuss the issues and seek action. Today, many look back at that Tanana meeting as marking the modern roots of the Tanana Chiefs Conference.

Testifying at a meeting in 1968, Al Ketzler described the significance of the Tanana meetings in 1962 and 1963: "Out of that first meeting of the Tanana Chiefs in 1962, and the second one in 1963, we have created a permanent organization, the Tanana Chiefs' Conference, of which Nenana is a member. The organization is now taking an active part with the other organizations of the native people of Alaska in trying to save our land before it is all gone."[104]

Tanana had particular significance to the delegates because it reminded them of the old days when people would gather at the confluence of the Tanana with the Yukon River shortly after breakup in the spring. The gathering was called "Noochu Loghoyet" and it took place at "Noochu Loghoyet Hʉt'aane" (Jones and Jetté 2000:491).[105] They met to trade and share information.[106] Some claim that the last time they met was in 1913.[107] The issues included: a call for citizenship, representation in Washington,

Conference Recess, Tanana, Alaska.
1-UAF-1992-202-1. Bear Ketzler Photograph Collection.
Alaska and Polar Regions Archive, Elmer Rasmuson Library, University of Alaska Fairbanks.

D.C., and recognition of the need to find a way to protect land and fishing sites (Sniffen and Carrington 1914:5, 16, 24). These were, of course, the same issues raised in 1915 and again in the 1960s.

The question of aboriginal rights remained unsettled, particularly since the Statehood Act provided both for state selection of land and, at the same time, disclaimed the State's right to claim lands that might be held by Natives.[108] Title 4 of the Alaska Statehood Act clearly protects lands held by the federal government for Alaska Natives from being selected by the State. The new state should have halted any land selection and development projects until the Native claims were settled. Instead, it took a federal action to stop state selections.

As the state ramped up its selections, the Native community organized at a statewide level, forming the Alaska Federation of Natives on October 18, 1966 (Arnold 1976:112–117). They actively protested the State's actions, and this led to Secretary of the Interior Stewart Udall's land freeze, virtually shutting down state selections until the issue of Native land claims was settled (Roberts 1970:1, 9); Federal Field Committee for Development Planning in Alaska 1968:440). These developments added momentum to land claims, but it would take something more, something like another gold rush to get action. It turned out to be an oil rush.

The discovery of marketable quantities of oil at Prudhoe Bay led to the question of how the oil could be transported to market. What was needed was a pipeline from the Arctic to an ice-free port. Once again, Valdez emerged as the ideal port. The proposed pipeline would have to cross hundreds of miles of federal and Native land and still there was no Native land settlement, but now the parties were eager to settle (Berry 1975). The Alaska Native Claims Settlement Act was finally passed in 1971.

Aboriginal Rights and Tribal Control

The passage of land claims legislation addressed land claims, but the more basic question of aboriginal rights and the achievement of services to tribal members remains. Health, education, management of fish and game, and control of community affairs are areas of concern that don't quite fit easily as Alaskans negotiate between cultures, systems of governance, and community values. It has been difficult for many Alaskans to recognize the role subsistence plays in Natives' lives.[109] Rightly or wrongly, this tension has played out in legal battles. For instance, it has been argued by some that the Alaska State Constitution prohibits preference to any segment of the population and this has created challenges to Native rural populations who seek subsistence preference in times of shortages. On this topic there have been legal differences in opinion.[110]

Beyond the legal questions that continue to cloud the issues of local control, there is societal friction between segments of the population that believe there should be no preferences given to Natives. On the other side, many in the Native community see issues such as rural preference for access to fish and game in times of shortage as a cultural right. In other areas such as local policing, child welfare, and tribal courts, the issues of aboriginal rights also remain under debate.[111] The modern Tanana Chiefs Conference is an active player in these concerns, representing forty-two villages and thirty-seven recognized tribes in the Interior. The old chiefs might be proud of what has been accomplished, but they probably would recognize the current struggles as part of an effort they initiated many years ago.

Many of us students of history are fond of pointing out the relevance of the past to current events. We are equally fond of pointing out the importance of historical context in our evaluations of the past. The 1915 meeting provides opportunity for both. How easy it is to marvel at the insight and skill of the old chiefs in 1915 calling for wage labor opportunities and education for their children even if it meant long periods of separation from their families. They recognized the need to change, yet it is so easy for us to forget how quickly change had come to their lives and to imagine the scope of their adjustment within their lifetimes. Hopefully, our discussion of transitions—from fur to gold and from Native country to white man's country—provide background to evaluate the changes. In the actual transcript of the 1915 meeting, the delegates tell us their questions and concerns. And in the events that have followed since then, we can see how their concerns are playing out.

The 1915 meeting is a touchstone to a tangible moment in time when we can almost hear and see the delegates describing their concerns. For that reason, it is an important window into the lives of Interior Native leaders seeking a place for their people in the white society that had so recently enveloped them. This immediacy is particularly true for those who trace their ancestry to the leaders who gathered in Fairbanks one hundred years ago. Their connections are personal and tangible. But, for all Alaskans, the issues raised by the chiefs force us to confront the challenges of living in a multicultural society and our responsibility to listen and try to understand each other. This is the fundamental message of the 1915 meeting; we need to hear each other, respect our differences, support, and learn to live with the diversity that is life in Alaska. For that reason alone, we should follow Will Mayo's lead and return to the transcript again and again to remind ourselves of the issues raised and the challenges that remain.

Postscript

by William Schneider

How the Story Unfolded

In this work there are plenty of references to the well-worn sources of Alaska history, but the story is also driven by a series of new opportunities and directions. For instance, the recording of Will Mayo's talk at the Tanana-Yukon Historical Society Meeting and the follow-up discussions and his editing led to the unique contribution of his perspectives in this volume. These perspectives are further developed in appendix 3, a discussion of the Treaty of Cession and the implications for Alaska Natives. The convergence of two important anniversaries—the 100th anniversary of the 1915 Tanana Chiefs meeting in Fairbanks and the 150th anniversary of the Purchase of Alaska in 1867—provided added focus to their relationship and the larger story of Native relations with the federal government.

Several key people helped shape this work. Ron Inouye lit our fire on the importance of recognizing the Tanana Chiefs anniversary; Ross Coen's work reminded us of how the treaty was important to the relationship of Alaska Natives and the federal government.[112] Kevin Illingworth provided the legal framework essential to describing the relationship and significance of the treaty and the chiefs' meeting to current legal issues and efforts. Extended correspondence with Lee Saylor led to the personal history of the Healy Lake and other Middle Tanana people who lived at the critical transition time between the fur-trapping era and the gold rush. Similarly, the Emmons Family Papers at the Beinecke Library revealed the plight of Copper River Natives during the gold rush and the impact Lieutenant Emmons had on President Roosevelt in getting relief for the Copper River people. So, for the rewarding new encounters, the reminders of anniversaries, and the opportunities taken to build on different streams of historical, legal, and local knowledge, it seems warranted to explain this book's journey.

Most students of Alaska history are introduced to the 1915 Tanana Chiefs Meeting by reading Stan Patty's 1971 article in *Alaska Journal*.[113] The piece was written at the time the Alaska Native Claims Settlement Act was passed by Congress. Patty, the ever sharp and opportune journalist, got a hold of the transcript from Ruth Allman, the niece of James Wickersham.[114] Patty's piece appropriately brought out how eloquently the chiefs' testimony spoke to their need for protection of the land that sustained their way of life. Patty's timing was perfect and the chiefs did not disappoint, but as we now know, land was only part of the story; there was much more that the chiefs said that needed to be remembered, talked about, and considered in light of the evolution of their relationship with the federal government. The transcript of the meeting is an opener to those ongoing discussions. In the best tradition of anniversaries, this anniversary has given us pause to explore a fuller range of the issues raised at the 1915 meeting.

This project really began after a presentation on Chief Joseph and Billy Mitchell at the Tanana-Yukon Historical Society. Ron Inouye reminded us that we were coming up on the 100th anniversary of the Tanana Chiefs meeting (July 5–6, 1915) and there should be some discussion of its significance. That led to a panel session that featured Tom Alton and Will Mayo. Alton was way ahead of us on his research. He had reported on the 1915 meeting and had a manuscript already on hand. We were also very fortunate that Will Mayo agreed to participate. Mayo's personal history of leadership in the modern Tanana Chiefs made him an ideal person to assess the issues raised back in 1915 and the progress since then. He made it clear that the old leaders and the 1915 event were still very much a part of his life and that of others in the Native community. He did this by pointing out how he and other members of the audience that evening are directly related to particular chiefs who participated at the 1915 meeting. These ties are reminders that the old leaders are important to their descendants and they are pleased to publicly acknowledge them. Mayo explained to me why he began his address this way. He said:

> It's cultural. Whenever two Native people encounter one another there is a rhythm and sequence to their greetings, if they have not met before. Identity and place are established up front and family linkages are made. Once families and communities are identified, the conversation can proceed. It was kind of like that. I also wanted to point out the continuum of then and now.[115]

As we know now, Chief Joseph, Billy Mitchell's traveling companion on the Goodpaster expedition, lived in both the white and the Native worlds, and he lived through the transitions that marked this time. These included the entry of the prospectors into the Tanana Valley, the move in trading focus from the Yukon to the Tanana, and the emerging role of chiefs as negotiators with representatives of the government, and he experienced mission life at the Episcopal Mission in Salcha. It was from there that he was chosen as a delegate to the 1915 meeting. Mitchell's account of the expedition sparked my questions about Chief Joe and life at the turn of the century (nineteenth to twentieth), but Lee Saylor was key to reconstructing the transitions people experienced, and his mother-in-law's photographic collection provided a visual record of the story. Without these sources, we wouldn't have such a personal and visual understanding of life during the transition period from pre–gold rush to the entrée of prospectors into the Tanana Valley.

At this point, several important threads were emerging. Most important was the realization that the legal history that defined how the government dealt with Natives was critical to the story, but the social attitudes of the white people were also a major force in shaping and interpreting the legal rulings. Kevin Illingworth and Will Mayo emphasized the chiefs' underlying call for clarification of their rights under United States law and their call for educational, medical, and labor opportunities in Western society. The leaders saw education as key to learning about opportunities for work and participation in the affairs of the territory. They saw reading and writing as key to understanding new opportunities, expressing their wishes, and establishing a record, the very same tools that were used by government

officials. As I later learned, Chiefs Alexander, Ivan, and William had experience with government officials prior to the 1915 meeting and early on
they employed writing as a way to present their concerns to the government.[116] It was becoming clearer that the chiefs were not only interested
in preserving traditional opportunities but actively acquiring access to new
ones as well.

One of the backstories in this work is the complicated relationship
James Wickersham had with Alaska Natives and that President Theodore
Roosevelt had with American Natives in general. Natives were subject
to two conflicting messages from the American public and the government: white society wanted them to give up tribal ways, but whites were
also fascinated with old Native art and other forms of expressive culture (Raibmon 2005:157–174). As for policies about land, by 1915 the
Puyallup Reservation in Washington State that Wickersham spoke of with
admiration to the Tanana Chiefs was largely a loss with the land divided
into allotments and sold off (Castile 1990), yet at the 1915 meeting, he
was still promoting reservations to Alaska Natives. In a strict reading of
the 1915 transcript, James Wickersham comes across as a man entrenched
in the legal and social constructs of the day. It is easy to forget that he had
met with some of the chiefs earlier; he had traveled to their camps, and
most important, he made the 1915 meeting possible. He later persisted in
Southeast Alaska to get a settlement for the Tlingit-Haida.

Roosevelt, as we have seen, was sympathetic to the plight of the Copper
River Natives and to some degree fascinated with Indian heritage and arts
in the country as a whole. Yet his push for allotments shows a callous dis-
regard for the cultural ways of Native people. Wickersham, Roosevelt, and
even Emmons probably couldn't overcome the Christian influences that
permeated government policy: "Family is God's unit of society" (Prucha
1984, vol. 2:622) and "Civilization was impossible without the incentive
to work that comes only from individual ownership of a piece of property"
(ibid.:639). I came to realize that this story is as much about white society,
its norms and laws, as it is about Native culture.

The Wickersham–Paul effort in Southeast Alaska prompted us to consider how the 1915 meeting fit into the chronology of events leading up to
the Alaska Native Claims Settlement Act. The history was easy to recon-
struct but, once again, we had to remind ourselves that the land issues so
essential to the chronology of events had blinded us to the deeper questions

of aboriginal rights that the Tanana Chiefs were striving to clarify. The chiefs wanted to preserve a way of life but also gain access to what the new order could provide. Perhaps in the reading and rereading and in the discussion that must follow, we can relate the leaders' concerns to the present challenges and achievements in intergovernmental relationships. The issues have not been fully resolved and that is why the transcript of the meeting has been reproduced in this volume, so that we can easily return to it again and again, to see how the leaders were struggling to understand and accommodate each other.

The 100th anniversary of the meeting passed with some public recognition but few in-depth explorations of the significance of the meeting for all Alaskans and few reflections on how the issues have been addressed. It does seem that each July 5 and 6 should be a time for further thoughts on the historic event, the record of Native leadership that followed in its footsteps, and the basic human challenges and responsibilities we have to understand each other.

Recognizing the 150th anniversary of the Alaska Purchase as an opportunity to reexamine Article III of the Treaty, we conducted the group interview with Kevin Illingworth, Natasha Singh, and Will Mayo. It was not surprising that the discussion brought us once again to the issues raised at the 1915 meeting about basic rights and opportunities under American law. As the participants pointed out, the story is not over; the issues still seek resolution. That is why it is important to continue to find ways to consider and evaluate the historical record that has brought us to this point.

Introduction to the Transcript of the 1915 Tanana Chiefs Meeting in Fairbanks

by Thomas Alton

The transcript of the July 1915 meeting of fourteen Tanana Athabascan leaders with Alaska's congressional delegate reveals, more than anything, two widely different views of the world of a century ago. To the indigenous peoples whose ancestors had lived on the land since time immemorial, the notion that land could be parceled and individually titled was foreign and nonsensical. The land was like the air they breathed. It belonged to everyone and no one. It was the world in which they earned their living, knowing and respecting other groups' hunting and fishing areas. The land they knew intimately defined who they were as a culture, and the prospect of accepting boundaries and being restricted within those limits was likened to a sentence of death. It would be the end of a way of life that had sustained them.

Meanwhile, the pioneers and settlers who in twelve years' time had built a small city on the banks of the Chena River and had created an economy based on farming and mining believed Interior Alaska to be a newfound place of wealth and opportunity. The future was limitless, especially now with a new railroad that would connect Fairbanks with the outside world and bring with it more prospects for development. But such a future also would usher in vast crowds of immigrants who would demand access to the same lands that had been occupied by generations of Athabascans.

These conflicting views represented an extension of the history of westward expansion. The wilderness of the contiguous United States had been tamed, and civilization had reached the Pacific Coast. Yet Americans still longed to conquer new frontiers, and they had turned their attention north. Just the day before the meeting with the chiefs was called to order in the log library building on First Avenue, James Wickersham delivered a speech at a ceremony laying the cornerstone for the new college that was to be built on a hill outside of town. Some, if not all, of the fourteen chiefs were present as Alaska's delegate spoke expansively about America's destiny and his hope that the federal land grant would convey to the college up to 200,000 acres of prime Interior territory.[117] What must the chiefs have thought as Wickersham declared this wish? And how did his statements influence what they had to say in the meetings held over the course of the next two days?

Certainly Wickersham was not the only representative of the federal government to express hopes for extensive development of the territory. President Woodrow Wilson himself made it a point in his 1913 State of the Union Address. "Alaska, as a storehouse, should be unlocked," he had told Congress. A railroad built and operated by the United States government was the means of "thrusting in the key to the storehouse and throwing back the lock and opening the door."[118] Wilson's secretary of the interior, Franklin K. Lane, told a congressional committee in 1914 that Alaska was a "great public domain" owned by the people of the United States and that its resources must be opened for their benefit and lands must be made available for settlement.[119]

This was the message that Wickersham wished to get across to the Native leaders, and he stressed the need for them to establish reservations to protect tribal lands. Also representing the federal government at the meeting were Alaska Railroad engineer Thomas Riggs and C. W. Richie of the federal land office in Fairbanks. All three men spoke of the certainty of extensive economic development and growth, and they were sincere in their desire to achieve the best outcome possible for the indigenous people. Above all, they sought to avoid seeing the ancient Athabascan homeland overrun and a way of life destroyed. But the chiefs were not ready to consider the choices the white men laid before them and, for better or worse, they made decisions based on what they believed was the best for their people and their future.

Will Mayo has speculated on what might have transpired over the years if the chiefs in 1915 had accepted Wickersham's concept and had gained title to tracts of land in the vicinity of Fairbanks. How differently things might have turned out for, say, the Chena band of Natives if they had established a reservation on the south side of the Tanana River across from the mouth of the Chena. Alfred Starr, the revered Nenana elder, who was instrumental in the land claims movement of the 1960s, believed that it was not the chiefs' intention to entirely reject the reservations. They only wanted to ensure that the land conveyances would be big enough for them to make a living. Alfred, who was the son of Jacob Starr, one of the fourteen chiefs present at the historic meeting, was sixteen in July of 1915. Late in life, he expressed his view of the event in a hearing before the Alaska Native Review Commission. "They didn't turn down the reservations," he testified. "The only thing they said was that we Natives live on a big tract of land. We've got to have quite a lot of land to live on if we're going to trap and hunt and gather game and fish."[120] The transcript reflects the lack of any discussion of what a reservation was or what it could be. The Natives reminded the white men present that government officials did not travel around Native country enough to understand the Natives' way of life. As we read the document, we can see the divide that existed between each party's understanding of the other.

The transcript that follows is the only record we have of the proceedings of those two days a century ago. As a historical document, however, it is not without its flaws. Paul Williams, the translator, was fluent in English and in some of the Athabascan languages spoken. He interpreted the words uttered by Wickersham and the other English speakers for the chiefs and then translated the Athabascans' statements back into English. The proceedings were taken down in writing by an English-speaking stenographer, who then transcribed his shorthand notes to produce the typescript we hold in our hands today. The archival copy is barely legible and appears to be a carbon copy. What most people work with today is an electronic scan produced by character recognition software. This last step leaves us with numerous minor errors that we have attempted to correct, and thus we have a version that is quite far removed from what the men present at the meeting might have heard.

Because of his abilities in English, Paul Williams had the strongest voice among the Athabascans in the room, and he gave his own opinion of the reservation idea directly to Wickersham, calling it "a fake" and stating that the Natives totally rejected it. Did Paul Williams translate that conclusion into the Native languages for the chiefs to understand? Did he interject his own opinions into the translations of the chiefs' words into English? And finally, how accurate were the stenographer's notes and his transcription of them to the typewriter? The transcript reflects unanimity among the chiefs, but Alfred Starr's comments in hindsight and his close connection to one of the participants open the door for the possibility that some opinions in favor of acceptance of the Wickersham agenda might have existed among the chiefs.

Wickersham himself left the meeting disappointed and perplexed about what avenue, if any, would now lead to a fair and humane end. His cover letter sent with the transcript to Interior Secretary Lane reflected his ambivalence, and he begged the secretary to solve the problem "before all the good land and fishing sites are taken up by the white men."[121] Perhaps he feared that despite his wishes and intentions, a just and humane settlement was nowhere in sight.

On the land issue, we are left with uncertainty about the level of understanding across the cultural divide. However, on other matters, the Natives' desires are quite clear. They wished to participate in the new order, to have a relationship with the government, and to acquire medical, educational, and employment opportunities. For all its problems, the transcript stands out as the first public voice for these concerns in Interior Alaska.

The Original Transcript of the 1915 Tanana Chiefs Meeting in Fairbanks

Fairbanks, Alaska, July 5th, 1915.

PROCEEDINGS OF A COUNCIL

Held in the library room at Fairbanks, Alaska, on July 5th,
1915, between the Chiefs and headmen of the bands of Indians
living along the Tanana River, and Delegate James Wickersham,
Thomas Riggs, Jr., Member Alaskan Engineering Commission,
and C. W. Richie and H. J. Atwell, Acting Register and Receiver of the United States Land Office, at Fairbanks, Alaska.

The following Indians were present at the said council:

Ka-da-tuts, or Chief Joe, of Salchaket,
Thla-den-no-duch, or Chief John, of Chena,
Be-yats, or Chief Thomas, of Nenana,
Do-no-hra-da-da, or Julius Pilot, of Nenana,
Yo-kah, or Chief Charley, of Minto,
Sit-tsu-dau-tuna, or Chief Alexander, of Tolovana,
Klewk-doo-aw, or Titus Alexander, of Tolovana,
Krux-ah, or Chief Ivan, of Crossjacket,
Yit-su-dad-a-kwot, or Alexander Williams, of Ft. Gibbon,
Sut-nal-nich, or William, of Fort Gibbon,
Nan-no-juk-thlit-lu-kwah, or Albert, of Ft. Gibbon,
Ba-cha-ta-naw-da-talth, or Jacob Starr, of Ft. Gibbon,
Johnny Folger of Fort Gibbon, and
Paul Williams, of Fort Gibbon, Interpreter.

There were also present:

James Wickersham, Delegate to Congress,
Thomas Riggs, Jr., Member Alaskan Engineering Commission,
C. W. Ritchie and H. J. Atwell, Acting Register and
Receiver of the United States Land Office at Fairbanks,
Guy H. Madara, Episcopal Minister, and
G. F. Cramer, Special Disbursing Agent, Alaskan Engineering
Commission.

Reverend Madara first addressed those assembled, saying that the
Chiefs and Headmen of the Indians present represented the Indians from
Salchaket down the Tanana River to Fort Gibbon, probably 1200 to 1500
Indians. He said these men had come to Fairbanks to discuss some
matters of interest to their people and that he desired that they be
given a hearing.

-2-

Delegate Wickersham then told the Indian Chiefs that Secretary of the Interior, Lane, in Washington, had charge of all matters connected with Indians and Indian lands in Alaska, that he knew Mr. Lane and that the Secretary was a good friend of Indian people and wished to protect them in all their rights. He asked the Indians to state fully what they wanted the Secretary to know and promised their words should go to Washington.

Some of the Indians then wished to talk and Paul Williams, from Fort Gibbon, a fluent speaker in both the Indian and English tongues, acted as interpreter at the request of the Indians.

Chief Ivan, of Crossjacket, through Paul Williams, Interpreter, says: That he is sick and hard of hearing. He was a young man when the United States purchased Alaska and that he has had no chance to talk to the United States officials or to appeal to the Government for help, and that this is the first time he can come to the officials to talk.

Chief Thomas, of Nenana, through Paul Williams, Interpreter, says: Long time since the United States got control of Alaska, but he now wishes to consult with the United States officials and that his main object in talking is to get better education for the Indians.

Here Delegate Wickersham arose and asked the Indians, through Paul Williams, Interpreter: "What do you want the United States to do for the Indians? What do they need the most to make them comfortable in their homes?"

Chief Charley, of Tolovana, through Paul Williams, Interpreter, says: That he wants advice from the United States. What can the United States do for us? We want many things but what can we get if we want it? When we know that we talk. Alaska is our home, we do not know where our people came from, but we are the first people here -- the white people came after us, and we want the white people to protect and to help us.

Chief Jacob Starr, of Fort Gibbon, through Paul Williams, Interpreter, said: We came up here today to talk to Delegate Wickersham because he talked to Chief Alexander at Tolovana, and we want to understand what he meant by that talk. What you told Alexander the natives did not believe and came here to find out. After we learn that we will talk.

Chief Alexander, of Tolovana, through Paul Williams, Interpreter said: That he told the Indians what Mr. Wickersham told him, but the Indians did not believe him, thought he did not understand. Hopes Mr. Wickersham will tell the natives so they will believe Chief Alexander.

Delegate Wickersham: Oh, Alexander told you the truth. I talked to him and told him about homesteads and reservations just as he told you I did. He told you the truth.

-5-

Delegate Wickersham said to the Indians, through Paul
Williams, Interpreter: "I am glad to see the Indian Chiefs here
from Salchaket, Chena, Nenana, Crossjacket, Tolovana, Fort Gibbon,
all up and down the river. I have been elected by the people of
Alaska, to go to Congress in Washington, to represent all the people
of Alaska, including the Indian people. I can say, as your friend,
that I want to do everything I can to help you. It is my duty to
help to make laws for the Government of the people of Alaska. Mr.
Riggs, here, is your friend, too. Mr. Riggs is the Commissioner in
charge of building the Government railroad from the Coast to the
Tanana River. He is a friend of Secretary Lane of the Department of
the Interior. Secretary Lane has charge in Washington of all Indian
lands and Indian matters. Secretary Lane has appointed Mr. Riggs
to have charge of the building of the railroad in Alaska. Mr. Riggs
and Mr. Lane are friends and Mr. Riggs is your friend. Mr. Richie,
here, is the Land Agent here in Fairbanks. He knows all about the
land laws. Mr. Richie was appointed to his office by Mr. Lane, or he
was appointed under Mr. Lane's general jurisdiction. Mr. Richie is
your friend and wants to help you. Now we three men know Mr. Lane
very well. Mr. Lane lived out on the Pacific Coast in the State of
California and in Washington State. He knows the Indian people and
knows what they want, and he is a good friend of the Indian people.
He wants to hear you just as we do.

"Some time ago I was down at Tolovana and I had a long
talk with Alexander. I told Alexander that the white people were
building railroads in this country now. White men are coming out
and taking up the land; they are staking homesteads, cultivating the
land, raising potatoes and all kinds of crops. Oh, there are many,
many white men in the United States, as many as there are trees on
the hills here, and in a few years many of them are coming to Alaska,
and they are going to take up land. Mr. Richie and the men employed
in the Land Office are surveying the land and they are going to
survey all the good land, they are running lines so that they can
tell where the good land is, and so they can tell how much 320 acres
are, on the ground. And the white men coming from the United States
are going to keep taking up this land until all the good land is
gone, and the Indian people are going to have to move over. The
white men are going to take all this good land, and when all the good
land is gone, the white men are going to keep on taking more land.
After while the Indian will have no land at all. He cannot live in
the water and he will have nothing to do, and this is what we want
to talk about. I told Alexander that Indian men can take land. I
told Alexander that the Indians were the first people here. I told
Alexander that the Government did not want to have the Indians pushed
off; that the Indians are good men -- I notice many of you have a
cross, that you belong to the white men's church, -- wear the white
man's clothes; that you are learning to talk like white men and are
sending your children to school to learn, and that you are learning
the law of the white men.

-4-

"We want you to have a home, we want your people to take land, we want you to take good land, and we do not want you to be just pushed aside. We are talking to you so you can understand, and we want you to do something before it is too late. Now, I told Alexander that there were two things you can do: First, you can take a homestead of 160 acres; you can pick out that land and stake on it, and live there forever with your children. You can always have your home there. The white man can come looking for land and you can tell him to go on, this is your land, he cannot take your land away from you. And you would be just equal to the white man. This is one thing you can do. Then I told Alexander that there is another thing you can do: You could ask the Government to give you an Indian reservation. The President of the United States and Mr. Lane, the Secretary of the Interior, can stake a big reservation for all the Indians to have together. The President or Mr. Lane could make that reservation at Salchacket, or at Nenana, or at Tolovana, or at Kantishna, or at Crossjacket, or at Fort Gibbon, anywhere in Alaska where the Indian people want it. If the President makes a big reservation, all the Indians can live there. You and your people could build an Indian town there. You could have a church, a school and an Indian Agent, an official agent of the President who would show you how to plow land and raise potatoes and other crops. And I told Alexander to talk with the Indian people and tell them these things and ask them what they want to do. And Alexander did that, and now you people are here to talk to us about it. Now, what we want to know is what you Indian people want. Do you wish to take homesteads of 160 acres apiece, or do you want a big reservation where all the people can come together. If you don't do something the white men will take all the best land for theirs. You can take land just like a white man, and you are just as good in the eyes of the law as a white man. You have just the same right under the law as a white man to take land. If you do not know the law you want to learn it. Now we are trying to tell you the law and trying to make you understand that you must take land so the white men won't get all of the best of it, and if you want a homestead of 160 acres for each one of you and for every Indian man over 21 years of age you can get it. Every Indian man in the Tanana Country over 21 years of age can take a homestead. You can take up homesteads side by side. Now, you ought to do something. You ought to either take homesteads or ask the Government to make you a big reservation. If you don't do this the white men will get the best of it. Now you can get the best of it. When the white men come into the country the land will all be taken up quickly, so we want to help you now. If any of you men, or any Indian man in the Tanana Valley, wants to take up a homestead, come to see Mr. Richie. Mr. Richie is the Land Officer and his office is in the Court House here in Fairbanks. He is your friend and wants to help you and he will tell you what to do. I will help you and will do anything I can to help you, and Mr. Riggs will help you too. We want you men to get your land before it is all gone, that is all."

-5-

Rev. Guy H. Madara: "Mr. Wickersham, what you say is all true. It has been done with the Indians Outside and it will be the same here. Forced back and back until there is no place to go. I am sure that the Indian chiefs have no idea of reservation. They may say a great deal about it. There is no use in my saying it. There is one objection to the present allotment that I want to speak of before they start to talk, and that is this: In my opinion, it does not fill the bill. It proposes that the Indian leave his tribal relations and live alone. I have had several allotments which were staked by the Indians and which are now in the process of being given them. The Indians live along the Rivers and when they come to Fairbanks it takes much time and expense. They cannot leave and go to town at any time because they must catch their fish, hunt, trap and otherwise make their living. Thomas, at Wood River, has staked an allotment. There are possibly a dozen more who have staked homesteads and when the Land Office investigates the claim they look to see if a cabin has been built and they look to see if a garden has been made, and if they find no permanent improvements they believe that the Indians do not intend to occupy it permanently. The Indians cannot do this because they have not the capital necessary to start. I think that most of the things I have said will be said by the Indians themselves with better grace, so I will wait until they have spoken, and then will possibly have more to say.

Paul Williams: If you gentlemen will kindly allow me to say a few words, I have been in the service among the Indians for the last fourteen years. I have worked as an Indian interpreter for the last fourteen years. And I have had a little knowledge from the civilized people, and lately have studied greatly the affairs of our people, and as I have listened, so far was very much pleased with the statements made by Mr. Madara, for the statements he has just made are what my people wish to say also. Now, about this homestead, there is, perhaps, this one objection that I think makes it rather impossible. If any Indian wants to take up a homestead and live there continually with his family and take himself away from his own people, there is only one thing I would suggest to you Government people. They do not have the money to build a cabin on the homestead and they cannot stay there continually for they depend for a living upon their fishing, hunting and trapping, and they have to travel far to do this. So if they should take up homesteads it would be rather impossible to have them live there on it permanently. Then, if they should make a big reservation, these Indians would have to move from their tribal relations, and not live where they have been used to and in the places which are their homes.

Delegate Wickersham: Suppose several smaller reservations could be made, say one at Salchacket, one at Nenana, one at Tolovana, and one at Fort Gibbon, and let them go on the reservations which are nearest where they have always lived.

Paul Williams: That would be about the same. It would take them away from the old homes and habits where they have been used to living, which is the same therefore as their native towns.

-6-

Chief Ivan, of Crossjacket, through Paul Williams,
Interpreter, says: "I remember ever since the ground was bought
from Russia by the United States Government when we used the stone
axe and the flint match, when I was a small boy. We have never
had a chance to see the Government officials and tell them what we
wanted. I have heard that the United States Government was supposed
to be a good Government, and according to reports that I have heard
they even protect the dogs in the street. And if the Government
is able to protect the dogs in the streets it should be able to
look out for us. I am the son of Old Ivan, and when he died long
years ago, I took his place, and have represented the people ever
since. I am an old man now and sick, and likely to pass away at any
time, so it makes no difference to me, but I am a friend of my
people and I want to look out for their interests, and this will be
the last time I will consult with the Government officials."

Paul Williams, Interpreter: "I think it would be wise,
as you have suggested, to talk over this thing you suggest, as to
whether we want to take up homesteads or whether we want one big
reservation. I will tell them of this, and we will wait until this
afternoon to answer, and decide among ourselves."

Delegate Wickersham: "I suggest that Mr. Richie explain
to them how to secure a homestead claim."

C. W. Richie, said to the Indians, through Paul Williams,
Interpreter: "The homestead allotment law, as approved by Congress,
gives every Indian who is 21 years of age or the head of a family
160 acres of non-mineral, unreserved land. In order to secure his
entry, he should stake the corners of his land, which should be as
nearly square as possible. The homesteads may be taken up anywhere
in the rolling lands, or facing upon a river, but if it is facing on
a river like the Yukon there must be a strip of land one quarter mile
wide between each homestead. After he stakes the land he may come to
the Land Office with two witnesses. If the Indian and his two
witnesses will come to the Land Office we will make out all the
papers necessary which will cost you nothing. We find out where you
want your land and get the correct description and protect you in
every way we can. There is no expense attached to anything the
Government does for you in the Land Office, everything is free. The
two witnesses you bring should know the same of the land as you know
yourself. And if you have used or claimed the land for a period
of years, the witnesses want to testify to that. The witnesses want
to know and should know that you are twenty one years of age or the
head of a family, and that you are an Indian of the District of Alaska.
This is all that the witnesses need know. Then when you come to the
Land Office a paper the same as this (showing blank application --
Form 4-021 G. L. O. series) is made out and filed with the Land Office.
It is then sent to Secretary Lane, your friend, and the land will be
reserved for all time for your use and for all time fro the family
that follows after you. The law provides that an allotment or a
homestead shall be occupied by the Indian. He need not live on it all

-7-

the time but it should be his home the same as the white man makes
a homestead his home. He may go fishing and hunting and visit his
neighbors and go to potlaches, but he should have this place as his
own home. It is desirable, that is, the Government would like to
have him cultivate the land of his homestead, but he is not expected
to work himself to death doing it." (Applause).

Thomas Riggs, Jr., told the Indians, through Paul Williams,
Interpreter: "Secretary Lane is a great friend of all the Indians
and he has charge of all the Indians in Alaska and in the United
States, and there are many, many thousands of them. In one of the
tribes in the United States they made him a chief they thought so
much of him. And he is trying to help the Indians all the time to
better their conditions in education and property. Secretary Lane
cannot make laws or change them but he can interpret the laws to the
best advantage of the Indian. If the laws are not suited to the Indians
of Alaska then new laws must be tried to be made although that may be
impossible, and that is where Judge Wickersham would try to help you.
The delegate has explained to you the two systems by which Indians can
take up property in Alaska and the Indians must take some action and
do it very soon, because after the railroad which we are building comes
into this country, it will be overrun with white people. They will
kill off your game, your moose, your caribou and your sheep. They
will run all of them out of the country and they will have so many fish
wheels on the river that the Indian will not get as many fish, so I
say the Indian must protect himself by one of the methods which has
been outlined under existing laws. If you ask Secretary Lane to put
aside reservations for you he will set aside large bodies of land for
your use and no white man would be allowed on them and the Indian would
hold them for all times. If the Indian, on the other hand, takes up
his homestead he must do a certain amount of work on it, but nobody
will be able to take his land from him, but you have got to make up
your mind what you want to do before Judge Wickersham or Secretary
Lane can take any action. And so you must get together and talk this
matter over and submit to either Secretary Lane or Judge Wickersham,
just what your opinion is and what you want done. When present conditions are changed, the Indian's livlihood will be taken away from
him by the killing off of the game and fish, but when you have land
either in reservation or homestead you will have something of value,
something that you can live on, something on which you can always make
a living by work, which need not be too hard."

Delegate Wickersham, to the Indians, through Paul Williams,
Interpreter: "Now, we will meet you men here again at 4 o'clock.
In the meantime you can talk it over among yourselves and tell us just
what you want to do. I have told Alexander just what you should do,
and told him that we are all your friends and that we want to help
you, and not take your lands away, and Alexander can tell you what I
said."

Paul Williams, Interpreter: "Alexander says that he believes
all you told him, and he will tell his people."

MS 107
Box 38 F-1
-7-

The meeting adjourned, and at 2 o'clock, the Indian Chiefs and Judge Wickersham, Thomas Riggs, Jr., C. W. Richie, Rev. Guy H. Madara and C. F. Cramer met at Johnson's Studio and had a picture taken of the group, the Indians dressing in their native clothes.

At 4 o'clock, the above mentioned men met the Indian Chiefs at the Public Library, to talk over the matter further. The Indian Chiefs gave two songs and a dance on the porch of the library, which was very much enjoyed.

The Council was then assembled in the Public Library.

Delegate Wickersham, to the Indians, through Paul Williams, Interpreter: "If these chiefs have talked this matter over and they want to say anything tell them to go ahead and tell us. This young man will take it all down just as it is said and then write it all out and it will go to Washington. Tell them to be careful what they say and say what they mean."

Chief Ivan, of Crossjacket, through Paul Williams, Interpreter: "I wish to state that I remember my conversation this morning. I may say some things that I should not say, but you must remember and excuse me if I do make such a break, but you people have a mind and have something to depend on, like books, which we do not have. We are ignorant, but we try to do the best we can. We don't want to go on a reservation, but wish to stay perfectly free, just as we are now, and go about just the same as now, and believe that a reservation will not be a benefit to us. We feel as if we always had gone as we pleased, and the way they all feel is the same. We don't want to be put on a reservation. Now what we wish you to do is — as you are here as Government officials and we know that you are the Government's representatives — now, we wish you to give your word. You tell us that you will be our friends, and it is for your people to promise us, so that we will have your words in mind when we leave Fairbanks. The only news we hear are generally some rumors, which we hear from some young ones, not from the old middle aged people, because they cannot speak the English language. But these rumors we wish you to give us in writing so that we will know ourselves what you people are going to do for us."

(Here some of the natives objected to the public place where the talk was being held, so all doors were closed.)

Chief Ivan, through the interpreter, then continued: "You must remember that I am making this statement in the name of the natives, all the natives that are in this district here. I am making this statement because I consider that all these natives that I represent I am sure do not want to be put on a reservation. They don't want to have one and therefore I am making this statement for the natives I am here to represent."

-9-

H. J. Atwell, to Paul Williams, Interpreter. "Can you tell us what tribes Chief Ivan represents?"

Paul Williams, Interpreter: "He represents Crossjacket, Tanana, Hot Springs, Kokrines. They have no Chiefs here."

Thomas Riggs, Jr.: "Is he the spokesman for all these tribes?"

Paul Williams, Interpreter: "No, he is the first one to speak, but these other chiefs present will talk after he does, in turn."

Chief Thomas, of Nenana and Wood River, through Paul Williams, Interpreter: "I won't say very much now because there are other people to say something too, so I won't have a composition here now, but, I am going to suggest, of course, on one point, and that is that all of us Alaska natives and other Indians will agree with us, that we don't want to be put on a reservation. That one thing, that you people of the Government, Delegate Wickersham, Mr. Riggs, and Mr. Richie, you people don't go around enough to learn the way that the Indians are living, so we want to talk with you to explain our living to you, for we are anxious to show your people. I wish to especially state that when I talk to you now, I wish to show you that you are touching my heart and at the same time I wish to touch your heart. Of course, we want to feel perfectly free when talking to you, and you must understand that anything we say if wrong, is meant the right way, and we want to feel that you are going to allow us to have just what we are asking for. We have perfect confidence in you and feel that you will be able to give us that we wish for."

Chief Alexander Williams, of Fort Gibbon, through Paul Williams, Interpreter: "This man that makes the speeches has said just what I want to say myself, so I don't want to say much more, but I am very thankful to you for paying so much attention to us in this manner. When the United States purchased Alaska from Russia, we heard that we were in somebody's hands that was to do us good. About the reservation business, I feel pretty strong against it myself. When the United States purchased the land this Government left us live by ourselves and did not interfere and I hope that the Government will not do anything to hurt us as we are the natives of the country. They left us alone before and we hope they will do so now. This will do for the present."

Chief William, of Tanana, through Paul Williams, Interpreter, said: "Us natives are an ignorant people as to the Legislature that is making laws for the natives, but now we feel that we have been awakened by you people and that is what we are here for. There are times when we cannot reach you people, the Government of this United States, and there is no way we can learn what laws have been made for us and what changes have been made regarding the lands of the natives. We ought to be notified in writing about these things. True, we cannot read it ourselves, but our young folks who are going to school can read it. We want to keep posted on such matters and wish that we would be able to be kept posted on the many matters going on. We are very glad that we have the oppor-

-10-

tunity to speak to your people, for we cannot reach your Capitol, but
we now have the opportunity to speak to you, as you have come here,
and we know that what we want shall be heard. Then you say to the
people here that the Government feels like sending the doctor here."

　　　　Delegate Wickersham: "Who does he mean by "the doctor"?"

　　　　Paul Williams, Interpreter: "A Government doctor to be sent
here".

　　　　Chief William, continuing: "We come here of course to get
help from your people and we expect to get it. We want you to give us
any advisement you can as to how to deal with this question, and all
advisements we will take at any time."

　　　　Chief Jacob Starr, of Tanana, through Paul Williams,
Interpreter: "The reason we came up was to find out about these rumors
we have been hearing, but what we heard was mostly rumor. Coming up
here at our own expense means a lot to us and we want to find out about
these rumors, some may be true and some not true, and we come here for
your advisement. You people must remember that now you are representing
up here all the Government. For years past we have been wishing to get
into the Capitol, to have a native represent us, but that we have been
unable to do. We have had no opportunity to speak for ourselves. We
know you people can go there and suggest anything you wish, and now we
are talking just as if Secretary Lane or the President was up here. Do
it for us and write it down clearly, so we can see what is being done,
and not have only rumors. We are ignorant of the law. The only law we
know, and the majority of us abide by it, is the Missionary. We listen
to our Missionary. By that you can see for yourself we are trying to
live up to some rulings, and if we could be posted on the laws, and the
United States will see that we try to live up to them like we do to the
Missionary's rulings. You gentlemen must remember that we have been
trying to go out and learn these things, but we had no way to enable us
to do it. Now we ask you to do your best for us. We come to you people
and we are appealing to you people ."

　　　　Chief Charley, of Minto, through Paul Williams, Interpreter,
said: "What the people had suggested is my wish, so I won't say much
about it now. You, Judge, are the elder brother and we natives are
your younger brothers, and we come to you for help. We have no strength
and we feel that you older brothers are strong and overpower us. You
are able to handle this, and we expect you to handle it for us. I wish
you to understand that what all my people have said I agree with. We
prefer to have homesteads and we do not want a reservation. Some of us
have already begun to take up land some time ago, and we want to get
these claims approved. The Missionaries are trying to help us and the
Missionaries have asked us to keep our places or homes in neatness, and
we are beginning to keep them so, and in order, and if the white people
are coming in here like the slush ice to cover all the villages, we
expect your people to protect us from them."

-11-

Chief Alexander, of Tolovana, through Paul Williams, Interpreter, said: "When I saw you down at Tolovana, you remember how much I thanked you for being able to see you there. Others have made the suggestion and I want you to understand that we all appreciate your being present. You told me that you were our people's friend, and you did not like to see us get into any kind of mischief. You stated to me that anything we want we shall talk to you about now. Therefore, the people now being present, I say that I feel the same way as I felt at that time, and I tell you that we are people that are always on the go, and I believe if we was put in one place we would die off like rabbits, and I told you also that if you wanted to do anything good for us here, you must select somebody for us who was truthful and not untruthful. I ask you now to let the white people come near us. Let us live our own lives in the customs we know. If we were on Government ground we could not keep the white people away. One more thing, from now on, I wish you would leave written instructions here with us, so we may know these things. This is all I want to say at the present time. I have more to say about some other things, but not at the present time."

Here Chief Joe, of Salchacket, was requested to speak, but he could not understand the native language spoken by Paul Williams, the Interpreter. He understands Wood River and Nenana dialect, but not Tanana. He was interpreted by two different Indians. He said:

"I am very thankful for being here. This is the first time I have been here and not much acquainted. I never have talked to the Government people before. This is the first time in my life I ever had the chance. Fortunately, I am able to speak to you on this celebration day of the U. S. Government, on what is supposed to be one of the biggest holidays in the United States. We people are depressed. Every one of us here are just like one man, and I feel as they all do. We are suggesting to you just one thing, that we want to be left alone. As the whole Continent was made for you, God made Alaska for the Indian people, and all we hope is to be able to live here all the time. And we wish to ask you to give us written instructions on our matters."

Chief John, of Chena, through Paul Williams, Interpreter, said: "Quite a while ago we sent for white people. At that time we felt that we would be able to have better living. I have heard that there is a Government which is ruling us, and I feel that I belong to some kind of a Government, but we want to know what this Government is. We wish that we could know just what it means. I have been in Fairbanks only this one time, and I have never been able to talk to any of these Government officials, but today on account of you people, who have listened to the talk of the Chiefs, we have been able to consult with the Government. For quite a while we have been expecting the Government to do something for us. There are times when we feel that we should have some assistance from the Government. Of course,

-11-

-12-

some day we may get help from the United States Government, but we do
not see any written instructions from the Government ourselves. 'Way
back in the early days there was no such a thing as a Chief, but lately
there are some, and we feel if the natives must have a chief, then the
white people surely must have something bigger than a Chief to rule."

Julius Pilot, of Nenana, through Paul Williams, Interpreter,
said: "This certainly is a good day for us to meet here, when all the
celebration is going on, and we wish you to know that we are pleased
to be here. We did not see the person who made this world, the man
who makes the sun shine on this ground. Perhaps this man that we have
heard so much about is God. We are the people that were put here by
God, the Person who made the world, so now it is just the same as if
we were talking to the Creator through the President of the United
States. Some day, we will expect that something will be accomplished
by this meeting here today. If it is accomplished, we want one thing,
and it is that the chiefs be notified. That means the same as inform-
ing all the Indians."

Titus Alexander, of Tolovana, through Paul Williams,
Interpreter, said: "I have nothing extra to say, but what the people
here and the Chiefs have said, I agree to. I will be very pleased
if the people will grant us the suggestions these chiefs have made,
and will feel that you people have accomplished what the natives have
asked for in the name of God. I have been wishing to know who these
gentlemen were we were coming up here to see, and just as soon as we
landed here this gentleman welcomed us with very generous words. We all
feel very pleased to see that you are all just as kind, and wish to
tell you so."

Alexander Williams, of Fort Gibbon, through Paul Williams,
Interpreter, said: "Every one of us have had a chance to say something,
now, we all must thank you for allowing us to make suggestions. I
wish to thank you for allowing us to be talking all this time, now that
we are here."

Delegate Wickersham: "It is now up to Paul Williams, the
Interpreter, to make his own statement".

Paul Williams said: "I made my suggestions this morning,
and I don't know as I care to say anything more regarding these affairs.
Judge Wickersham, Mr. Riggs, Mr. Richie and Mr. Atwell, as I said this
morning, I have had a chance to work among my people, my own people, for
the past 14 years, and I also stated this morning that I was glad to say
that I was able to know more about their living than you do, and I always
feel that at any time I should advise you Government officials or our
Missionaries, and that my advisements would mean a great deal because of
the experience I have had with the native people. Therefore, I wish
you to take this in mind, that about this reservation, I think it is a
fake.

-15-

"It is along this line that I will mention. For this one reason, Alaska is a cold country and I don't think it would ever do for a reservation. In the states your Government reserves for the Indians and gives them a good start. First, the Government purchases their ground for them and puts it in good condition for raising vegetables and making farms and raising cattle. That is different from here. Of course, the Government could raise cattle here and grow vegetables for the people to live on, but we natives of Alaska are different from that. We feel that just as soon as you take us from the wild country and put us on reservations that we would soon all die off like rabbits, just as the chief has said. We live like the wild animals, -- in long times ago our people did not wear cotton clothes and clothes like the white men wear, but we wore skins made from the caribou. We lived on fish, the wild game, moose and caribou, and ate blueberries and roots. That is what we are made to live on, -- not vegetables, cattle, and things like the white people eat. As soon as we are made to leave our customs and wild life, we will all get sick and soon die. We have moved into cabins. There is no such thing now as the underground living, and as soon as we have done this the natives begin to catch cold. You used to never hear anything of consumption or tuberculosis. The majority of people say that whiskey brings tuberculosis to the Indians, but this is not true. It is because we have changed our mode of living, and are trying to live like the white men do. I feel that the natives are entitled to their own land, and should not be put on a reservation. If the homestead is allowed, I think that the natives should be permitted to take up their own homesteads, but I think these people have told you just what they want. There is one more subject that I want to talk on which I will hold until you people answer what we have to say. There is one here we have not heard from. Our missionary, Mr. Madera, may suggest something."

Reverend Guy H. Madera, Missionary, said: "I cannot say much more than I said this morning. The question is a hard one to settle. We don't want a reservation, but will be glad to have allotments. In a very few isolated cases we can take up allotments. The majority of the Indians cannot do this. There is in the Indian life one very sweet feature -- that is, their mutual helpfulness. There is no such thing in an Indian village as one person having plenty and others being hungry. If one person has luck and gets a black fox and sells it, he has plenty of grub. He stores it in a tent or cabin and everybody goes in and eats. If one man kills a moose, this moose belongs to the whole village. That is what we call a community life. It would be too bad if that were taken away, which it certainly would be if they had to all live on separate allotments. The reservation would result in the Indian soon perishing for they could not live in one place. Today the Indians are self-supporting and independent. They do not bother anybody to give them grub. They do not ask the Government for anything. They keep the law, unless they are given whiskey. They are wards of the Government, and this is the same as children of the Government. They have many traits that I would like to see perpetuated. Between the reservation and the allotments, Delegate Wickersham prefers the reservation. The Tanana

-13-

-14-

River runs all the way down this valley and about 55 miles on each side
are the foothills of the Alaskan Range and about 40 miles on the other
side of the Tanana Hills.　All that country is hunted by the Indians.
To give them a reservation big enough for them to live on like they do
at present, would mean several hundred miles and I don't think the Government can afford to give them that much ground.　A smaller reservation
would help them, if there could also be a hunting reservation made,
extending to the foot hills.　This would help them and not interfere
with development.　I think it best to set off a large tract of land
where only Indians could hunt and trap."

　　　　Chief Alexander, of Tanana, through Paul Williams, Interpreter,
said:　"I am very thankful to Mr. Madern for giving an address like that."

　　　　Delegate Wickersham:　"Mr. Riggs, do you want to make some more
observations for their benefit?"

　　　　Thomas Riggs, Jr., to the Indians, through Paul Williams,
Interpreter:　"As far as I can make out, from what the chiefs have said,
the Indians want certain things, and I want to know if I have understood
it rightly.　They want to keep their present villages free from encroachment by the white men.　They want freedom to come and go as they want to,
fishing and hunting, and if they take up their allotments, they don't want
to have to live on them perhaps all the time that the law demands, but if
they do take up allotments they will build cabins and call them their homes.
Is that the opinion of the assembled chiefs?"

　　　　Unanimous answers from the Indians:　"Yes".

　　　　Paul Williams, Interpreter:　"I think, gentlemen, that as far
as these natives taking up homesteads, they want to do this at present,
but they also want to maintain their villages.　Would it make any
difference to the natives if they did take up allotments -- could they
still hold their villages?"

　　　　Thomas Riggs, Jr.:　"I think that is a question for Mr. Richie
of the Land Office to answer".

　　　　Paul Williams, Interpreter:　"At present they have their
native villages.　What we want to know is if we are entitled to take up
homesteads, could we still maintain our villages and take up homesteads
at the same time?"

　　　　C. W. Richie:　"As the law is at present, a native does not
have to take up an allotment, that is simply a privilege the Government
gives him if he wishes to take a certain piece of ground, it will be held
to him and from all white men.　If he wishes to live in a village or
if he wishes to live on his homestead he can do so.　He does not have
to take his allotment, it is simply an offer the Government makes.　The
law also provides, and Mr. Atwell and myself and all Government men in
our service, are instructed to see that the Indian villages are not
encroached upon.　Any village or homestead cannot be encroached upon
by the white men."

Ms 107
Box 38 F1
-14-

-15-

Thomas Riggs, Jr.: "Can an Indian live in his village and have an allotment at the same time?"

C. W. Richie: "This has not been decided by the Department. If an Indian has an old fishing site he cannot live in his village all the time and still keep his fishing site. The allotment proposition implies use and occupancy in order to hold it, and you must use and occupy it. If you do not, you cannot hold it."

Delegate Wickersham: "I want to talk to them about reservations. The Chiefs say they want to hold their village sites. Under the law the Secretary of the Interior or the President can mark out a big tract of land around one of their village sites, maybe ten miles square, or may be a hundred miles square, or one mile square. Any amount that the Secretary of the Interior or the President thinks is necessary for their use. If he did that, there would be a reservation, but they would continue in that case to live in their own homes and villages. Of course, the President may make a large reservation and ask all of them to move to one place, but I do not think he would do that now that you have all expressed opposition to it. The Secretary of the Interior would want to do the best thing for them, and he might think it was necessary to mark out a reservation, one or more of them. If he did that he would make all reservations, undoubtedly, around their villages. Now, if they make a reservation at Tolovana, say, two miles square, that would be around Chief Alexander's house, and Chief Alexander and his people would continue to live there. They would be just as free as they now are. They could go fishing whenever they pleased and could go hunting whenever they pleased. They could go south and hunt and could go up the Tolovana and they could go up to Fairbanks and they could go anywhere they pleased. A reservation is not a prison. A reservation is more for the purpose of helping the Indians. It is made to help them, and if a reservation is made at any place, the Government would appoint an agent there to help the Indians. They would start a school for the children and would build a church, and the Indians would be just as free as they are now. I want to say again that a reservation is not a prison. A reservation would not be made for the purpose of limiting the people, but to help them. On the other hand, the people can take up homesteads and go fishing from their homesteads, and they may go to the Kantishna or up the Tolovana, just as they do now. A homestead is not a prison either. Both the homestead and the reservation would be simply a piece of land set aside by the Government for their use. The only difference is that in the case of a homestead, each man has his piece of land, but if it is a reservation they all have an interest in it. But after a while the Government might survey the reservation and deed each one of them a part. Now, I lived, long ago, down at Puyallup. For twenty years there was an Indian reservation there, and the Indians were my friends and I was their attorney. I helped them many times. They had a big reservation there. A great many of them lived on the reservation, and a great many of them had homesteads on this reservation. Some time ago the Government surveyed

-16-

the reservation and gave each one of them 160 acres of land, some 80 and some 160. The Government had a big school there, and churches. These Indians were perfectly happy and perfectly free, and went hunting. They were good people and now they own their reservation. Some of the land has been sold. I don't agree with the people here. They think that a reservation is a bad thing. I think that a reservation is excellent and the best thing that can be done for the Indians, but we want you people here to say what you want, and we take it down in this book and we are going to have it all written out and send it to the President and to the Secretary of the Interior, and when they consider about you they will read that and will understand what you people say. Now, I cannot make a reservation, I cannot give you a homestead. These other gentlemen cannot make a reservation, or give you a homestead. None of us can make you do anything. Nobody can force you to do anything but the President of the United States, and the President of the United States can make you move on. Now, we are going to tell him just what you are saying, and we don't know what he will do. We are going to try and get him to help you. I am going to be your representative in Congress for two years, and I will help to make laws, but we don't have to make laws about reservations and homesteads. But I am going to live here for many years and I want you men to know that I am your friend and if I can be of any service to you I am going to do it, and don't you believe that the Government wants to do anything to hurt you. The President and the Secretary want to try to help you. They want you to have homesteads. They want you to have homesteads, where they can keep bad people away from you. If it is on a homestead or a reservation, they will keep the white people away, and they will protect you and help you in either place, but all this talk today I hope you will take to your hearts, because Mr. Riggs here is going to build a railroad and these gentlemen are going to continue to survey these lands, and when Mr. Riggs' railroad is built, the white people are going to come in here in great numbers, and push, and push until the Indians are clear off the best land and you people must do something. If you don't you won't have any homesteads, for the white people will get all the best lands. This is what I want you to see. And you must not put it off too long. You must not put it off until it is too late. Of course, there will be plenty of land in this country one hundred years from now, but it will not be the best hunting and fishing grounds. All the land on the river will be gone. Then where will you live? The white man knows just as much about taking good land as you do and he is going down to the Land Office and take this land, so we want you people to beat him there and get your homesteads. The Government will protect you either on a homestead or on a reservation. Let me tell you again, I want you to do something and do it soon. The white man has already been taking these lands. He has been backing the Indians up and has been getting the best places. You have got to do something soon or there won't be anything left. You don't want to be left out. What I am trying to do is to make these Indian Chiefs see that there is going to be a change and I want them to get homesteads before they are too late."

-17-

the Indians were advised by Delegate Wickersham to talk the matter
over with

Chief Ivan, of Crossjacket, through Paul Williams, Interpreter: "I have misunderstood you and would like to say something
now. I have a village of about 12 cabins, 14 or 15 families there.
A very important place for the natives. It is where the road goes
into the Kantishna, into Fort Gibbon and up to Fairbanks. We live
there during the winter and during the summer are in the woods hunting
and fishing. Now, what I wish to know is what should we do to hold
that ground?"

Delegate Wickersham, through Paul Williams, Interpreter:
"Well, that would depend upon how good this place is. If you wanted
to you could have a large reservation taking in your village and the
country around it. Under the law, the white man when he takes a homestead must live on it as his home. He must live on it under the white
man's law. Where you have your 12 cabins owned by Indians no white man
has a right to go into those cabins. No white man has a right to live
on that ground. That ground and the cabins and everything around them
belong to the Indians, and if a white man goes there and the Indians
will come up here and tell the Land Office men they will see that the
white man is put off the land. There is nothing about a reservation to
be scared of. A reservation is a good thing for the people, for all
your people and all your families. I think it would be a good thing to
make a reservation five miles square and keep the white men off. Long
time ago, there was some of your people and they went over on the headwaters of the Fraser. They kept on traveling far away, on and on, and on,
till they got to Mexico. They talk the same language you do. They are
descendants of the same people as you are. They are three thousand
miles away but they talk your language just the same, and all these
people are your people. They have horses and cattle and sheep and farms
and all kinds of implements to work with. There are reservations of
your people in Oregon. They live on reservations all through the
country. It is a mistake to be afraid of reservations. Your villages
are reservations now, and the Government will help you to keep these
villages and protect them from the white man. And if you want homesteads
and schools and churches, the Government will make them for you and
protect them. They are your friends and are trying to help you and not
to hurt you."

H. J. Atwell, through Paul Williams, Interpreter, said to the
Indians: "Two years ago there were reservations five miles square
proposed around certain villages on the lower Yukon, that is, below the
mouth of the Tanana. The recommendation was that the Indian be kept on
the reservation and the white men be kept from coming there. The recommendation was sent up here to us to make a report on, as to whether it
would be good or bad for the Indians. We reported that such a reservation
would be bad for the Indians. We reported that the Indians were used to
roaming over the country, hunting and fishing everywhere and that they
would go a long way up and down the river to do this. The proposed reservations have not been made."

After a vote of thanks from the Indians for allowing them to
express their wishes to the officials of the Government, and with the
statement that they knew everybody was tired, the meeting was closed and

-18-

the Indians were advised by Delegate Wickersham to talk the matter
over thoroughly among themselves and let him know just what they wanted.

On July 6th, at 4:00 o'clock P. M., at the Public Library,
in Fairbanks, Alaska, the Council reassembled, the same persons being
present.

Paul Williams, Interpreter: "Well, I guess we are through
with this reservation business. We have decided about that."

Delegate Wickersham: "You don't want a reservation?"

Paul Williams: "We don't want a reservation.

Delegate Wickersham: "How would you like a withdrawal of
the land around your villages for the use of your Indians?"

Paul Williams: "What do you mean, a line around the villages?"

Delegate Wickersham: "No, a withdrawal of the land several
square miles around the villages for the exclusive use of the Indians?"

Paul Williams: "Couldn't they do that themselves by allotments?"

Delegate Wickersham: "They could take homesteads."

Paul Williams: "Yes, they could take homesteads, and another
thing I am going to ask: If the natives take up homesteads or allotments
do they have to have a quarter of mile strip around their ground between
the homesteads or can they have homesteads right close up to each other?"

C. W. Richie: "Only where the land is near a river, like the
Yukon or Tanana, a river that is traveled by boats and launches, they
have to have strips between the homesteads; where the allotments are
taken up back from the river they can be up close against each other with
no space between the allotments."

Paul Williams: "Then, if we had these homesteads where the
town is, could we claim that if somebody had it for a homestead, one
chief's homestead, like one big family and all live there like we do
now? Could we hold it that way?"

C. W. Richie: "No. The patent would issue to the man or
chief who took up the homestead and it would belong to him."

Paul Williams: "Then in such a place as Crossjacket, where
we have claims for two miles square which haven't been recorded there.
We could take that as a homestead in the name of Chief Ivan Henry --
suppose Chief Ivan takes that as a homestead, couldn't the natives come
back and use that village just as they do now?"

C. W. Richie: "They could if Chief Ivan Henry would let them,
and if he agreed to it, yes, but the Government would finally issue the
title to the homestead to Chief Ivan Henry alone, and he would then be
the owner of the ground, but if he wished the other natives to come there

-19-

they could come, but the chief's homestead couldn't be two miles
square, it could only be 160 acres, or half a mile square."

Paul Williams: "But right back of Chief Ivan couldn't
somebody else take up a homestead, and on each side of him, enough
to cover the two miles square?"

C. W. Richie: Where the village is on the river these homesteads would have to have quarter of a mile strips between them.
That would cut the two miles of shoreline into four claims with strips
between the homesteads.

Paul Williams: "And these strips between, some white man
could come in there and start a store or something on those strips?"

C. W. Richie: "The strips between the homesteads are
reserved by the Government. Nobody could take the strips that are
reserved."

Paul Williams: "This place then, Crossjacket, -- I am referring to Crossjacket, because it is held by natives alone and the white
people have been trying to get in there for so long -- if we threw it
open for homesteads, and took up the two miles square in homesteads,
cut up by the strips between, won't the white people get in there, on
those strips, and start a store, and live on the quarter mile strips?"

C. W. Richie: "Nobody could live on the quarter mile strips.
The Government reserves these strips. And even now no white man can
take the Indian villages. They are now reserved and are safe. Nobody
can take the Indian villages away from you. But this protection is
only for just what the villages cover, and what is actually needed for
the villages. It doesn't give the Indian any right to the timber that
he will need for his firewood in the years to come, or any hunting
ground, but the villages themselves nobody can encroach upon."

Paul Williams: "That is what I wanted to find out. I am
especially referring to Crossjacket because it has been marked for two
or three years and has always been held by the natives and the white
people kept out."

Delegate Wickersham: "Who marked it -- you say it has been
marked?"

Paul Williams: "The natives themselves marked it, but it has
never been recorded, but the village has been there from generation
to generation.'

Delegate Wickersham: "Well, for further advice on this you
can always see Mr. Richie, and I think it is best that you consult
with him about this.

C. W. Richie: "Paul, you can tell your people that at any time
they want to know anything about taking up the homesteads or allotments,

-20-

or any time they want advice about their land matters, if they will
come to me, I will be very glad to tell them what they want to know
and to advise them the very best that I can."

Paul Williams: "Then, you people will understand that we
natives have decided to keep off the reservation, and do not wish to
go on a reservation at all. But our next suggestion, that we wanted
and of course which we shall wish the Delegate to bring up for us and
see what he can do for us about it, after we have discussed the matter
among ourselves we have decided that we are going to ask the Government
to see what it could do for us. It has been so long ago now since
the Mission came, in fact the Missionaries have been with us longer
than this Government has, and they have always done all they could for
the natives, but somehow or other they have always been pretty short
on workers or on money so that they couldn't very well accomplish what
the natives have needed, on account of being so short of funds or of
workers; so now, we have decided that we all wish to ask the Government
if they couldn't get us some industrial schools. If they wish to help
the Indians, the natives, that is the best thing the Government could
do for us, and I think it is about time for the Government to look
after us. So I think the best thing we can ask for is an industrial
school."

Delegate Wickersham: "You want to learn trades?"

Paul Williams: "Yes. As you told the Chiefs here yesterday,
you said this country would be all crowded with people coming in, and
of course, I know that is going to happen too, in my own knowledge, and
the game will be short, the fishing will be short, the fur will be
short, and everything will be short that the natives are using now, and
in time it is going to take money for the natives to live, and we all
realise that, so I think it is time for the Government to give assistance
to the Indians, either by themselves, or through the Missionaries who
have been with us so long but cannot do so much for us because they are
short of funds and workers. So far as we know the Government has done
nothing toward assisting the natives' education. Of course, the Bureau
of Education has got schools here and there, but they are public schools
and the natives practically live from hand to mouth and are out rustling
for their living mostly. They have villages, of course, but they only
live there for a week or two weeks and then go on a fishing or hunting
trip, and take the children with them, and so they cannot go to these
schools the Bureau of Education has established and live with their people."

Delegate Wickersham: "How are you going to make these native
children go to school then if the Government builds an industrial school?"

Paul Williams: "If they put up an industrial school, with a
boarding school or anything, then they can keep the native children there.
That would be different from public schools for the children would stay
there and would not be with the older natives fishing and hunting so much.
Of course, if you think I am bringing up something impossible, it is for
you to say so."

-21-
-11-

Delegate Wickersham: "It isn't impossible. It is quite possible. If the Government builds an industrial school here these native children could go and learn trades. Paul, do all these natives here want such an industrial school?"

Paul Williams: "They say that is the way they all see it, and that they all want it."

Rev. Guy H. Madara, Missionary: "Five years ago, the Mission sent a half breed boy out to educate him, Arthur Wright, who has been at Mount Herman Mission. He came in last summer, and he has the ability and enthusiasm necessary to do good work. At the present time, the Mission has the logs up at Nenana for an industrial school building, which they expect to finish this fall. That is the present plan. The great trouble we have found is that the only way to get the children in school and keep them there is to take them and board them and keep them. With their people, the children do not live in one place long enough to go to school, and when they do Indian customs are such that the life of the Mission, being orderly, is not in line with the life of the native villates, and it is hard for the children to come. For instance, I don't think there is an Indian at the village -- I don't think there is an Indian in the Tanana Valley -- who goes to bed three nights in succession at the same time. Now, school children have to do that if they are going to get any good out of school. Some of these men have children at Nenana, now, others have not. But there are some present, who will send their children this fall to begin learning this industrial work. Our capacity, at Nenana, is at the most about thirty five or forty children, girls and boys together. Unless there be a boarding school, there is no use attempting any industrial work. There are a great many more children in this section of the country, that want to come to school, that we cannot take care of. We want to take care of all we can, but sometimes it is quite a strain on our resources to take care of them, and I think it might be a good plan to ask the Government to establish a school at Tanana, or possibly at Crossjacket, either by aiding the Mission financially and letting them do it or by doing it themselves, through the Bureau of Education, but without a boarding school in connection, there is no use of attempting it. The natives have to follow the game and the fish already. He couldn't stay in one place and live. So the only thing to do is to establish a boarding school, probably at Crossjacket."

Upon Paul Williams interpreting to the Indians what Reverend Madara said, there was unanimous approval, and Paul Williams said: "They say 'Really, what we wish very much'."

Delegate Wickersham: "Let me ask you some questions, Mr. Madara. What arrangement has been made for doing anything for the Indians at Salchaket, by the Mission?"

-22-

Mr. Madara: "We have at Salchaket two workers. They belong to the Episcopal Mission. One is a trained nurse and the other one has charge — both ladies. They have day school for the children and at present they have two children living in the house with them and when the boys are home from hunting they have night school for the boys."

Delegate Wickersham: "Who built the school building?"

Mr. Madara: "The Mission".

Delegate Wickersham: "What did it cost, approximately?"

Mr. Madara: "I couldn't tell you now".

Delegate Wickersham: "About how much per annum does it cost for the maintenance of the school at Salchaket?"

Mr. Madara: "It cost us last year in the neighborhood of $5500.00, paid for entirely through the Episcopal Mission by money gotten from people in the East, with absolutely no help from other sources."

Delegate Wickersham: "No National or Territorial aid given it?"

Mr. Madara: "No."

Delegate Wickersham: "Where is the next mission?"

Mr. Madara: "Chena village, fifteen miles from Salchaket. We have no workers there at present, although we hope to have one this summer."

Delegate Wickersham: "What is being done there for the Indians?"

Mr. Madara: "The only thing I am able to do now is to give them Sunday services and sometimes occasional services during the week."

Delegate Wickersham: "Where do you live, Mr. Madara?"

Mr. Madara: "At Chena, proper. Three miles above the Indian village. You understand that my work is the supervision of all the whole Tanana Valley Missions."

Delegate Wickersham: "What other effort is being made by any other persons or churches to help and to educate the Indians?"

Mr. Madara: "None".

Delegate Wickersham: "Below Chena Village, where is the next mission?"

Mr. Madara: "The Nenana Mission."

-25-

Delegate Wickersham: "That is the point where the Government Railroad is supposed to cross the Tanana River, isn't it?"

Mr. Madera: "Yes".

Delegate Wickersham: "How far from where the railroad work will be carried on is your mission established?"

Mr. Madera: "Adjoining it."

Delegate Wickersham: "What have you there?"

Mr. Madera: 'We have a large two story hall, a two story hospital, a large school room, and an industrial building in the process of erection, a two story cache, stables, outbuildings, and also two cabins."

Delegate Wickersham: "How many teachers or other employees do you have there?"

Mr. Madara: "Seven."

Delegate Wickersham: "By whom are they maintained?"

Mr. Madara: "The Episcopal church."

Delegate Wickersham: "And they get no assistance from the Government or Territory?"

Mr. Madara: "None."

Delegate Wickersham: "What was the expense of maintaining this plant last year?"

Mr. Madara: "Between $11,000.00 and $11,500.00."

Delegate Wickersham: "Where did you get the money?"

Mr. Madara: "From voluntary gifts and from grants from the Board of Missions."

Delegate Wickersham: "How many Indians, children and adults, are they given assistance there, either by way of education or in any other ways?"

Mr. Madara: "In the neighborhood of three hundred."

Delegate Wickersham: "And what bands or tribes do they belong to, mostly?"

-24-

Mr. Madara: "Wood River, Nenana, Minto, Tolovana. In addition to which we have children from all along the Tanana and the Yukon Rivers in the schools conducted there."

Delegate Wickersham: "Where is the next place below that where you have a mission?"

Mr. Madara: "There is nothing between there and Tanana."

Delegate Wickersham: "What is there at Crossjacket?"

Mr. Madara: "An Indian village."

Delegate Wickersham: "No school or mission of any kind there?"

Mr. Madara: "No. Crossjacket has been a growing village for several years, gradually growing larger through the coming of the Indians from Tanana to Crossjacket. It has now reached proportions where it is necessary to do something, and it is the intention of the Mission to establish a mission there as soon as it can possibly do it."

Delegate Wickersham: "Where is the next mission?"

Mr. Madara: "At Tanana. There is a large hospital and it is just in process of erection. There are two resident workers there with a resident priest coming in this summer, which will make three. At the Indian mission, we have in addition to the hospital, a school and a shop."

Delegate Wickersham: "What kind of a shop?"

Mr. Madara: "A carpenter shop and a sawmill plant."

Delegate Wickersham: "To whom does the sawmill belong?"

Mr. Madara: "To the mission."

Delegate Wickersham: "Is there a Government building there?"

Mr. Madara: "The Government has a public school building there, right across from the Mission, which was erected by the Government through the Bureau of Education."

Delegate Wickersham: "How many children are there at that place, either in the Mission schools or at the Government school?"

Mr. Madara: "Altogether there must be about thirty or forty children going to the two schools."

-25-

Delegate Wickersham: "How long has that Mission been there?"

Mr. Madara: "Since 1900".

Delegate Wickersham to Paul Williams, Interpreter: "Where were your born, Paul?"

Paul Williams: "At Mike Hess Creek, above Rampart."

Delegate Wickersham: "How far from Gibbon?"

Paul Williams: "About a hundred miles."

Delegate Wickersham to Mr. Madara: "Has the Bureau of Education any schools of any kind in the Tanana country?"

Mr. Madara: "Nothing at all. They built the school building at Nenana and for one or two years supported a teacher there, but the Mission, about five years ago, took this over from the Government and has ever since supported the work there.'

Delegate Wickersham: "Why did the mission take it over rather than let the Bureau of Education maintain it?"

Mr. Madara: "Largely through friction between the teachers and the mission employees."

Delegate Wickersham: "And it was turned over so that it would be under one head."

Mr. Madara: "Yes ."

Delegate Wickersham: 'Are there any more missions in that country?'

Mr. Madara: 'In addition to these there is a mission at Tanana crossing which of course will not be affected by anything we do here, but which is a part of the work being done by the Church in the Tanana Valley."

Delegate Wickersham: "How many Indian people are there in the valley above Salchaket?"

Mr. Madara: "There are about 400 who center at Tanana Crossing and there are tribes up on the Nebesna and Shushana which I have never even seen and know nothing of. It is impossible to carry the mission work to them. It is almost impossible to take the work to Tanana Crossing.'

-26-

Mr. Riggs: "Is the work between the Bureau of Education and the Mission, as a rule, harmonious?"

Mr. Madara: "I would rather not answer that, because I have had no personal experience with the Government school teachers."

Delegate Wickersham, to Paul Williams, Interpreter: "Ask these Chiefs if they would prefer to have the industrial school located at Crossjacket or at Tanana, or at Salchaket, or any other place on the river."

Chief Alexander Williams, of Fort Gibbon, through Paul Williams said: "We expect the Government to establish the school where it will be the center for the Tanana Valley and the Yukon River and the Koyukuk river and down river."

Chief Jacob Starr, of Fort Gibbon, through Paul Williams, Interpreter, says he thinks it is right that it should be in the center.

Delegate Wickersham: "They want the school centrally located. Now, will they all support the school and send their children there if there is one established by the Government?"

Chief Alexander Williams, of Fort Gibbon, through Paul Williams, Interpreter, said that if any of his people objected to sending their children to the school when it was established that he would make them come.

Chief Alexander, of Tolovana, through Paul Williams, Interpreter, says that he has his child now in care of the Mission school and that you can see for yourself that he is anxious to get his children educated and if there is an industrial school put up, he will be willing to put his child there, and see that his people send their children there.

Delegate Wickersham: "Ask them, Paul, if there is any one of them here who will object to sending their children to school if an industrial school is established, either by aiding the Mission or by establishing an independent Government school."

Paul Williams, Interpreter: "Chief Jacob Starr says he is willing, and Chief Alexander, and Chief Thomas says he won't agree because he has got one of his own children now in the Mission at Nenana."

Delegate Wickersham: "He wants to send his children to the mission school at Nenana?"

Paul Williams, Interpreter: "He says that as long as the school is there so close he would prefer to send the children there."

Ms 107
Box 38 F1
-26-

—27—

Delegate Wickersham: "But they all favor the establishment of a centrally located industrial school?"

Paul Williams, Interpreter: "Yes."

Chief Ivan, of Crossjacket, through the interpreter, said: "I am willing. I haven't got a child of my own of course but that cuts no figure with me, I am the head of the other natives, and of course if a school is established he is going to see it supported. I want the school and any time I get any advice from the Government or the mission I will see that the children do go to the schools. It is for the benefit of my people and I wish it would be established."

Delegate Wickersham: "Well, do they all feel that way about it?"

Chief Julius Pilot, of Nenana, through the interpreter, said: That he agrees to it. That an industrial school ought to be established by the mission or the Government. He says the railroad is coming through to Nenana and they don't know whether the mission ground is liable to be taken away by the Government and if so the mission would have to remove its buildings and take their schools to some place where they could stay and it would be wasting time, and for that reason he prefers to see the school some other place."

Delegate Wickersham: "Paul, how many Indians, men, women and children, old and young, are there at Tanana, and from there up to Salchaket, altogether?"

Paul Williams: "I don't know anything about the people up at Salchaket. Mr. Madara would know".

Mr. Madara: "Over two hundred Indians."

Delegate Wickersham: "How many at Crossjacket?"

Mr. Madara: "About sixty."

Delegate Wickersham to Chief Charley, of Minto, through Paul, the interpreter: "Chief Charley, how many Indian people, old, young, and middle aged are there at Minto?"

Chief Charley, through Paul, interpreter, said that he had never taken a census and did not know.

Delegate Wickersham: "Mr. Madara, how many Indian people are there at Salchaket, altogether?"

Mr. Madara: "About sixty."

-28-

Delegate Wickersham: "How many at Chena?"

Mr. Madara: "Forty."

Delegate Wickersham: "At Minto?"

Mr. Madara: "The total of Nenana, Minto and Tolovana, is about three hundred and fifty."

Delegate Wickersham: "How many do you think there are altogether, between Salchaket and Tanana, counting both these places?"

Mr. Madara: "The population is somewhat floating, but I would say about seven hundred to eight hundred, and possibly more."

Delegate Wickersham: "And about how many are children not over twenty one years of age -- from babies up to twenty one?"

Mr. Madara: "A rough estimate, well, I think there would be about 40%."

Delegate Wickersham: "Then, Paul, the short of it is that the Indians all want an industrial school for the young Indian people to be located at some central point and to be controlled either by the mission or by the Government, or by both. All of them are in favor of that, aren't they? Tell them if they are to hold up their hands."

Unanimous approval, all of them holding up hands.

Delegate Wickersham: "You tell, the Indian people, Paul, that I went to school when I was young and Mr. Riggs went to school and got a good education, and Mr. Richie and Mr. Madara and Mr. Atwell all went to school, and we all favor schools. We can't establish the school you want, but we will do what we can to help you to get schools. We will send this paper in which you have all said that you want schools to the Secretary of the Interior and ask him to help you. The Secretary of the Interior is a good man. He is strongly in favor of schools for the Indians, and we are sure that he will do something to help them, but we don't know what."

Paul Williams, Interpreter: "They want to talk about some labor now. Some labor that they want the Government to allow them to do."

Chief Alexander Williams, says: "Us natives are self-supporting people, of course, and in order to support ourselves we have to work for a living. Therefore, although we got the land, they wish the Government to allow them to work whenever they have anything to do. That would be a help to them just as much as the schools would. There are quite a few things that they are able to do that other people do."

-29-

Delegate Wickersham: "The Indians want a school and they also want a chance to work, is that it?"

Paul: "They all feel that way. They don't want to get up and talk about it because it takes so long, so I asked them if they all felt that way and they all said they did."

Delegate Wickersham: "How do you mean that they want to work?"

Paul: "I might explain that. The army has posts in different places. Each telegraph station lets out contracts for wood. Each telegraph station lets out contracts for fish each year. This would mean quite a bit of money for the natives if they could get the contracts, but they never are able to get the contracts."

Delegate Wickersham: "Why, Paul?"

Paul: "The white men get the contracts because they can read and write and the white man gets it before the Indians know that there is a contract to be let."

Delegate Wickersham: "Can the natives cut the wood as cheaply as the white men?"

Paul: "They could and would if they knew anything about them wanting the wood cut."

Delegate Wickersham: "Can the natives cut the wood as cheaply if they had a chance?"

Paul: "Yes."

Delegate Wickersham: "Can the natives put up the fish as cheaply and as well as the white men do, if they had the chance?"

Paul: "The native puts up a better fish than the white men do, because that is his native food and he has to put it up the very best way he can."

"There are so many white people here, and the natives altogether depended on their trapping, hunting and fishing, but the game laws are enforced now and they are not supposed to sell meat or fish or anything, and so they must have some way to get money, and they think it is time to ask for labor. Now on the railroad, they could go on the line just as well as the white people with a pick and shovel but they never have an opportunity, but even so, I believe the natives could do just as well as the white people on the railroad work."

Delegate Wickersham: "But if they were given work would they stick to it, or would they want to go hunting and fishing?"

-30-

Chief Alexander Williams, of Fort Gibbon, through Paul Williams, Interpreter, said: "Any time the natives get a job that they are able to handle they will handle it. I am an Indian and I had a job from the white people for 34 years."

Delegate Wickersham: "Doing what?"

Chief Alexander Williams: "Piloting boats."

Delegate Wickersham: "On what boats?"

Chief Alexander Williams: "Mostly all the company boats. The A. C. Company, and the N. L. T. T. and the N. N. boats, on the Yukon river."

Delegate Wickersham: "For how many years?"

Chief Alexander Williams: "Thirty four."

Delegate Wickersham: "Have any of these other men worked as pilots?"

Paul Williams: "Julius Pilot did."

Delegate Wickersham: "For how long?"

Paul Williams: "Seven years."

Paul Williams: "You see when there is any market or any demand for meat, the Indian has got meat and the white men got meat, the white man's meat is bought first always, and if the Indian got a fish to sell and the white man got a fish to sell, always the white man's fish is bought."

Delegate Wickersham: "Why?"

Paul Williams: "I don't know. The white people patronize each other, but are always down on the natives, that is what it is."

Delegate Wickersham: Don't you think Paul that the reason is because the Indians have never gone to school and don't understand things?"

Paul: "Yes, that is why we want the schools to learn these things."

Chief Alexander Williams, of Fort Gibbon, through Paul Williams, Interpreter, said: "If there is an industrial school started for the Indians, will you have a doctor there?"

-31-

Delegate Wickersham: "Do they need a doctor there?"

Paul: "Chief Alexander Williams says little as they get it they need the doctor just as bad as they need the schools."

Delegate Wickersham: "When their people get sick where do they go for help?"

Paul interpreting for Chief Alexander Williams: "Down at Gibbon there is a Government doctor, the army doctor, and they depend on him, but other places they go to the mission for medicine but there are places where there is no mission or Government doctor and anyway it is only those who have money who can go to the doctor."

Delegate Wickersham: "What do they do when they have no money and are sick?"

Paul: "Then they are helpless and can't do anything."

Delegate Wickersham: "Are there many who need doctors and can't get them?"

Paul: 'Yes, lots of them". All the Indians answered that question promptly in the affirmative.

Chief Ivan, of Crossjacket, through the interpreter, says: "I was pretty sick this winter and they took me down to the army doctor at Fort Gibbon and the doctor said he was to far gone and there was no hope for him. But anyway the doctor gave him some medicine and he paid him $2.50 but the doctor said he couldn't do anything for him. He says the medicine froze in the bottle and that it was mostly water."

Delegate Wickersham: "But he got well".

Paul: "No, he never was affected at all by the medicine. He says this is the last time he will talk now so he is going to talk away. He wants you to understand that he thinks it is very simple for the Government to do anything when it wants to, because the Government has a good people and citizens to support it, but the chiefs have people who cannot support them if they want to accomplish anything so they cannot do these things, but the Government can. So they came all the way up here at their own expense to show you how anxious they are to have the Government help them."

Paul: "They are very anxious to have three things, school, a doctor and some labor."

-32-

Thomas Riggs, Jr.: "About the labor on the railroad we will
have to wait and see what we can do. When the railroad starts next
year, if the Indians want to work and will work earnestly and
steadily, I will give them a show, but as a rule the natives have not
been very reliable about working. I landed once at an Indian village
and it happened that I had about a hundred tons of supplies and the
Indians were sitting around there in the village. I tried to hire
them, paying them big wages, to put that stuff in a warehouse and I
couldn't get any of them to work. That was at Rampart House. So any
Indians that went to work would have to understand that it would have
to be in earnest and that they would have to stay with it. But we
will give them a trial next year, if they want to work. If they will
work good the Indians can get work next year when the railroad construction starts. All we are doing now is surveying."

Chief Jacob Starr, of Fort Gibbon, through Paul Williams,
Interpreter, said: "We are not asking for labor for ourselves. We
are asking it for the whole of our people."

Paul Williams: "Now all these Indian Chiefs have come all
the way up the river in order to interview you gentlemen here and they will
hope very much that you will be able to accomplish something for them so
that when they go back they will be able to say it paid them to make
the trip to Fairbanks, and so that the people will see that it meant
a great deal to send their chiefs up here."

Delegate Wickersham: "Paul, you tell them I say I think it
has done a great deal of good. We have seen them now and know them
and are acquainted with them, and have written down all they said and
will send it to the Secretary of the Interior, and a copy of their
pictures too, so that the Secretary of the Interior will look at their
picture and look into their faces and see what kind of looking men
they are, and he will read here about what they want, about them wanting
schools and work and that they want to make homes and want to become
like white people and want to learn to talk the white men's language,
and to work like the white man. The Secretary of the Interior has
charge of all these matters you have brought up. He has charge of the
railroad and of the lands and I think he will feel very friendly to
you. But you tell them, Paul, that it all depends finally upon the
Indians themselves. If they work good they will be employed. If they
work bad they won't be employed. So it all lies with the Secretary of
the Interior and the Indians."

Paul Williams: "The Indians say that next time you run for
a Delegate you want to be sure and notify us and be sure you accomplish
this before you run again for Delegate."

Mr. Madara: "If they ever get to vote there will be enough
of them to settle the delegate question all right."

Delegate Wickersham: "I want you to say to them, Paul, that
I am glad to hear the Indians say that they are going to be interested

-33-

in who shall be elected Delegate from Alaska. It sounds good to me.
You tell them that as soon as they have established homes and live
like the white man and assume the habits of civilization, they can
have a vote."

       Rev. Guy H. Madara: 'A suggestion in regard to the doctor.
We have had so many Government officials in this country who don't
officiate, that I would like to make this statement right at the
start. We have had Government officials here who were supposed to
work, who were supposed to look after the preservation of game and
of fur, and who stayed in Fairbanks. We do not need that kind of a
doctor. If there could be a doctor appointed to look after the
health and sanitation among these Indians it would be a great thing,
but he would have to have an expense account large enough to allow him
to make regular visits up and down along the river, so that he could
go up and down the river and keep on moving at regular intervals from
place to place, and not just have an office in Fairbanks and expect
the Indians to come, because they can't do it.'

       Unanimous approval from the Indians.

       After the meeting, the Indians formed in two lines and shook
hands with the white men present, expressing their gratitude at being
allowed to state their case.

The Alaska Purchase
and Alaska Natives

The 150th Anniversary of the Alaska Purchase gave the contributors to this volume a chance to reflect on how the treaty set parameters for the legal discussions at the 1915 Tanana Chiefs meeting. What follows here are observations on how interpretation of the relationship between Native tribes and the federal government has evolved over the years, both in terms of legal rulings, expression of tribal leadership, and issues of sovereignty. Because this document is derived from an oral recording of discussion between four people who are intimately familiar with the history and the issues and know each other, the tone is both informal but also content rich in legal detail, understanding, and opinion. The transcript has been edited for a reading audience with an effort to retain the meaning but also the informal interaction between the participants.

A Group Discussion
Including excerpts, edits, and additional commentary

Natasha Singh, Kevin Illingworth, and Will Mayo are interviewed by William Schneider in Fairbanks, Alaska, on December 20, 2016, on the 150th Anniversary of the Alaska Purchase. Recording 2016-20-01, Parts 1 and 2. Oral History Collection, Alaska and Polar Regions Collections and Archives.

William Schneider: We have the pleasure of a group discussion about the Alaska Purchase. And it's particularly timely because we're celebrating the 150th anniversary, and so we'll try to get into some of the implications of that treaty on the Tanana Chiefs 1915 meeting. Our discussion of the treaty establishes some of the background for our understanding of the 1915 Tanana Chiefs meeting, so it is particularly appropriate that we take time to explore the treaty and its implications for Alaska Natives. Leslie McCartney, the Curator of Oral History at the Alaska and Polar Regions Collections and Archives, has agreed to videotape this so that we can create a record,[122] and I'm hopeful that this will lead to more investigations in this particular year, because I think there's a danger that this aspect of the purchase could get neglected. So here today is Will Mayo, who's Executive Director of Tribal Government and Client Services, and Kevin Illingworth, who is a professor at the University in Native Tribal Law, and Natasha Singh, who is the Legal Counsel for Tanana Chiefs. Thank you all for making time to do this. I know that you all have incredible schedules, and I'm glad we could have this happen. So, I think the way I'd like to start, if it's okay with you guys, is just to open up the question of "Why is the Alaska Purchase important to Alaska Natives?" And I think we can go from there.

Kevin Illingworth: So, I would say that the simplest way to say why the Alaska Purchase is so important to Alaska Natives is because it created such a profound change in the legal rights of Alaska Native people's sovereignty. I guess I would even say, it just changed with the stroke of a pen. For the vast majority of tribes in Alaska, there was no significant contact with Russian people—certainly not under the realm of dominion.[123] There were vast stretches of Alaska where Russians had no presence or influence. So what Russians sold was their interest—but yet when the United States purchased Alaska, the United States saw it more in the realm of manifest destiny and the continued expansion of the United States, control and influence over all of Alaska. So while Russian control may have been very small and dominion very small, the United States immediately started acting as if all of the territory that they purchased was then under the dominion of the United States.

William Schneider: And I guess as a backdrop to that we would say that particularly for Interior Alaska Natives that the Russian influence was particularly less than the coastal groups.

Kevin Illingworth: Certainly, but there were also many coastal groups not under any definition of what we would consider under Russian control. So you went from all these independent nations having 100 percent absolute sovereignty—not encroached upon at all, to at least under the United States understanding of the law—that was immediately eroded.

Immediately just taken away with the stroke of a pen. And there was no notice, certainly no choice in the matter. It wasn't whether people were given a vote: yes or no— how would you like this to happen? And we heard the Native response that was expressed even down in Southeast, right? The Tlingit say that this land wasn't the Russians to sell, that we allowed the Russians to be here for our own benefit, but it wasn't that Russians owned this. Up in the Copper River region where they drove out the Russians, they probably had even less feelings that they were under the control of the Russians before and at the time of purchase.

Natasha Singh: So for me, I guess I find the Alaska Purchase interesting because it brings up all these legal questions that Alaska Native tribal leaders had—always have had. There were all those legal questions of whether it was valid that the Russians owned the land. That wasn't only in 1867. Our tribal leaders *still* question that. It's still an open question. And all of the assertions that these, governments, Russia and the United States, have in terms of their perceived ownership and rule aren't accepted by the tribes. They're not fully accepted by our tribe—tribal leaders. They weren't fully accepted by our tribal chiefs a hundred years ago, and they're not gonna be accepted now. And there are still valid legal questions. The Alaska Purchase is interesting and relevant because that's when the United States and everything that it is, good and bad, started on our land. And while the U.S. Constitution creates a relationship with tribes and this nation, it also brings with it this view that tribes are domestic dependents.[124] And it's from this manifest-destiny[125] type of view that the body of federal Indian law is developed. So, that's why I find it interesting, because it's still so relevant to Indian law and there are still so many questions and things are so undecided.

Will Mayo: So, I think then the one thing that stood out to me was the language in the Treaty of Cession that acknowledged aboriginal claims and reserved that for a future date and which in just and honorable circumstances could have resulted in a more acceptable, realistic settlement. But as we know, the United States' treatment of the tribes that was going on at that time was one of warfare, of looking upon the Native American or indigenous nations as hindrances that had to be overcome. The West had to be won. And that was the flavor of things in 1867. Native rights were just sort of put on hold at that time, nationally. That period of time was just after the Civil War. And it was after that, that the nation began to turn its attention more specifically towards the issue of their Indian problem. What do we do? How do we deal with this situation? We want to punch these railroads through. We want to get access to resources. We need land because our population's growing, and they (the Natives) need to move. And the West was the ticket we had to get there.

So I guess I'm just setting kind of the backdrop nationally. And so in the middle of this, this harebrained idea of buying Alaska from Russia came up, and the secretary of interior, Seward, was ridiculed for wasting Congress's time and money. But then shortly after that, with the Klondike gold rush,[126] then everybody stopped arguing. They said there's money to be made up there and there's untold potential, so the whole thing changed. And we became then a part of the westward and northward movement of resource-hungry visionaries. And that just did not, it just did not go well for Natives. And the United States acted as if there was really nothing to stop them from ignoring Native land claims and they would have continued if it were not for the oil on the North Slope and the need for a right-of-way to transport it out, forcing a claims settlement. So, those are just thoughts that I've had.

William Schneider: So when does the treaty or the acknowledgment of aboriginal claims become an issue?

Kevin Illingworth: Well, I think building on what Will was saying, first, there was this competing idea of Alaska as some sort of frozen wasteland, the ice box, and at the same time there was this idea of Alaska as a big storehouse of wealth. And both of those are competing and conflicting imagery at the time of purchase. I think, weirdly, the first thing that really influenced the Interior was actually the commercial fisheries that happened on the coast. You already had overfishing of the Pacific Northwest, and Alaska was seen by fishermen right away as this great source of wealth, and so all the commercial fleet, all those who had experience fishing down south, came up here. I don't think it's by chance that Klawock was the location of the first cannery.[127] The commercial fishermen knew how to find the best rivers; it was where the Indian villages were. You moved there, displaced all the people that were there and set up fishing for your own wealth. I think that's when you started to see conflict occur. So the impact on the Interior was that commercial fishing was so successful and widespread that starvation started to hit before you even had mining and the gold rush in the Interior. The mining and the gold rush just severely compounded the scarcity even more.

The *Berrigan* case was the first time a case was brought that upheld the aboriginal land claim of Alaska Native people. It basically said that Alaska Natives had an aboriginal land claim to their entire territory. We have conflicting legal cases coming out of Southeast Alaska. There, the court ruled that the Tlingit held their land as private land, therefore the Court held that there was no responsibility of the federal government to protect their interests. So you saw in a sense this conflict of what was happening in Southeast Alaska and what was happening in the Interior. And then that's even compounded by the language coming from the Treaty of Cession where they're talking about the uncivilized tribes. I think people within the United States were trying to use that language to form some sort of third category under federal law that had never existed, where you had Indians with no recognized land rights or sovereignty. And I think that's why this continues to be such a big issue today. There was just such an effort to disenfranchise Alaska Native people of their land, of the value of the resources.

William Schneider: Would you say that despite Wickersham's ruling that Chief Jarvis's land couldn't be taken, couldn't be sold?

Kevin Illingworth: Yeah, I would say—

William Schneider: —in the *Berrigan* case?

Kevin Illingworth: Yeah, I would, and I guess to me the way that it most obviously plays out is that the Salchaket tribe is *not* federally recognized today, despite the fact that they won in court; they *were* ultimately removed from their land; everybody ended up dispersed. There is not even a Native allotment. There is nothing there in the place where the *Berrigan* case happened.

Natasha Singh: Where they won.

Kevin Illingworth: Where they won.

Will Mayo: Just a cemetery.

Kevin Illingworth: Yes. But the people, Salchaket people, still exist. The people that identify as Salchaket exist up the Copper and the Upper Tanana area and elsewhere.

William Schneider: And, Will, you've talked about the irony of that situation.

Will Mayo: Yes. So, I think about the effort that Judge Wickersham made to warn the tribes that more white men were gonna be coming. He said that they would number "more than the trees on the hills." He used this language. And when they came, they would start taking the land. And after they had taken the good land, they would take the remainder of the land. And he said this will happen. And it was very, almost poetic language that he used. It was actually one of the engineers, the land guys, that used this language. But it didn't sink in. The chiefs didn't hear that. They did not fathom what he was saying. They had no frame of reference.

William Schneider: This is in the 1915—

Will Mayo: Nineteen-fifteen meeting. And here you had the Salchaket leader, and the leaders from Chena, Nenana, Tolovana, Minto, Cosjacket, and Tanana. They were being invited to look at protecting a land base. But as I was rereading the text this week of that 1915 meeting, and it sounded to me like what I would've taken away from that meeting if I were William the interpreter, is: it sounds like they want to give you a little land around your community that will always be yours. And they all knew right away that that wouldn't work, because it would take a massive slice of land to sustain their wild-resource economy. And they just could not envision placing themselves in these little stamps, postage stamps of land, and expect to make a living. So, I sometimes wonder if we'd had a negotiator there who was familiar with land rights and claims and reservations and someone who realized that if those groups of tribes had united, they could've carved out a piece of land from the Ray Mountains, down to the Novi, out to the Alaska Range, and over to Delta. They would've included all those areas and Salchaket would've existed today along with Chena and Tolovana and Cosjacket, all places that don't exist as Native communities. They no longer exist as peoples.

And so I think about that. I think that way sometimes and wonder what it would've looked like today. But of course, it didn't go that way.

Kevin Illingworth: But I do want to say I think it is really a legitimate thing to think that way, because that's the way land claims were supposed to have been settled. If you're following the legal pattern of land claims, then we should've had the treaties and negotiations, certainly as we're talking about the purchase of the territory, and as soon as possible after the purchase of the territory, certainly prior to statehood. And I think, in that sense, when you see where the federal government did follow through, and I'm thinking of during the IRA period[128] here in Alaska, in the case of Venetie and Arctic Village, to me these closest represent what it would've looked like if the federal government had sooner followed through with their responsibility to settle Native land claims. The settlement would have more closely represented the actual tribes and actual aboriginal land claims.

William Schneider: Do you think the chiefs were asking that question when they said it's been so many years since the purchase, and no one has come to us? We don't know what our relationship is with the U.S. government. Do you think that they were looking for that type of clarity about governmental relations?

Kevin Illingworth: Yeah, I do because they said it in a couple of different ways. They said that, you know, we'd love to follow the law, if you'd just write it down for us, tell us what the rules are. And so much of that conversation was forward thinking, but also to me, it was governmental in its terms, too, as in the idea of giving notice. You supposedly purchased this however many years ago and you never even notified us. We've not had any opportunity to be heard. And if you put this in modern terms or legal phrases that we recognize today, we see they were asking for due process. I very much think so. There was no due process in the purchase of Alaska, I guess is what I would say, and no due process in the government-to-government relationship that the chiefs obviously recognized and pointed out. I don't think anybody would have ever used terms like that at the time, but I think when you're talking that conversation between sovereigns, that's what they were saying.

William Schneider: I think oftentimes that you kinda opened my eyes, Kevin, to the notion that the Tanana Chiefs meeting sometimes gets overshadowed. We think of it as a land-based meeting. But really there was this more fundamental question of what's our relationship to each other as government-to-government bodies? And that has tremendous implications, the types of things you were talking about, Natasha. We see it down the line through history in the struggle to establish a relationship that is satisfactory.

Natasha Singh: Yeah, to me in reading the transcript, the chiefs held themselves out to be leaders of sovereigns, and that is how they communicated in their requests, their demands. And I believe that's how they demonstrated that they are leaders of governments. And I don't know if it was thought of on the other side that way, but it seems like they got the message, the government representatives.

Will Mayo: Yeah, so the consultation was very strong, the desire for a meaningful consultation was set out very early in their dialogue in the 1915 meeting. And the chiefs wanted more clarity. There was no treaty, but there was still the avenue of creating a reservation. And with a little bit different education, I think Paul Williams could have led the chiefs in an entirely different way. As the interpreter, he was the one who could relate to them a path forward. And though he learned the other language (English), his vision was never extended to include one whereby a large land base could be obtained. But anyway, that was kind of my feeling that came out of it. They did not feel that there was enough, they could get enough land to really make it worthwhile, and they thought that it was going to be a small individual thing.

William Schneider: Going back to this government-to-government relationship and the role of tribes, how much of a leap is it to talk about the recognition of tribes today and the importance of that in terms of the strategies such as Land in Trust to acquire more civil control within the communities,[129] within the tribes? Natasha, you've talked about this tribal concept.

Natasha Singh: So, I'm thinking about the period from 1915 till today. In 1915, these chiefs were very strong at that time. And whatever happened after that, the sicknesses, epidemics that blew through our territory, all the efforts to intrude on our territory, all the military bases, everything, history happened. And these events began to erode the tribal governments of the time. And yet tribal leadership never went away. And in all parts of Alaska, but particularly in the Interior, chiefs were there. And they would make important decisions. They continued despite lack of recognition. They would have a meeting with a judge or the representative from the Senate, or anyone else. They continued despite any recognition from anyone. And they continued to resolve internal issues. The leadership would talk about whatever issue, and they would make a decision for the people. I guess when you want to fast-forward to today, what do our tribes look like? Our tribes in the Interior are recognized. There's thirty-seven federally recognized tribes, and are they accurate reflections of the tribal governments of 1915? No. Absolutely not. They're very different. History happened and it changed them significantly. Our federal relationship developed, and it changed our tribal governments significantly. But there are pieces that remain constant throughout, and I think that those are still there. And while before we had contact with outsiders, there wasn't thirty-seven different tribes in Interior Alaska. There absolutely wasn't. I don't know what it would have been, and it's definitely not perfect with how it is now. But are these tribes, tribal governments? They're tasked with the well-being of their people. The leadership are asked to make decisions in the best manner for people in the same way as earlier leaders, decisions about land resources, health care, economy, jobs. So there are these remnants of what they were. And I believe that, tribal governments were based in faith. They were based in the spiritual connection, in our beliefs as Native people. And I think that somewhere in there, that has continued and it still has a spark in our tribes present today. And I think that gives us hope as Native people that our tribes can once again be the strong governments that are making the best decisions for their people. But there's a lot of criticism, particular in Alaska from the people who deny that tribes exist, who basically are denying the U.S. Constitution and case law and everything else. Their criticism is that there are no real tribes because they were either extinguished somehow or they ceased to exist. I just reject that thought, because they did continue to exist. And it was just not in a way that you could write it on paper sometimes, but usually you can show, you can prove in history how the tribes of the Interior continued to exist. Official federal recognition happened in 1994 (1993, and 1994) with the Federally Recognized List Act that Congress passed.[130] Well, the secretary of interior came out with a list and then Congress passed the Act, and so for Alaska, when that happened we had tribes who were doing what they've always done, looking out for their children, making sure they're safe. And when they were tested and it came out in the state courts that, yes, you guys do exist after all, that little flicker or whatever we had, kinda got blazing again. And I think where we are now is we have thirty-seven federally recognized tribes who have inherent powers, that are recognized by outsiders as the strongest to control their internal affairs, meaning they control their own tribal membership, control their domestic relations; they have those authorities. Those are their strongest authorities. And with those authorities, recognized authorities, we have a lot of room to develop into and find our way back to the tribes that were, the larger tribes that existed.

Kevin Illingworth: So I just wanted to point something out just thinking about what Natasha's talking about and your previous question about the meeting in 1915 and how people perceived the meeting and maybe it wasn't just about land. In fact I think that perhaps from the perception of Wickersham, it was about land, and from the land office people that were there, it was about land. But I think clearly when you hear Natasha talk about the responsibilities that the tribe has, you realize land was only one of the concerns. There was economic development. There was food. There was, you know, all these things that were brought up by the chiefs. The more I read the transcript of the 1915 meeting, the more it becomes clear and what probably should be obvious, that land in the abstract was not what the chiefs were talking about. They were talking about very tangible things. The most abstract sentence, but one that I still think is very tangible, was that the rest of the United States was made for white people. Alaska was made for us Natives. If people were looking for a land claims statement, the statement was "Well, this is our land." And then, "Now let's talk about everything else." We're not interested in reservations or homesteads. Now let's talk about everything else that's actually more important, the things that are impacting people's lives, that people can't get, such as contracts with steamboats to cut wood or contracts to sell fish. So, it just really struck me that the chiefs felt a governmental responsibility to speak for their people. Clearly it was unbroken. And then as far as federal recognition goes, it is so confusing and I really want to put the onus on the federal government because one of the ways you can get recognition is through a court decision, a positive court decision like the Salchaket did in *Berrigan*. So they *were* federally recognized from the moment that decision came out. You know, same with Arctic Village and Venetie when their reservation was established, that was federal recognition. And right now—there's three federally recognized tribes in Arctic Village and Venetie because of the remnants of the IRA reservation. So federal recognition happened at different points for different communities. But I keep coming back to, and something that I just didn't understand myself until learning more about the *Berrigan* case with you, is that Wickersham understood that the only way that every single tribe was going to get that same recognition was if they brought their own lawsuit. So basically you're leaving it up to the rest of the tribes to bring their own actions for their own recognition. And I feel like that was the big problem for Wickersham, in the sense of you are gonna have some tribes that are left out because they don't see this happening and some tribes that do. And I think that that was what finally happened in 1993–1994. The secretary of interior and then Congress just said, "Listen, you can't have some tribes federally recognized and some tribes not, we're going to have federal recognition in Alaska." And it finally got rid of an imaginary third class of Alaska tribes, those with no recognized rights. I also think that purposefully made false narrative because some people claimed there were no tribes in Alaska, therefore no federal responsibility. And again, I just keep coming to that, because I don't believe that it was accidental. I don't believe that it was because of the lack of clarity in the law. But I think it was because there were people that had their own individual agendas and they wanted to follow them through, to extinguish the claim that there are any tribes in Alaska.

William Schneider: But with this federal recognition of tribes, how does that become important in terms of working with parts of the federal government to gain more community control of different services and things that you want to provide for the community, whether it's police, whether it's social services, or whether it's child welfare?

Natasha Singh: So I guess when you're federally recognized, it comes with this body of law that has been developed where the courts and Congress, they recognize tribes as having these inherent powers, that tribes have these sovereign powers. If they've never explicitly been taken away by Congress, then they still possess these powers. And this authority includes their domestic relations, and that's the strongest in Alaska, because they have no land base right now. And with that you have recognized power to fix internal problems. So if you have issues, whatever your issues are with your tribal membership, the tribal government can deal with it. And how they deal with it is going to be recognized by the state and the federal courts. In terms of government-to-government relationships with federal agencies, when you are a federally recognized tribe, your relationship is rooted in the United States Constitution, in the Treaty Clause.[131] And that's the basis for the government-to-government relationship, and the federal agencies take it seriously. And the past eight years under President Obama have probably been the best years for tribal recognition in terms of his demand on the federal agencies in his executive order to provide that government-to-government relationship. Each agency was directed to create a consultation policy with the tribes, which they did. So it gets you in the door with agencies. It gives you backing in the courts on how to deal with your own problems if anyone wants to test your powers. It provides a mechanism to contract with the federal government to implement programs for your tribes in terms of health services or social services. President Nixon signed into law the Indian Self-Determination Act,[132] which has been the most successful Indian policy. "Self-determination" gave control to the tribes, where as before, Indian Health Services or the Bureau of Indian Affairs provided services from Washington, D.C., to all the five hundred federally recognized tribes in how *they* thought would be a great way to implement programs. With self-determination policy, it's given back to the tribes. They're allowed to contract with the federal government to be the service providers. They're in control. And federal recognition gets them in the door for that.

William Schneider: And that's something that Will has been involved with, isn't it, with the medical delivery here?

Natasha Singh: Yes. The Alaska Native Health Care system is a unique one in that we have one agreement with the federal government. All two hundred and thirty-one tribes have one agreement with the federal government, and that was really Will's brainchild. And we definitely have the best tribal health care in the nation. We have the highest-quality rural health care in the world. And it's because we have tribes working in unity. All the tribes in Alaska are working in unity with one voice when we negotiate with the federal government.

Will Mayo: So on sovereignty, I think historically the tribes demonstrated sovereignty in a lot of different ways, very firmly with their foreign policy, with their enforcement of land sovereignty. And I remember stories that my mother told me. Her grandfather was, according to the stories that they told me, he was an enforcer of the tribal law in the Koyukuk River area when they set controls in place to keep Russian trappers from going wherever they wanted to. The manner of enforcing came from Chief Red Shirt's edict enforcing his law on the Russians at Nulato.[133] Chief Red Shirt established enforcement that was done by specifically assigned people who carried out that task. And so my mother's, I guess it'd be my great, my great-great-grandfather. I'm a little foggy on that. He was one of those. And the stories they tell are about his enforcement efforts and how he handled intrusions by Russian trappers into the area past the Koyukuk River, mouth of the Koyukuk River. We also maintained at key locations our land boundaries with the Inupiaq Eskimos. And that's all well documented in our stories. And we have both the stories of the Unalakleet–Kaltag trail and then the Hog River interaction point. So it all became blurred with the coming of more people from outside. After the Russians, the miners started showing up in huge numbers. People started coalescing around communities where there were trading posts, in some cases with medical services, churches, and schools, where their children could get training for the future. That created a lot of changes in the expression of sovereignty. And there was a time when it waned. But it never really went away. And so I think when ANCSA (Alaska Native Claims Settlement Act) was created, that members of Congress from Alaska wanted it to be tribal-free. I firmly believe this. They wanted it to be sovereignty-free, tribal-free. They did not want Indian law to apply to Alaska the way it does to tribes in the other parts of the nation. And I believe that it was very *intentional* to write that language the way it was written, whereby they said that this act will be carried out without the creation of any racially defined bodies, any reservations. And all of that was all very specifically designed language to try to kinda forestall the reemergence of active sovereignty, because it had never been explicitly extinguished. They were hoping that the Native Claims Settlement Act would become that termination law. And in fact, you'll still hear today where some attorneys are still arguing that ANCSA was a termination law, terminating tribal jurisdiction.

William Schneider: This evolution of tribes is taking us back to the Alaska Purchase where the term *uncivilized tribes* is used. The government must have had some recognition, although it certainly wasn't an understanding, was it, of the needs and nature of the people?

Will Mayo: So I believe ANCSA was really the hope of some people that tribes were extinguished. But of course that didn't happen, and the list of federally recognized tribes had an Alaska section that contained corporations, and at no time did it say tribes. It said communities and even referred I think sometimes to municipalities. My village had three designations in that list, three separate ones, the corporation, some vague community of Tanana, and something else. I remember because I looked it up. But once it was straightened out, it helped. But the fact that the land was separated from the tribes is still hindering the full expression of tribal sovereignty. But that has become a reopened discussion because of the lands into trust possibilities. So if you carry out the land into trust scenario and you say that a tribe manages to place land into trust, then it becomes arguable that they can exert jurisdiction over a land base. And this is where you get the full expression of nationhood. This is where you're no longer separated from your land base. And so you not only would be talking about sovereignty over membership matters, citizen matters, but now you're talking about expressions of sovereignty over the land base. That opens that whole possibility. And so we're on the cusp of something exciting. But also we take warning because we're concerned about what the blowback will be from this decision. And people are thinking about that. In other words, will steps be made to limit the effects of tribes being rejoined to their land base?

William Schneider: And then what are the implications for the regional corporations? How would that work?

Natasha Singh: I don't think there's a lot of implications right away, because for tribes to put land into trust they have to own the land. And tribes don't own very much land right now. Ownership is in private landowners in the towns, in the villages. The cities own some land. Village corporations own some land in the villages. But the regional corporations don't own much land in the villages. The land in the villages would be of most interest to tribes to put into trust. And as far as hunting and fishing, we've heard people talk about land into trust as an answer to hunting and fishing. But I go back to the 1915 chiefs saying, "Well, guess what? One little piece of land around my village is not going to feed the community and provide for what we need. So we're not going to get enough land into trust in order to have enough land to regulate our hunting and fishing for it to matter. There's just not enough land for us to put into trust." I guess having a really open mind, could our regional corporations give us all their land? Yeah. But that would be a vote of the shareholders, who don't have an interest so much in doing that right now. Maybe they would in the future. Maybe if we could educate our shareholders and maybe if our tribes develop in a way where they could see that connection is important. But right now there's not a huge interest I don't think, on the part of the regionals. The regional ANCSA corporations are so scared about land into trust because they fear it'll interfere with our resource development. And, you know, a lot of the federal agencies do interfere with resource development. All those land selections in Alaska, it's all overlapping and there's easement issues, and it's a huge headache for anybody who's trying to pillage the land.

Kevin Illingworth: I think that for me a big concern is asking what people really want. Is it a reservation, or is it to be able to hunt and fish? You know, I don't know the answer, but I don't think what people really think is "Geez, we really want a reservation." People want to be able to do things that they should be able to do . . . to feed their family.

Natasha Singh: They want safe communities. They want a say in the management of fish and game. They want some self-determination. And I think trust lands has been that possibility. But, really, trust lands is just to save the land, put it in a very, very safe place so nobody's gonna mess with it. And it's this weird federal process that the BIA came up with to have all these federal protections so nobody can mess with the land. I think Kevin's absolutely right. I think we can get what we want, what the tribes want, safe communities. We can do that without trust lands. We can do it without a land base. And we probably have to, because our tribes, the two hundred and thirty plus tribes, most of them they don't own the land in their villages. There's gonna be some that do—maybe a dozen, maybe a couple dozen.

Will Mayo: To a large degree neither do the corporations because of the 14C provisions,[134] which set aside about what, 1,280 acres for future municipality, for a municipality.

Natasha Singh: Mm-hmm.

Kevin Illingworth: I think it all spins around or comes back to this idea of sovereignty, what that means, and is that being recognized. And I think we know the answer to the last part. It has not been recognized here in Alaska. So when we're talking about tribal sovereignty and this inherent sovereignty that Natasha brought up that attaches itself to federal recognition. Inherent sovereignty is a recognition that the sovereignty has always been there, that it's never been extinguished, legally speaking. And what it does is it turns the question you're asking almost opposite of what you're asking. Faced with the question what powers do tribes have? Well, what powers don't tribes have? They have all the authority that wasn't specifically taken away by Congress. The basic limitations are on your ability to declare war, enter into treaties, and print money. These are the original limitations on inherent tribal sovereignty. Sovereignty should include everything, the authority over the people, authority over the land. In Alaska the land was separated, legally, with the Alaska Native Claims Settlement Act. With the decision in the *Venetie* tax case they said, well, the tribes have sovereignty, but they don't have the authority over the land.[135] And with the authority over the land comes very clear jurisdiction to, among other things, regulate hunting and fishing. These are just some of the aspects that are tied to the control, so to speak, of the land. But the most important attributes of sovereignty aren't necessarily control of land. I've always really been intrigued by the language that we heard people use after the *Venetie* tax case in saying that Alaska tribes are sovereigns without territorial reach, meaning that they're sovereigns, but over what territory? But the very next year, we had *John v. Baker*,[136] which really turned that upside down and said that tribes are sovereigns without territorial bounds. Tribes have authority over and responsibility to protect tribal members everywhere, not just on the reservation, not just on the Indian lands. I think that, in that sense, so many of the issues that we have and that we consider village issues really come from lack of state recognition or even federal recognition of the local governing authority of tribes. Whether you say that's tied to the land, whether that's over people—these individual subjects aside—it seems like it's been, and I think Will was absolutely right, the Alaska Native Claims Settlement Act was an effort, by some people, to just extinguish that sovereignty.

Natasha Singh: But they forgot a critical part.

Kevin Illingworth: It was unsuccessful, yeah. The fact that termination has to be explicit. It has to use the terms *terminated, termination*. And the United States had passed the termination era at that point and was not going to use that language, so they tried to backdoor a similar thing without actually terminating tribes.

William Schneider: Well, let's conclude with my original question. Here we are at the 150th anniversary of the Alaska Purchase. From the standpoint of the impact of that purchase on Alaska Natives through the years, what should the American public remember? Is there one thing they should remember?

Natasha Singh: I think they should remember that at the time of the purchase, we had strong tribal nations in Alaska that were functioning as sovereigns to protect their people and their land, and that has often been ignored. It was unclear and it was unrecognized. Those governments then have persisted, throughout backdoor termination, through missionaries raping our children, and now throughout our own Alaska Native people seeking to make profits off of fossil-fuel industry in the name of Alaska Native corporations. Our tribes still, with no legal jurisdiction over their own lands, seek to be stewards of the land. They seek to continue a relationship with the land and the animals and each other in a way that is good. I say that is in a way that is good, because that is what a government should be, good for the people. I think now, 150 years later, we've gone through all that and we still remain, and it's only going to get stronger. The tribal governments are going to get stronger.

Kevin Illingworth: You know, I think that it does come back to recognizing that there were indigenous governments, cultures, societies that were here first, that still continue to exist today, and that we as American people do owe a debt to them, and a legal obligation too, for a variety of different reasons. But I think that I would say even more poignantly, the Alaskan experience really highlights a time when the United States decided that certain outcomes were more important than following the rule of law and people exploited this lack of clarity in the law for their own outcomes. And I really think that this whole discussion is focused around the impacts that it had, and still have to this day. As one-sided and colonial as the system of federal Indian law is, if it would've been consistently applied here in Alaska, we'd be in a far better world. We'd be in a far better place. We would see a lot more self-determination. We would see a lot more local control over issues like drugs and alcohol and violence that we talk about as if they're village issues, but they really are issues that came from outside the Native community from non-Native society and now Native communities are left trying to figure out how do we deal with this.

Natasha Singh: And I completely agree. I think some people who don't involve themselves with Natives or don't go to villages, they kinda think, wow, what's wrong with them? Like, why do they have these high rates of crime? Why do they have low rates of graduation? People need to understand our history. For 150 years outsiders have been telling tribes either: you don't have the power, or you don't exist. You can't fix your own problems because you don't have the authority to do that. And when you're told that, after 150 years you're going to find yourself in an area where you start to believe it, that the answer is not within us, it's outside of us. The educational system doesn't teach our Native children what really happened, colonialism. This is why we are where we are today. And if we as tribal citizens begin to understand *the factual history* (because we're not even told our own history—our schools are controlled by the State of Alaska), *we will be empowered to find solutions to the impacts of colonialism.* Give us back those authorities and empower our tribes and our tribal communities through self-determination policies. That's how we're going to emerge as healthy communities and individuals. And until that really happens, we might be struggling. And if those who don't involve themselves in Native issues and kinda wonder about our struggles, I think the one takeaway would be that we *do* need their help. We do need them to be educated on *the real history of Alaska*, as Kevin was saying, and recognize that we need their help in this recognition and empowerment so that we can have healthy communities.

William Schneider: Well, I hope if there is talk about the Alaska Purchase that people talk about Alaska Natives and they talk about tribes and they talk about self-determination and they talk about getting the rights that people really want and deserve to grow and emerge.

Appendix 4

Timeline of Important Laws and Events Impacting Tribal Governments in Alaska

by Kevin Illingworth

The Early Years

Time Immemorial: Alaska Native tribes reside in what we now call Alaska.

1493   Papal Bull and the Rule of Discovery.
Early epidemics of small pox, measles, flu.

1741   "Discovery" of Alaska by Vitus Bering.

1743   Russian commercial fur voyages to Alaska begin.

1763   Unungan (Aleut) retaliation for Russian attacks and enslavement results in destruction and sinking of four Russian ships.

1766   Tsarina Catherine declares Aleut/Alutiiq to be Russian subjects in order to force them to work for the Russian American Fur Company.

1784   Shelikov assault on Refuge Rocks. Massacre marks the decline of Unungan independence.

1784   Russian colony is started in Three Saints Bay, Kodiak Island. Russians begin expansion into the Southeast.

1794   Russian exploration into Copper region. Russians are killed by Ahtna people.

1802   Battle of Sitka~Kiks.ádi. Tlingit destroy Russian fort at Sitka.

1824　First Russian–American Treaty: agreement between both nations to commercial fish and trade with Native people in Alaska.

1848　Beginning of Yankee whaling in Alaska.

1855　Russian coal mine is established in Cook Inlet.

1865　Start of survey of Overland Telegraph Route through Alaska.

1865　Last shot of Civil War fired in Alaska, months after official end of U.S. Civil War.

1867　Treaty of Cession/Quit Claim purchase of Alaska by United States.

1867–1884　Department era: Army, Treasury, Navy authority in Alaska.

1867　Letter describing U.S. Indian Policy in Alaska calls for "vigilance in dealing with Tlingit, always have guns ready to fire, hold entire tribe responsible for crime of individual" (McClanahan 2001:204).

1869　Secretary of Interior Seward tours Alaska with military commander of Alaska, General Jefferson Davis, who reminds Sitka that "with only 2,000 whites and 25,000 Indians in Alaska, a display of military force is needed" (ibid:179). U.S. Navy bombards and burns Kake and later the same year the Army bombards Wrangell.

1870　Testimony expressing dissatisfaction of tribes over the sale of Alaska: "The dissatisfaction among the tribes on account of the sale of the Territory did not arise from any special feeling of hostility, but from the fact that it was sold without their consent, they arguing that their fathers originally owned all the country, but allowed the Russians to occupy it for their mutual benefit, in that the articles desired by them could be obtained from the Russians in exchange for furs; but the right of the Russians to sell the Territory, except with the intention of giving them the proceeds, is denied" (Report of Captain Charles Bryant to the secretary of the Treasury, 1870, referred to committee on Territories and ordered to be printed, Senate Document 32, 41st Cong., 2nd sess., p.14).

1871　Letter from Aleuts of St. George Island complains of slavery under the federal government's leasing of the island to the American Fur Seal Company.

1873　Sale and importation of alcohol in Alaska is made illegal. The law declares all of Alaska to be Indian country for the purpose of that law.

1875　Sale and importation of breech-loading firearms in Alaska is made illegal.

1877   Administration of Alaska is transferred from Department of War to Department of Treasury, citing the need for the Army in fighting the Modoc and Nez Perce tribes.

1878   Commercial fishing in Alaska; first salmon canneries are established and commercial salmon traps become widespread.

1879   Osprey Affair: white residents of Sitka (U.S.) request help of British government because they feel the United States is not protecting them from the Tlingit.

1882   U.S. Navy bombards and burns Angoon.

1884   Alaska District Organic Act: creation of Alaska's first civil government. Calls for Alaska Native "use and occupancy" to be protected, for education without regard to race, and the creation of commission to report on needs of Alaska Native people.

1887   General Allotment (Dawes) Act passes. It never directly applied to Alaska, but signaled a shift in U.S. policy to take more Indian lands and an assimilationist purpose reflected in future laws.

1888   First Alaska Native children arrive at Carlisle Indian School in Pennsylvania ("Kill the Indian, Save the Man" was the school motto).

1889   President Harrison Inauguration Address supports allotment and assimilation policy through the Dawes Act and says that it is fortunate that the United States has not extended reservation policy into Alaska, because the reservations were seen as limiting western expansion by the United States.

1889   US Congress passes first Act limiting Native fishing in Alaska.

1890   Wounded Knee Massacre: After members of the Lakota tribe surrender to the U.S. Army, a massacre ensues in which more than 150 Lakota men, women, and children are killed.

1890   Tlingit clan leaders send a letter to President Harrison, followed the next year by a petition to Congress asking for the protection of fishing and hunting areas.

1891   Alaska Townsite Act: allows for non-Native ownership of townsites in Alaska.

1891   Establishment of first Indian Reservation in Alaska, with over 150 reservations eventually formed, many with the express purpose of protecting subsistence resources.

1898   Alaska Homestead Act: allows non-Natives to own homesteads in Alaska.

1898   Klondike gold rush: over 100,000 people flood to the Yukon region searching for gold, with more to come to Nome and the Interior. Widespread commercial hunting (market hunting) wipes out wildlife resources.

1900   Pneumonia epidemic: the "Great Sickness" strikes Aleutians and Southwest Alaska particularly hard, with as many as half perishing.

1900   "Carter Code" passed by Congress extended civil laws of Oregon to Alaska.

1901   U.S. Army builds Valdez to Eagle Trail.

1902   Congress passes Alaska Game Law. It allows for subsistence hunting and fishing.

1903   St. Lawrence Island is set aside as a Native reservation in order to provide reindeer to prevent starvation.

The Middle Period

1905   *Berrigan* case: Judge Wickersham holds that Alaska Tribes hold title to their traditional lands as Aboriginal Title, but only way to enforce is through individual lawsuit.

1905   *Report to Congress on Conditions and Needs of Alaska Natives*, in noting that the "rush of prospectors has literally *swept the country clean, denuding it of life* . . . leading to destitution and semi-starvation," calls for modification of game laws and a moratorium on commercial fishing north of Aleutians, due to importance of Yukon and Kuskokwim fisheries to the interior, as well as the Copper River (never implemented) (Emmons 1905).

1905   Creation of Tongass National Forest with no compensation for Aboriginal Title.

1905   Alaska Native Brotherhood (ANB) sues United States in 1929 but loses: not a tribe. 1935 Act recognizes Tlingit-Haida allowing for suit. 1959 Tlingit-Haida win, 1968 United States pays $7.5 million.

1905   Nelson Act: segregation in Alaska. Territory schools only allow Native students if "civilized" and no tribal ties. U.S. federal government takes over Native education.

1906   Letter from Chief Ivan and Chief William (Tanana area) to U.S. Secretary of War complains of "troubles we are having with white people since 1898" (Chief Ivan and Chief William to secretary of war, 1906). Focus is on hunting, fishing, commerce and justice.

1906   Alaska Native Allotment Act (1906–1960 only 80 approved, 1960–1980, approximately 10,000).

1910   After being nearly commercially hunted to extinction, sea otter hunting is banned in Alaska by the Fur Seal Act.

1912   First Native advocacy group in the state, Alaska Native Brotherhood, forms in Juneau.

1913   Gold is discovered on the Chisana River. That first winter, more than 2,000 Dall sheep and even more caribou are killed to support the new miners.

1915   Territorial Act: Alaska's first civil government.

1915   Native Citizenship Act (modeled after Dawes Act).

1915   Women's Suffrage.

1915   Wickersham meeting with Tanana area chiefs.

1916   Migratory Bird Treaty closes the harvest of migratory birds during the only season in which birds are in much of Alaska.

1917   Chief Goodlataw files complaint about commercial fishing on Copper River leading to starvation.

1918   Worldwide influenza epidemic hits Alaska.

        End of World War I.

1924   Indian Citizenship Act extends citizenship to Alaska Natives without terminating tribal rights/identity. Among other rights, extends the right to vote.

1924   The "White Act" effectively ends subsistence fishing in Southeast Alaska. Native fish traps were prohibited while cannery traps were encouraged.

1925   Alaska Voter Literacy Act is passed by Territorial legislature. Requires literacy test as a way to limit Native voting. A similar literacy requirement is later enshrined in the Alaska Constitution.

1925   Alaska Game Act creates five non-native Game Commission, imposed seasons and bag limits on Alaska native hunting. Allowed for subsistence taking only when in absolute need (starvation).

1926   Alaska Native Townsite Act: allows for formation of Alaska Native townsites.

1926   William Paul is the first Alaska Native elected to Territorial Legislature.

1930   Formation of Tetlin Indian Reserve, as a Public Purpose Executive Order Reserve "to promote the interests of the Natives . . . in restocking the country and protecting the fur bearing mammals" (Executive Order 5365, June 10, 1930).

1931   Alaska Native programs are transferred from Bureau of Education to BIA.

1936   Indian Reorganization Act (AK): expansion of reservations in Alaska.

1942–1945   Aleut (Unungan) residents are removed from their homes on the Aleutian Chain and imprisoned in internment camps in Southeast Alaska during World War II.

1943   Venetie Reservation sets aside 1.8 million acres to protect hunting/trapping and fishing rights.

1943   Karluk Reservation is formed. The USFWS opposes creation of Native fishing reserves in Alaska and refuses to enforce the reservation. *Grimes Packing* case holds that reservation can only be enforced through trespass action brought by Department of Justice. Failure of reservation policy in Alaska.

1945   Territorial legislature passes Alaska Anti-Discrimination Act. Legal segregation in Alaska ends.

        End of World War II.

1957   Project Chariot is proposed. The project entails using atomic explosions to create a harbor near Point Hope in northwest Alaska.

1959   Tlingit-Haida win federal court case.

1959   Alaska Statehood Act: State is allowed to select 120 million acres of land:

1959   "As a compact with the United States said State and its people do agree and declare that they forever disclaim all right and title to any lands or other property . . . (including fishing rights), the right or title to which may be held by any Indians, Eskimos, or Aleuts (hereinafter called natives) or is held by the United States in trust for said natives" (Alaska Statehood Act).

1960   The Federal government transfers the authority to manage fish and wildlife in Alaska to the new State government. Uncompensated taking of aboriginal hunting and fishing rights. Fish traps are made illegal in Alaska.

1961   "Barrow Duck-in": one hundred thirty-eight people present themselves for arrest for shooting ducks in violation of the Migratory Bird Treaty.

1961   State starts selecting lands in the Minto Flats and Wood-Tikchik area.

1962   Douglas Indian Village is burned to the ground to make room for new Douglas City harbor and park.

1962   First issue of *Tundra Times* is published. This was a statewide Native paper reporting on issues of concern to the Native community.

1963   Rampart Canyon Dam and Reservoir is proposed, raising protests by Stevens Village and other Yukon River villages.

1965   U.S. Interior Secretary Udall issues a preliminary injunction freezing land conveyances to the state.

1967   First Alaska Native Land Claims Settlement bill is introduced in Congress by Senator Jackson of Washington.

1968   Oil is discovered at Prudhoe Bay.

1968   Tlingit-Haida are awarded $7.5 million for suit against the federal government.

ANCSA to the Present

1971   Alaska Native Claims Settlement Act (ANCSA): extinguishes aboriginal land claim, ends the Alaska Native Allotment Act, leads to formation of ANCSA corporations.

1973   "Limited Entry" restricting number of eligible fishermen passed Alaska legislature.

1975   Voting Rights Act is extended to Alaska due to long history of discrimination and literacy tests.

1976   Federal Land Planning and Management Act repeals the Alaska Native Townsite Act.

1979　In *Frank v. State*, Alaska Supreme Court rules that the U.S. Constitution guarantee of free exercise of religion protects taking of moose for potlatch.

1980　Congress passes Title VIII of the Alaska National Interest Lands Conservation Act (ANILCA), which protects the subsistence needs of rural Alaskans. It began as a Native Priority, but was changed to a "Rural Priority" as a *compromise* between the federal government and the State of Alaska, which promised to administer a Rural Priority on ALL lands and waters in Alaska.

1993　Federal recognition of tribes in Alaska.

1993　Federal takeover of subsistence on federal lands.

1998–1999　*Venetie* tax case and *John v. Baker*: tribal sovereignty without territory.

2000　Administrative Order 186 and the Millennium Agreement.

2001　*Katie John* case expands federal authority to include "reserved waters." Governor Knowles declines to appeal. In 2005, Governor Murkowski challenges rules implementing the ruling. Katie wins. In 2010, Parnell appeals. In 2014, U.S. Supreme Court rejects Alaska appeal.

2009　Secretary of the interior announces the *failure* of the federal government in its legal obligation to protect Alaska Native subsistence and orders a comprehensive review of the Federal Subsistence Management Program.

2013　*Akiachak* case and Land into Trust. *Akiachak* decision holds that it is unlawful to discriminate against Alaska Tribes. State of Alaska appeals, loses June 2016. State declines to appeal loss.

2017　Alaska attorney general releases legal opinion, at the request of Governor Walker, stating, "The law is clear. There are 229 Alaska Tribes and they are separate sovereigns with inherent sovereignty…" (State of Alaska, Attorney General to Governor, letter, October 19, 2017).

Notes

Kevin Illingworth provided footnote commentary in italics.

Introduction

1   Jane Galblum, "A Short Tour of Historic Fairbanks," *Alaska Journal* 10 (Spring 1980): 60; Mary Mangusso, Interview on Judge Wickersham and the Wickersham House, September 20, 1999, Oral History Program, Oral History tape number 99-29-01, University of Alaska Fairbanks.

2   Wickersham's house is now preserved and maintained by the Tanana-Yukon Historical Society at Pioneer Park. Set amongst the log cabins of the park, it still represents the Wickersham family's desire to see Fairbanks become a modern town.

3   Wickersham State Historic Site, Manuscripts, 1884–1970s, Proceedings of a Council, Held in the Library Room at Fairbanks, Alaska, on July 5, 1915, between the chiefs and headmen of the bands of Indians living along the Tanana River and Delegate James Wickersham, 28, ASL-MS-107, Alaska State Library, Historical Collections, Juneau, http://library.alaska.gov/hist/fulltext/ASL-MS-0107-38-001.htm (hereafter cited as Wickersham State Historic Site, Proceedings of a Council).

4   At this time, there was an emerging fascination with certain aspects of Indian life, the pageantry, the art, the song (Hallowell 1957). The very presence of the chiefs, shocking to some at the time, was an invitation to find value in past Indian life.

5   At this point in history, establishing new Native reservations in the continental United States had gone out of vogue and the thinking was that "civilization was impossible without the incentive to work that comes only from individual ownership of a piece of property" (Prucha 1984, vol. 2:639). The push for private ownership was, in part, based on the notion that "the family is God's unit of society" (ibid: 622).

6   Certainly land was what was on the government officials' minds at the 1915
     meeting because they knew the railroad was coming and they predicted many
     settlers would want land. The other more recent factor influencing depiction
     of the meeting is Native land claims and the publicity surrounding the enact-
     ment of the Alaska Native Claims Settlement Act in 1971. However, a reading
     of the transcript demonstrates that there were other issues of concern to the
     Native leaders.

7   Will Mayo has played a direct role in the growth of the modern Tanana Chiefs
     Conference. This is the nonprofit Interior Native organization responsible for
     delivery of social services, medical and dental care, and advocacy for villagers
     on issues of subsistence, tribal development, legal matters, and public safety.

Chapter 1: From Fur to Gold

8   Hence the Organic Act of 1884 recognized the government's responsibility to
     Natives by stating that they were not to be disturbed in their use of the land.
     Native land rights were legally tested in 1904 in the *Minook* case and in 1905
     in the *Berrigan* case. In all of these cases, the frame of legal reference was Title
     III in the Treaty of Cession.

9   For the Russians, the uncivilized tribes were not people they directly con-
     trolled. Writing about Russian administration of Russian America, Vladimir
     Gsovski states: "The relations of the colonial administration with the inde-
     pendent tribes were 'to be limited to the exchange of European wares for
     furs and other native products.'. . . These provisions may be construed as a
     recognition by implication, of the integrity of land possessions of both the
     not wholly dependent and the independent natives" (Library of Congress
     1950:23).

10   Shortly after the purchase, in 1869, Captain Charles P. Raymond was sent
     up the Yukon River to document the location of Fort Yukon and determine
     whether the Hudson's Bay Company was operating on newly acquired
     American soil (Raymond 1900:19). On that trip he found that Fort Yukon
     was in American territory and so he instructed the Hudson's Bay Company to
     vacate their holdings. But even more important was the fact that the trip was
     made with a steamboat. This marked a big change. Soon the early American
     traders came to depend on steamboats to get their goods upriver and to move
     to other trading locations as new opportunities developed. This gave greater
     access to more goods and mobility to move easily to new sites.

11   *United States law had held that Natives could not have a legitimate mineral
     claim, and this would have been common knowledge to any miner with experience
     in the West.*

12   Melody Webb noted that Minook's father was Ivan Pavaloff, a half-Russian
     and half-Koyukon Native who worked for the Russian American Company
     before the Treaty of Cession (Webb 1985:62–64).

13   William Schneider, "On the Back Slough," in *Interior Alaska: A journey
     through time*, ed. Jean Aigner et al. (Anchorage: Alaska Geographical Society,

1986), 162; Alaska Mining Hall of Fame Foundation website http://alaska-mininghalloffame.org.

14   Berrigan Collection, Report of Referee for *USA v. Berrigan et al.* (1905), Case 270F, Alaska District Court, Third Division (Fairbanks), Box AS 30921, Alaska State Archives. Order of Injunction for *USA v. Berrigan et al.* (1905), Case 270F, Alaska District Court, Third Division (Fairbanks), Box AS 30921, Alaska State Archives (hereafter cited as Berrigan Collection).

15   Berrigan Collection, Report of Referee 270F.

16   Berrigan Collection, Report of Referee 270F.

17   At roughly this same time, May 11, 1906, a hearing was held in Sitka, Alaska, initiated by a petition from Rudolph Walton to Governor John Brady. Walton was the stepfather of two mixed-blood children, and he wanted them to be able to attend the public school. The Nelson Act had passed the year before, creating a provision for white and mixed-blood children to attend one school and Native children to receive separate schooling. In the hearing that followed, the proceedings revolved around whether the mixed-blood children and their family were civilized. Title 7 of the Nelson Act provided that "children of mixed blood who live a civilized life" (Raibmon 2005:176) could attend school with white children, but those who did not qualify would have to attend the Native school. The judge ruled against Walton and the other parties, concluding that they were not civilized and in the case of Walton and his children that mixed bloods "partake of the character of the tribes with which he lives whether it be civilized or otherwise" (ibid:195).

18   Berrigan Collection, Report of Referee 270F.

19   *This was a legal recognition of an aboriginal land claim that the government had both the legal responsibility to settle, as well as a duty to protect until the claim is settled (see also Case, David. 1984. Alaska Natives and American Laws. Fairbanks. University of Alaska Press.).*

20   James Wickersham Family Papers, 1884–1970s, Phyllis J. DeMuth Movius (archivist). Diary transcripts, March 5, 1905. Alaska State Library, Historical Collections, http://library.alaska.gov/hist/fulltext/ASL-F909.W52-2000.htm (hereafter cited as Wickersham, Diary transcripts).

21   *The Berrigan case is so significant because it is the application of that treaty (Treaty of Cession) in the legal system—the recognition of an aboriginal land claim that only the United States government can settle, with the accompanying duty to protect until that settlement occurs.*

22   Frederica de Laguna, *Tales from the Dena: Indian Stories from the Tanana, Koyukuk, and Yukon River* (Seattle: University of Washington Press, 1995), 20.

23   In reconstructing Native life in the Middle and Upper Tanana region, I have benefited immensely from Lee Saylor. He came to Alaska in 1964 and married his first wife Stella Healy in 1966. She was the daughter of Jeany and John Healy. John Healy was the son of Chief Healy. Jeany shared her knowledge of the early years with Lee, including stories, genealogy, and an extensive photographic collection that now resides at the Archives, University of Alaska Fairbanks.

24 An example of this is taken from Mertie Baggen writing about the Salcha band, where she describes how Bessie Barnabasses's father was a chief at Salchaket. When he died the family moved to Goodpaster, where her father's brother lived. When he died, they moved back to Salchaket (Baggen Collection, box 1, folder 11, p. 10). In another example Lee Saylor recorded how Chief Joe's mother was originally from the Middle Tanana but was married downriver. When her husband died, she moved back upriver (Saylor 2013:7–8).

25 William Simeone notes, "In the case of Lieutenant Allen, the Ahtna were suspicious of him until they realized he had not come to revenge the early killing of Russians by the Ahtna" (Simeone, personal communication, August 10, 2016).

26 Patrick H. Ray, "Relief of the Destitute in the Yukon Region, 1898," in *Compilation of Narratives of Explorations in Alaska* (Washington, DC: Government Printing Office, 1900b), 524–528.; letter from Ray written from Fort Yukon, September 15, 1897.

27 The fish were particularly plentiful during their yearly migration. For instance, a short ways downstream from where the Ketchumstuck Natives might have been fishing, Chief Healy had a fish camp on the Healy River. Saylor recounted:

> They occupy it in the late summer when the whitefish were really coming through there and also it was used as a caribou camp to hunt caribou from. And it was just down river from there, there is a lot of lakes and potholes and the ducks nest pretty heavily there. Healy Lake there is whitefish coming through in May and go up the Healy River and they stay up there and spawn and they come back through in September and they draw up on that end. (Saylor 2013:5)

28 Charlene LeFebre, Field Notes, July 7, 1949, Kantishna Oral History Project Records, 1910–1984, box 1, folder 54, page 3, collection assembled by Dianne Holmes, Consortium Library, Archives and Special Collections Department, University of Alaska Anchorage.

29 At first, the idea these were ownership marks seemed highly unusual, but there is testimony from 1905 alleging Chief Jarvis requested that ground be staked near the Little Delta River (Berrigan Collection, Document 7890). Chief Jarvis did stay at Goodpaster before moving to the mission at Salcha, and the cache in question may have belonged to him, but this is speculation at this point. Whoever was the owner of the cache at the mouth of the Goodpaster River (mislabeled on the photograph as Volkmar River) may have been influenced by watching prospectors in the Forty Mile Country mark trees to signify their claims and adopted the practice, knowing that white men might soon be in the country and would recognize the effort. Of course, at this point this is unknown.

30   Farnsworth Family Papers, 75-175-267, Alaska and Polar Regions Collections, University of Alaska Fairbanks; identification of people in the photograph by Lee Saylor.

31   "Family at Winter Camp," UAF-2000-0181-00245.

32   We still don't know how McKennan knew this picture was taken at Joseph, but the genealogical and photographic connections seem to point to this conclusion and Andrews reports that Farnsworth identified the site (Andrews n.d.:19, and photograph, 20). The village of Joseph is associated with Chief Joseph but according to Silas Solomon, who was interviewed by Elizabeth Andrews, it is also associated with Sam, presumably Old Sam (ibid.:23). Another person associated with the camp was Belle Sam's first husband, whom Lee Saylor identified as Tseyh. It makes sense that Old Sam, Belle's second husband, and his family would be pictured at this good caribou and fishing site.

33   Chief Joe was Belle Sam's brother and was a contemporary of both Belle's husband, Old Sam, and Chief Healy, Jeany Healy's father-in-law. Chief Joe's position in the band is not clear, and it is even questionable whether he held the power of a chief. What is known is that Joseph Village on Joseph Creek, a tributary of the Middle Fork of the Fortymile River is named for him (ibid.:42), that he accompanied Billy Mitchell on the telegraph line survey down the Goodpaster River, and that he would in a later chapter play a prominent part in the 1915 Tanana Chiefs meeting.

34   Saylor, personal letter.

35   William Mitchell Collection. Manuscript. Alaska Microfilm 3637, box 20. University of Alaska Fairbanks Archives.

36   This seems to indicate Chief Joe was directed to go by someone else, perhaps Chief Healy, who would have been the most prominent leader in the band, although both men were of the same generation, so the reference to "son" would seem to diminish this possibility.

37   Robert McKennan Collection, box 3; undated letter from Paul Kirsteatter to McKennan saying that Chief Healy was given his name by prospectors who said he resembled someone they knew from Dawson area.

38   Jarvis was the military officer who conducted the famous reindeer drive to assist stranded miners off the coast near Barrow in 1897, and was in 1903 serving as custom agent in Eagle, a position he had held for a year. Previously, he was in Nome and St. Michael on government assignment (U.S. Department of the Treasury 1899; U.S. Congress, Senate Subcommittee of Committee on Territories 1904:79).

39   *Yet in the formation of the Tetlin Reservation, Hadjukovich professed to oppose the potlatch system and saw the reservation as the best way to destroy potlatch culture (Brown 1984:94, 99).*

Chapter 2: From Native to White Man's Country

40　Wickersham to Witten in Report of the Secretary of the Interior for 1903
　　(Witten 1903:278); Bishop Rowe in Emmons Family Papers, box 23, folder
　　411, manuscript call number Wa Mss S-1306, Beinecke Rare Book and
　　Manuscript Library, Yale University; Elliott on cannery operations in Prince
　　William Sound 1900:738.

41　Chief Ivan and Chief William to the secretary of war, written and posted from
　　Fort Gibbon, August 18, 1906, box 9, folder 47A, record group 22, entry
　　UD-91, records of the U.S. Bureau of Fisheries, Division of Alaska Fisheries,
　　Reports and Related Records, 1869–1937. National Archives and Records
　　Administration, College Park, Maryland, August 18, 1906 (hereafter cited as
　　Chief Ivan and Chief William to the secretary of war).

42　*In reality this meant that the same body of Federal Indian Law that had developed
　　in the lower 48 to protect tribal interests was to apply to the "uncivilized" tribes.
　　As imperfect as this was, it was better than the* fantasy *frontier that had begun to
　　emerge in Alaska, a frontier where Natives had no rights.*

43　The impact of the Western legal system was felt in other ways. In 1906, in
　　Sitka, Rudolph Walton petitioned Governor Brady because his daughters
　　had been denied entrance to the Sitka school. Under the Nelson Act of 1905,
　　"children of mixed blood who live a civilized life" (Raibman 2005:176) could
　　attend the white schools. The proceedings of this case scrutinized the family,
　　their home, their relations, activities, and associations. In the end, the judge
　　ruled they had not attained a civilized life (ibid.:175–197).

44　U.S. Congress, *Alaska Organic Act*, Section 8, 23 Stat. 26, May 17, 1884.

45　Perhaps this philosophy is also imbedded in the words of Thomas Jefferson
　　who had admiration for the independence and virtue of the yeoman farmer.
　　He contrasted the independent tiller of the land with the plantation farmer
　　who depended on slaves and readily available supplies (Kennedy 2003:11–12).

46　Bruce L. Gardner, *American Agriculture in the Twentieth Century: How It
　　Flourished and What It Cost* (Cambridge: Harvard University Press, 2002), 1;
　　reporting on a *New York Times* article dated January 1, 1900.

47　Walter Goldschmidt described this pattern for the villages of Tanacross,
　　Northway, and Tetlin in his 1946 study of Athabascan possessory rights
　　(Goldschmidt 1946:56).

48　Secretary of the Interior, *Report of the Secretary of the Interior* (Funsten
　　1903:271).

49　Secretary of the Interior, *Report of the Secretary of the Interior, Exhibit H*
　　(Witten 1903:275–279).

50　Emmons Family Papers. Manuscript call number Wa Mss S-1306, box 23,
　　folder 417. Beinecke Rare Book and Manuscript Library. Yale University, New
　　Haven, CT.

51　Emmons Family Papers. Letter from Dept. of Education, Bureau of
　　Education, Alaska Division, June 1, 1904, box 23, folder 412.

52　Emmons Family Papers, box 23, folder 417.

53   Emmons Family Papers, box 23, folder 408, "Food Supply for Indians; President Calls Attention to Report on Conditions in Alaska."

54   Emmons Family Papers, box 23, folder 408.

55   Michael C. Brown, 1984, *Indians, Traders, and Bureaucrats in the Upper Tanana District: A History of the Tetlin Reserve*, 62, Alaska State Office and Alaska Resources Library and Information Services, Bureau of Land Management, Anchorage, AK; referencing National Archives, Office of the Secretary of the Interior, RG 48, NA Microfilm Publication 430, roll 7, frames 518–520.

56   Illingworth, personal communication. See appendix 4 "Timeline of Important Laws and Events Impacting Tribal Governments in Alaska."

57   Prucha notes that this powerful wording was actually first used by Merrill Gates one year before Roosevelt's address (Prucha 1984, vol. 2:671).

58   These included the requirement that an applicant for citizenship be examined by school teachers to determine if he could meet the "obligations of suffrage," that he had abandoned "tribal customs and relationships," and that he had adopted the "habits of a civilized life." Further, he had to be represented by five white citizens who would state the applicant met the requirements of the law. Only then could the applicant appear in the district court and state that he was living "separate and apart from any tribe of Indians" (Alaska Humanities Forum; Illingworth n.d. "Timeline of Important Laws"; Alaska State Library, ASL-KFA1225.A3-1915-p52).

59   By the turn of the century, Natives were no longer considered a threat to settlers in the West and there was a growing appreciation for certain aspects of Native culture. Native arts and stories were gaining recognition in American culture (Hallowell 1957). Paige Raibmon, writing about the Tlingit in Sitka has portrayed the tension between the tourist trade, with its interest in "authentic" Native cultural items, and the mission, whose goal was to "civilize" and demonstrate the advancement of Native students under their care. The contrasting images of women selling berries to tourists and the students at the mission school are striking and portray some of the conflicting attitudes of white society at this time in history (Raibmon 2005:157–174). Another example of the complexity of the times comes from President Theodore Roosevelt, who appointed Francis Ellington Leupp to the post of commissioner of Indian Affairs. In a 1905 statement Leupp is credited with pointing out that "the Indians have qualities and a heritage of art and music that should be preserved and cultivated, not eradicated" (Prucha 1984, vol. 2: 767). The picture is obviously confounded by conflicting attitudes. We have Roosevelt's 1905 inaugural parade with war chiefs and Carlisle Indian School students side by side, and there are other examples of the president's interest and appreciation of Native arts. For instance, he wrote a preface to Natalie Curtis's book on Native art, music, and stories in which he said: "These songs cast a wholly new light on the depth and dignity of Indian thought, the simple beauty and strange charm—the charm of a vanished elder world—of Indian

59   (*continued*) poetry" (Curtis 1907). Despite these sentiments, Roosevelt, like Emmons, saw the need to extinguish tribal ties. It is as if they could appreciate the artifacts of Native culture but not the reality of Native lives. In white minds, there was still just one way to be American. Faced with these confusing and conflicting visions of what white society wanted of Natives, it is not surprising that in the early years of the Alaska Native Brotherhood, members agreed to renounce their cultural ways and adopt white society (Drucker 1958). Ironically, this organization went on to become a powerful supporter of Native cultural ways.

60   Emmons Family Papers, box 23, folder 408.

61   There is a tradition of Native river pilots going back even earlier and is one of the few areas in which Native expertise continued to be valued by white society. This was a job they were uniquely qualified to do based on their knowledge of the rivers.

62   Wickersham State Historic Site, Proceedings of a Council.

63   Frederica de Laguna estimates this was around 1910 (de Laguna 1995:8).

64   Wickersham State Historic Site, Proceedings of a Council, 32–33.

65   It should be noted that there were two meetings before the 1915 meeting in which Indian leaders spoke out about issues. One was in the Interior, one in Southeast Alaska. In 1913 or 1914, Interior Indian leaders met in Tanana. The leaders were concerned about impacts on fishing sites and reports about the possible impacts from the planned railroad to the Interior. They called for citizenship and a representative in Washington to represent their interests (Sniffen and Carrington 1914:16, 24; also Ketzler, Alfred R. Sr. Alaska Native Land Claims Settlement Collection, 1961–1977, "The Tanana Chiefs Conference, Tanana, Alaska, June 24–26, 1962"). I have not located an official report or transcript of the meeting, and it is not evident that government officials were present. The second meeting was in Southeast Alaska in 1898 and featured Tlingit Chiefs and Governor Brady. The governor invited the chiefs to meet and to discuss their grievances. The chiefs were concerned because white men were taking over their fishing streams and hunting grounds. There is a transcript of this meeting that demonstrates very similar concerns as those expressed by the Tanana Chiefs. The government's response was also similar (Hinckley 1970).

Chapter 3: July 1915: Wickersham Meets the Tanana Chiefs

66   "The Indian Conference," *Alaska Citizen* (Fairbanks), July 12, 1915.

67   James Wickersham's Diary (1900–1939) is available on the Alaska State Library website at http://library.alaska.gov/hist//hist_docs/wickersham/ASL-MS0107-diaries1900-1941.pdf.

68   The full transcript, "Proceedings of a Council held in the library room at Fairbanks, Alaska, on July 5, 1915," can be found in appendix 2. It is also available on the Alaska's Digital Archives website vilda.alaska.edu. Hereafter, all quotes attributed to the speakers at the July 1915 meeting are from that

source. See also Stanton H. Patty, "A Conference with the Tanana Chiefs," *Alaska Journal* 1 no. 2 (Spring 1971): 2–18.

69   Peter Trimble Rowe to James Wickersham, November 22, 1908; Wickersham to Rowe, December 18, 1908. Episcopal Church Records, Correspondence, Bishop Rowe, box 102, Alaska and Polar Regions Archives, Rasmuson Library, University of Alaska Fairbanks.

70   Rowe to Wickersham, June 5, 1909. Episcopal Church Records, Correspondence, Bishop Rowe, box 102, Alaska and Polar Regions Archives, Rasmuson Library, University of Alaska Fairbanks.

71   U.S. Congress, House of Representatives Hearings Before the Committee on the Territories on Conditions in Alaska, 62nd Cong., 2nd sess., January 16, 1912 (Washington, DC: Government Printing Office).

72   Wickersham, Diary transcripts, January 16, 1912.

73   See Francis Paul Prucha, *The Great Father: The United States Government and the American Indians,* vols. 1 and 2 (Lincoln: University of Nebraska Press, 1984), 759–762.

74   Frederick Drane to R. B. Drane, September 12, 1915. Episcopal Church Records, Frederick Drane Collection, box 1, folder 3, Alaska and Polar Regions Archives, Rasmuson Library, University of Alaska Fairbanks.

75   Rowe to John Wood, July 22, 1910. Episcopal Church Records, Correspondence, Bishop Rowe, box 102, Alaska and Polar Regions Archives, Rasmuson Library, University of Alaska Fairbanks.

76   Hudson Stuck to John Wood, June 19, 1909. Episcopal Church Records, Correspondence, box 105, Alaska and Polar Regions Archives, Rasmuson Library, University of Alaska Fairbanks.

77   "Alaska's New Era," *Alaska Citizen* (Fairbanks), October 12, 1914.

78   *Descriptive of Fairbanks "Alaska's Golden Heart."* The Fairbanks Commercial Club, 1916. p. 7.

79   U.S. Congress, House of Representatives, Alaska Railway Bill, Speech of Hon. James Wickersham, January 14 and 28, 1914, 6, 63rd Cong., 2nd sess.

80   Ibid., 7.

81   Wickersham, Diary transcripts, April 17, 1913.

82   Drane to Arthur Wright July 1, 1929. Episcopal Church Records, Frederick Drane Collection, box 1, folder 3, Alaska and Polar Regions Archives, Rasmuson Library, University of Alaska Fairbanks.

83   While this was the stated conclusion, one wonders if the two parties (Native and government officials) weren't separated by a deep cultural gulf. The government officials knew very little about the subsistence life of the Natives and how it would be negatively affected by a reservation. The Native leaders had little time to think about what to them was a new concept. With more time to consider, the chiefs might have opted for a large segment of land set aside and maybe this would have been acceptable to the government.

84   James Wickersham to Franklin K. Lane, July 22, 1915. Alaska State Library, library.alaska.gov.

85   U.S. Congress, House of Representatives, Committee on the Territories Report No. 92, 63rd Cong., 1st sess., November 26, 1913.

86   James Wickersham, "An Address Delivered at the Laying of the Cornerstone [July 4, 1915]." Rasmuson Library, University of Alaska Fairbanks (hereafter cited as Wickersham, "An Address Delivered at the Laying of the Cornerstone").

87   Wickersham, Diary transcripts, May 19, 1915.

Chapter 4: Alaska Leader Will Mayo Shares His Perspective on the 1915 Tanana Chiefs Meeting

88   Natasha Singh, legal council for the Tanana Chiefs points out that Congress has amended the Alaska Native Claims Settlement Act each Congress since passage (Singh, personal communication, September 9, 2016).

Chapter 5: The Fester

89   U.S. Department of the Treasury, Letter of the Secretary of the Treasury, communicating, in compliance with a resolution of the Senate of December 20, 1869, the reports of Captain Charles Bryant, late special agent of the Treasury Department for Alaska, and H. A. McIntyre, special agent for the Treasury Department, 14 (41st Cong., 2nd sess., Senate document 32, p. 14, 1870).

90   The Alaska Native Brotherhood developed out of local church societies established by the Presbyterian missionaries. At the Sitka Society the participants had Bible study, discussed social problems, and advocated abolishment of aboriginal customs and alcohol use (Drucker 1958:17). While the Presbyterian missionaries influenced the development of the church societies, the Brotherhood was nonsectarian, and members called on different denominations to give invocations at their meetings (ibid.:73). The ANB and the Alaska Native Sisterhood (ANS) became strong social and political advocates for their members.

91   Wickersham State Historic Site, Proceedings of a Council, 32–33.

92   November 19, 1929, Alaska Native Brotherhood Grand Camp Meeting Notes, reported in *Gastineau Heritage News*, "Wickersham's Juneau Part 6: James and William (1921–1929)", vol. 20 no. 2, August 24, 2015, (pp1-17)." August 24, 2015, p. 13.

93   Page 11 of the transcript of the meeting that is reproduced in Appendix 2 of this volume.

94   *I truly believe that the* Berrigan *case was the first piece of the puzzle, establishing the aboriginal land claim that the federal government had a duty to protect and settle. The meeting in 1915 was, I think, his attempt to follow through with the duty (as the federal commissioner), that he had established while he was judge. While he was not able to follow through with that duty then, in a broad way, he finally did with the pursuit of the Tlingit-Haida litigation.*

95 In testimony to the Alaska Native Review Claims Commission in Anchorage on February 28, 1984, elder Alfred Starr told the gathering how he tried in the late 1950s to get Native people to talk about their land claims (Oral History Collection Tape number 86-33-11). The State's plan to build a recreation area in the Minto Flats with road access raised the ire of villagers in Minto and led to their filing a protest. Their chief, Richard Frank, testified concerning the impact this would have on their subsistence (Arnold 1976: 100–101).

96 Alfred R. Ketzler Sr., Alaska Native Land Claims Settlement Collection, March 11, 1962, box 6, folder title "Nenana meeting of chiefs, 11 March, 1962," page 2, Alaska and Polar Regions Collections. University of Alaska Fairbanks Archives (hereafter cited as Ketzler, Nenana Meeting of Chiefs).

97 Ketzler, Nenana Meeting of Chiefs, page 1; see also article by Tom Snapp, *Fairbanks Daily News-Miner*, March 14, 1962:1. "Interior Indian Chiefs meet in Nenana: Plan Session" p. 8.

98 Ketzler, Nenana Meeting of Chiefs, page 3; Toghotthele Corporation, Nenana Denayee (Nenana, AK: Toghotthele Corporation, 1983), 60–76; Stephen Haycox and Alexandra J. McClanahan, *Alaska scrapbook: Moments in Alaska history, 1816–1998* (Anchorage: CIRI Foundation, 2007), 93–94.

99 Riggs was in Nenana representing the government's Engineering Commission that was charged with laying out and building the railroad.

100 U.S. Congress, *Alaska Organic Act*, 23 Stat. 24 [48th Cong., 2nd sess.], May 17, 1884.

101 Ketzler, Nenana Meeting of Chiefs, 8.

102 Paul Brooks, "The Plot to Drown Alaska," *Atlantic Monthly*, May 1965 (article in the Northern Alaska Environmental Center (NAEC) archival collection, at the UAF archives, box 52, series 2, folder 40).

103 Fortunately, the plan was opposed in June 1967 by then secretary of the interior Stewart Udall (Coates 1991:153).

104 Alfred B. Ketzler Sr., William Paul Collection, "Statement of Alfred R. Ketzler, Spokesman from Nenana, Alaska, February 8, 1968," The Tanana Chiefs Conference, June 24–26, 1962, box 7, page 3 (hereafter cited as Ketzler, "Statement of Alfred R. Ketzler").

105 Special thanks to linguist James Kari for assistance in reference and for correct spelling.

106 Athabascan elder Alfred Starr described the ancient site and the large gatherings that were held there, and he said that his mother remembered that when she was a little girl, there was a large gathering at the ancient meeting site. The discussion is from an oral recording: 00-00-178-06 P4. Recorded June 9, 1972. Alaska and Polar Regions Collections, UAF, Oral History Recording.

107 Ketzler, "Statement of Alfred R. Ketzler". The reference to the 1913 meeting is on page 2. Bear Ketzler Collection, Box 1, pamphlet titled, Chiefs' Conference, Tanana, Alaska, June 24–26, 1962. Matthew Sniffen and Thos. Carrington representing the Indian Rights Association did an investigation of Indian conditions in Interior Alaska in 1914. In their report, they mention a meeting in Tanana from July 2 to July 6, 1914. There is also reference to a

107　(*continued*) 1913 meeting in the *Fairbanks Daily News-Miner*, April 14, 1967. Despite the discrepancy in years, we are probably talking about the same meeting referenced by Ketzler.

108　U.S. Congress. *Alaska Statehood Act.* 72 Stat. 339, Public Law 85-508, 85th Cong., H.R. 7999, July 7, 1958, amended June 25, 1959, Public Law 86-70, § 2(a), 73 Stat. 141; and Article 12, Section 12 of the Alaska Constitution.

109　Natasha Singh points out that Alaska Natives were promised protection of subsistence and this hasn't happened. She states that this is important because "one of the only ties the current tribes and Alaska Natives have with their indigenous existence is their spiritual connection to the land and animals that is practiced through traditional hunting and fishing"(Reviewer's Report, September 9, 2016).

110　Kevin Illingworth argues that there is no legal conflict over the State's right to allocate preferences:
I consider this an overly broad statement because the Alaska State Constitution states under "Common Use": wherever occurring in the natural state, fish, wildlife, and waters are reserved to the people for common use. Until the McDowell *case, this had never been interpreted as prohibiting hunting and fishing preferences. There is nothing in the Constitution that "prohibits a preference to any segment of the population" and of course all sorts of segments of the Alaska population have preferences and rights in a number of ways. In fact, the next section of the Constitution specifically endorses them. Under "Sustainable Yield" the Constitution states: Fish, forests, wildlife, grasslands, and all other replenishable resources belonging to the State, shall be utilized, developed, and maintained on the sustained yield principle, subject to preferences among beneficial users"* (Illingworth, personal communication).

111　The Federally Recognized Indian Tribe List Act of November 2, 1994, affirmed that Alaska Native communities are tribes with legal government-to-government relationships with the United States government. Tribal recognition of communities affirms their rights to negotiate with the federal government for services much like Native tribes in the rest of the United States. The State's decision not to appeal the federal government's Land Trust ruling (*Fairbanks Daily News Miner*, August 16, 2016) opens up opportunities for Alaska tribes to gain jurisdictional authority in their communities (Illingworth, personal communication, September 7, 2016, see also Case and Voluck 2012:388-397). See also "AG Says Alaska's Tribes Have Legal Sovereignty," *Fairbanks Daily News Miner*, October 21, 2017, Parts 1 and 3.

Postscript

112　Ross Coen, "A Statue of Seward in Juneau Would Also Honor Painful History in Alaska," *Alaska Dispatch News*, Commentary, March 31, 2016; and Alaska Historical Society, Message from the President, "The Past Is Never Dead. It's Not Even Past," *Alaska Historical Society Newsletter* 44 (Spring 2016).

113　Patty, *Alaska Journal*, 2–18.

114 Alaska State Archives, Tanana Chiefs Council, 1915, and Native-Related Material. ASL MS107 038 001, box 38, 4 folders.

115 Will Mayo, personal communication, February 20, 2017.

116 Chief Ivan and Chief William to the secretary of war. Chief Alexander wrote to Judge Wickersham from Tolovana in 1910 describing his people's need for medical assistance and schooling (Chief Alexander to James Wickersham 1910).

Appendix 1: Introduction to the Transcript of the 1915 Tanana Chiefs Meeting in Fairbanks

117 Wickersham, "An Address Delivered at the Laying of the Cornerstone [July 4, 1915]."

118 Woodrow Wilson, State of the Union Address, December 2, 1913, accessed at teachingamericanhistory.org./library/document/state-of-the-union-address-102/.pdf.

119 U.S. Congress, House of Representatives Hearings before the Committee on the Territories on H.R. 15763, 63rd Cong., 2nd sess., June 3 and 5, 1914.

120 William Schneider, "Elders' Voices Echo Links to Land," *Heartland* magazine, *Fairbanks Daily News-Miner,* February 11, 1990, H-5.

121 James Wickersham to Franklin K. Lane, July 22, 1915, accessed at http://www.library.state.ak.us/goldrush/ARCHIVES/manu1/077_013.JPG.

Appendix 3: The Alaska Purchase and Alaska Natives

122 Natasha Singh, Kevin Illingworth, and Will Mayo are interviewed by William Schneider in Fairbanks, Alaska, on 12/20/16 on the 150th Anniversary of the Alaska Purchase. The recording is 2016-20-01, parts 1 and 2 in the Alaska and Polar Regions Oral History Collection.

123 Dominion: *As used in international law, the term refers to the economic and political control of a discovering nation, dominion being a requisite of ownership.* As used here, the term refers to power over land and people and is how the United States government saw its relationship with the "uncivilized tribes" designated in the Treaty of Cession.

124 Domestic dependents: *In* Cherokee Nation v. Georgia, *Chief Justice Marshall referred to tribes as "domestic dependent nations," a change from their previous status as foreign nations.* With respect to the United States and Alaska Natives, it refers to the government's responsibility to meet the material, health, and educational needs of tribes until such time as this relationship is legally terminated.

125 Manifest destiny: In the latter half of the nineteenth century, with European powers and American industrialists expanding their financial empires in search of raw materials, they came in contact with Native people around the world whom they viewed as "less developed" and inferior in their knowledge and lifeways. Manifest destiny was the philosophy that the "great powers" had a

125 (*continued*) divine right to expand and take over these lands and subject the populations to their values and standards of acceptable lifeways. The philosophy also reflected a paternalistic responsibility of the conquering powers to show the light and way to the less informed they encountered.

126 Klondike gold rush: The discovery of gold near present-day Dawson City, Canada, in 1896 created a stampede of gold seekers to the Yukon. A large number of the prospectors quickly spread to Alaska to find gold-mining opportunities.

127 Klawock Cannery: The Klawock Cannery incident of 1878 is recorded by Penelope Goforth in an Alaska Historical Society blog post (alaskahistorical-society.org). See also Steve Henrikson, "History in a Can," Alaska Canneries Blogspot (alaskacanneries.blogspot.com).

128 IRA Period: *The Indian Reorganization Act of 1934, also referred to as the Indian New Deal, ended the diminishment of reservations, reversed the U.S. policy of assimilation, and had a goal to strengthen tribal governments and culture. The act gave the secretary of the interior power to acquire land for "landless" Natives. The act was amended in 1936 for Alaska to allow establishment of reservations (Case and Voluck 2012:28–29).*

129 Land in Trust: *In 2013* Akiachak v. Salazar *held that it was unlawful to discriminate against Alaska tribes by not allowing land in Alaska to be taken into trust. In 2017, the Department of Interior began taking land into trust, creating opportunities for Alaska tribes to obtain "jurisdictional control" over lands held in trust with the federal government. These could include increased public safety, and judicial authority as well as regulatory control of environmental and natural resources.[partial list] (Illingworth, personal communication, September 7, 2016).*

130 Federally Recognized List Act: In 1993, the Tribal Recognition Act established that Alaska Native communities were "tribes" with legal government-to-government relationships with the federal government. The Federally Recognized Indian Tribe List Act of 1994 recognized the official tribes in Alaska. Tribal recognition of communities offers them rights to negotiate with the United States government for services much like Native groups in the rest of the country.

131 Treaty Clause: This refers to Article II, Section 2, Clause 2 of the United States Constitution. This clause allows the president to make treaties with other countries, but they must be confirmed by the Senate. Since Native tribes are sovereign, they were party to treaty making until 1871 when the United States ceased making treaties with Natives (Arnold 1976:51; Prucha 1984, vol. 1:531).

132 Indian Self-Determination Act: The Indian Self-Determination and Education Assistance Act of 1975, Public Law 93-638, gives tribal entities the opportunity to contract for Bureau of Indian Affairs services (Case and Voluck 2012:338–339).

133 Frederica de Laguna 1995:197. She documented his presence at the time of Russian occupation. Chief Red Shirt: A picture of Chief Red Shirt appears in Edward Schieffelin's archival collection at the Huntington Library in San

Marino California, PhotCL264(12). Schieffelin was a prospector who came to Alaska for a prospecting trip in 1882 and is reported to have prospected around the mouth of the Tanana River (Brooks 1973:327).

134 14C Provisions of ANCSA: *This provision requires Alaska Native Corporations to convey land to other individuals and groups. The most controversial provision, 14(c)(3) requires the corporations to convey land to "future municipalities" rather than local tribal government.*

135 *Venetie* tax case: *The Ninth Circuit held that land that was conveyed through ANCSA was not considered to be Indian country for jurisdictional purposes* (Case and Voluck 2012:390).

136 *John v. Baker*: This was an Alaska Supreme Court child custody decision that sided with a tribal court. The Alaska Supreme Court found that the tribal court had authority to regulate "internal and social relations," even though the parents in question were not living in Indian country (Case and Voluck 2012:401–402).

References

Abercrombie, W. R. 1900. A military reconnaissance of the Copper River Valley, 1898. In *Compilation of narratives of explorations in Alaska*, 563–591. Washington, DC: Government Printing Office.

———. 1900. A supplementary expedition into the Copper River Valley, 1884. In *Compilation of narratives of explorations in Alaska*, 383–408. Washington, DC: Government Printing Office.

Alaska Department of Fish and Game. 2005. Wheels spin into second century in Alaska. In *Subsistence Management Information* Vol. 5 (March): 6.

Alaska Historical Society. 2016. Message from the president: "The past is never dead. It's not even past." *Alaska Historical Society Newsletter* 44 (Spring). Anchorage, AK.

Alaska Humanities Forum. Alaska History and Cultural Studies. "Native Citizenship and Land Issues."

Alaska Mining Hall of Fame Foundation website. http://alaskamininghalloffame.org.

Alaska State Archives. Tanana Chiefs Council, 1915, and Native-related material. ASL-MS 107, box 38, 4 folders. Alaska Organic Act 1884. 23 stat. 24. May 17, 1884.

Alaska State Constitution. Accessed at http://ltgov.alaska.gov/services/alaskas-constitution/.

Alaska State Library, Historical Collections. "An Act to Define the Political Status of Certain Native Indians within the Territory of Alaska." Alaska Legislature of the Territory of Alaska. S.B. 21. April 27, 1915. ASL-KFA1225.A3-1915-p52. 24 SLA 1915. http://library.alaska.gov/hist/fulltext/ASL-KFA-1225.A3-1915.htm.

Alaska State Library, Historical Collections. Wickersham State Historic Site. Manuscripts, 1884–1970s. ASL-MS107-38-001.

Alaska Territorial Legislature. 1915. An Act to Define the Political Status of Certain Native Indians within the Territory of Alaska. S.B. 21 (Alaska Native Citizenship Act).

Allen, Henry T. 1900. A military reconnaissance of the Copper River Valley, 1885. In *Compilation of narratives of explorations in Alaska*, 411–488. Washington, DC: Government Printing Office.

Andrews, Elizabeth. n.d. *Native and historic accounts of some historic sites in the Tanacross-Ketchumstock area.* Report prepared for Cemetery and Historic Sites Committee, Doyon, Limited. Fairbanks, AK.

Arnold, Robert. 1976. *Alaska Native land claims.* Anchorage, AK: Alaska Native Foundation.

Berrigan Collection, Report of Referee for *USA v. Berrigan et al.* (1905), Case 270F, Alaska District Court, Third Division (Fairbanks), box AS 30921, Alaska State Archives.

Berrigan Collection, Order of Injunction for *USA v. Berrigan et al.* (1905), Case 270F, Alaska District Court, Third Division (Fairbanks), box AS 30921, Alaska State Archives.

Berry, Mary. 1975. *The Alaska pipeline: The politics of oil and native land claims.* Bloomington: Indiana University Press.

Blackman, Margaret. 1989. *Sadie Brower Neakok: An Inupiaq woman.* Seattle. University of Washington Press.

Bonnell, Ray. 2011. Salcha Native Cemetery: A people and place worth remembering. *Fairbanks Daily News-Miner.* January 9, E2.

———. 2013. *Interior sketches: Ramblings around Interior Alaska historic sites.* Fairbanks, AK: Pingo Press.

Brewster, Karen. 2013. Interview with Lee Saylor on June 5. Oral History Collection, number 2013-14-01, parts 1 and 2. Online at https://jukebox.uaf.edu/site7/interviews/2016.

Brooks, Alfred Hulse. 1898. Journal of trip to Alaska, 1898. United States Geological Survey Office Files. Anchorage, AK.

———. 1900. A reconnaissance in the Tanana and White River Basins, Alaska, in 1898. Extract from the twentieth annual report of the survey 1898–99, part VII, Explorations in Alaska in 1898. Washington, DC: Government Printing Office.

———. 1973. *Blazing Alaska's trails.* Fairbanks: University of Alaska Press.

Brooks, Paul. 1965. The plot to drown Alaska. *Atlantic Monthly*, May. Northern Alaska Environmental Center Collection. Box 52, series 2, folder 40. Alaska and Polar Regions Collections. University of Alaska Fairbanks.

Brown, Michael C. 1984. Indians, traders, and bureaucrats in the Upper Tanana District: A history of the Tetlin Reserve. Alaska State Office and Alaska Resources Library and Information Services. Bureau of Land Management. Anchorage, AK. (Also available from Consortium Library in Anchorage.)

Callahan, Erinia Pavaloff Cherosky. 1975. A Yukon autobiography. *Alaska Journal* 5 (2): 127–128.

Callaway, Donald G., and Constance A. Friend. June 2007. Mendees Cheeg Naltsiin Keey'; or, An oral history of the people of Healy Lake Village. Interviews and manuscript prepared with support from Tanana Chiefs Conference, the Alaska Systems Support Office, and the Alaska Humanities Forum.

Case, David. 1984. Alaska Natives and American laws. Fairbanks, University of Alaska Press.

Case, David, and David Voluck. 2002 and 2012 editions. Alaska Natives and American laws. Fairbanks, University of Alaska Press.

Castile, George Pierre. 1990. The Indian connection: Judge James Wickersham and the Indian Shakers. *Pacific Northwest Quarterly* 81 (4): 122–129.

Castner, Joseph C. 1984. *Lieutenant Castner's Alaskan exploration, 1898: A journey of hardship and suffering.* Ed. Lyman L. Woodman. Alaska Historical Commission Studies in History. No. 125. Anchorage, AK. Cook Inlet Historical Society.

Chief Alexander. 1910. Chief Alexander to James Wickersham. "A Preliminary Inventory of the James Wickersham Papers 1884-1970s." Wickersham Collection. Ms. 107, rev. 2005, p. 57. ASL-MS-107. Alaska State Library. Historical Collections. Juneau. http://library.alaska.gov/hist/fulltext/ASL-MS-0107-38-001.htm.

Chief Ivan and Chief William. 1906. Chief Ivan and Chief William to the secretary of war, written and posted from Fort Gibbon, August 18, 1906, box 9, folder 47A, record group 22, entry UD-91, Records of the U.S. Bureau of Fisheries, Division of Alaska Fisheries, Reports and Related Records, 1869–1937. National Archives and Records Administration, College Park, Maryland.

Coates, Peter A. 1991. *The Trans-Alaska Pipeline controversy: Technology, conservation, and the frontier.* Bethlehem, PA: Lehigh University Press.

Coen, Ross. 2011. *Long view: Dispatches on Alaska history.* Ester, AK: Ester Republic Press.

———. 2016. A statue of Seward in Juneau would also honor painful history in Alaska. *Alaska Dispatch News.* Commentary. March 31.

Cohen, Felix S. 1986. *Felix S. Cohen's Handbook of federal Indian law.* Five Rings Corporation.

Cole, Terrence. 1981. *E. T. Barnette: The strange story of the man who founded Fairbanks.* Anchorage. Alaska Northwest Publishing Company.

———. 1989. Historic resources of the Minnie Street Corridor. Final report for the Alaska Department of Transportation and Public Facilities, Northern Region. Fairbanks. Department of History, University of Alaska Fairbanks.

Cook, John P. 1989. Historic archaeology and ethnohistory at Healy Lake, Alaska. *Arctic* 42 (2): 109–118.

Curtis, Natalie. 1907. *The Indians' book: An offering by the American Indians of Indian lore, musical and narrative to form a record of the songs and legends of their race.* New York: Harper and Brothers.

Dall, William H. 1870. *Alaska and its resources.* Boston: Lee and Shepard.

Dean, David M. 1988. *Breaking trail: Hudson Stuck of Texas and Alaska.* Athens: Ohio University Press.

de Laguna, Frederica. 1975. Matrilineal kin groups in Northwestern North America. In *Proceedings: Northern Athapaskan Conference, 1971*, vol. 1, 17–145.

———. 1995. *Tales from the Dena: Indian stories from the Tanana, Koyukuk, and Yukon rivers.* Ed. Frederica De Laguna, Norman Reynolds, Dale DeArmond. Seattle: University of Washington Press.

Doogan, Sean. 2013. Katie John, noted Ahtna elder and Alaskan icon, has passed. *Alaska Dispatch News.* May 31.

Drane, Frederick. Frederick Drane to R. B. Drane, September 12, 1915. Episcopal Church Records, Frederick Drane Collection, box 1, folder 3. Alaska and Polar Regions Archives, Rasmuson Library, University of Alaska Fairbanks.

Drane, Frederick. Drane to Arthur Wright, July 1, 1929. Episcopal Church Records, Frederick Drane Collection, box 1, folder 3, Alaska and Polar Regions Archives, Rasmuson Library, University of Alaska Fairbanks.

Drucker, Philip. 1958. *The Native brotherhoods: Modern intertribal organizations on the Northwest Coast.* Bureau of American Ethnology, Bulletin 168. Washington, DC: Smithsonian Institution.

Elliott, Charles P. 1900. Details of a visit to the fishing grounds and canneries from and including Prince William Sound to Nushagak. In *Compilation of Narratives of Explorations in Alaska,* 738–741. Washington, DC: Government Printing Office.

Emmons Family Papers. Manuscript call number Wa Mss S-1306. Beinecke Rare Book and Manuscript Library. Yale University.

Emmons, G. T. 1905. *Conditions and Needs of the Natives of Alaska,* 1–23. 58th Cong., 3rd sess. Document 106. Washington, DC: Government Printing Office.

Emmons, George Thornton. 1991. *The Tlingit Indians.* Ed. Frederica de Laguna. Seattle: University of Washington Press.

Endicott, Henry W. 1928. *Adventures in Alaska and along the trail.* New York: F. A. Stokes Company.

Fairbanks Commercial Club. 1916. *Descriptive of Fairbanks "Alaska's Golden Heart."*

Fairbanks Daily News-Miner. 1962. Chief's parley shows stature, clear purpose. April 14, 4.

Fairbanks Daily News-Miner. 2016. State will not appeal federal land trust ruling. August 16, 1.

Fairbanks Daily News Miner. 2017. "AG says Alaska's Tribes have legal Sovereignty." October 21, 2017, P1 and 3.

Farnsworth Family Papers. Charles and Robert Farnsworth Papers. Alaska and Polar Regions Department Archives. University of Alaska Fairbanks.

Federal Field Committee for Development Planning in Alaska. 1968. *Alaska Natives and the land.* Washington, DC: Government Printing Office.

Federally Recognized Indian Tribe List Act of November 2, 1994. Pub.L no.103-454 103d Congress.

Fischer, Victor. 1975. *Alaska's constitutional convention.* National Municipal League State Constitutional Convention Studies. No. 9. Fairbanks: University of Alaska Press.

Fish, Oscar. 1900. Oscar Fish to the secretary of the interior, 1900, NA Microfilm Publication 430, roll 7, frames 518–520, record group 48. Records of the Office of the Secretary of the Interior.

Fitch, Edwin. 1967. *The Alaska railroad.* New York: Frederick A. Praeger.

Funston, Frederick. 1903. *Report of the Secretary of the Interior for the Fiscal Year 1903,* 269–275.

Galblum, Jane (Haigh). 1980. A short tour of historic Fairbanks. *Alaska Journal* 10 (Spring): 56–63.

Gardner, Bruce L. 2002. *American agriculture in the twentieth century: How it flourished and what it cost.* Cambridge: Harvard University Press.

Garner, Bryan. 2009. *Black's Law Dictionary.* St. Paul, MN: West Publishing Company.

Gastineau Heritage News. 2015. November 19, 1929, Alaska Native Brotherhood Grand Camp Meeting Notes. Reported in *Gastineau Heritage News*, vol. 20, no. 2., pages 1–17.

Gastineau Heritage News. 2015. August 24, 1–17. Wickersham's Juneau, part 6: James and William (1921–1929). Juneau: Gastineau Channel Historical Society.

Goforth, Penelope. 2014. Klawock Cannery, 1878. *AHS Blog.* Alaska Historical Society. July 17, 2014. http://alaskahistoricalsociety.org/klawock-cannery-1878-2/.

Goldschmidt, Walter. 1946. Possessory rights of the Athabascan Indian Natives of the villages of Northway, Tanacross, and Tetlin in the Interior of Alaska. *Report to the Commissioner of Indian Affairs.* Washington, DC.

Goodrich, Harold. 1898. History and conditions of Yukon Gold District to 1897. In *Eighteenth Annual Report of the United States Secretary of the Interior, 1896–97, Geology of the Yukon Gold District, part III: Economic geology.* Washington, DC: Government Printing Office.

Griese, Arnold, and Ed Bigelow. 1980. *O ye frost and cold: A history of St. Mathews Episcopal Church.* St. Mathews Episcopal Church. Fairbanks.

Haigh, Jane. 1996. . . . And his native wife. In *Preserving and Interpreting Cultural Heritage.* Papers given at the annual meeting of the Alaska Historical Society. Anchorage. October 9–12, 39–54.

Hallowell, A. Irving. 1957. The backwash of the frontier: The impact of the Indian on American culture. In *The frontier in perspective*, 229–258. Ed. Walter D. Wyman and Clifton B. Kroeber. Madison: The University of Wisconsin Press.

Haycox, Stephen. 1994. William Lewis Paul / Shgu'ndi [Shquindyl], May 7, 1885–March 4, 1977, Raven; Teeyhittaan [Tee-hit-ton]. In *Haa Kusteeyí, Our culture: Tlingit life stories*, 503–524. Ed. Nora Marks Dauenhauer and Richard Dauenhauer. Vol. 3. Seattle. University of Washington Press.

———. 1996. Economic development and Indian land rights in modern Alaska. In *An Alaska anthology: Interpreting the past*, 336–363. Ed. Stephen Haycox and Mary Childers Mangusso. Seattle: University of Washington Press.

Haycox, Stephen, and Alexandra J. McClanahan. 2007. *Alaska scrapbook: Moments in Alaska history, 1816–1998.* Anchorage: CIRI Foundation.

Healy, Jeany. Collection. Alaska and Polar Regions Collections. University of Alaska Fairbanks Archives.

Henrikson, Steve. 2014. History in a can. *AHS Blog.* Alaska Historical Society. July 17, 2014. http://alaskahistoricalsociety.org/history-in-a-can-2/.

Herron, Joseph. 1909. *Explorations in Alaska, 1899: For an All-American Overland Route from Cook Inlet, Pacific Ocean, to the Yukon.* Washington, DC: Government Printing Office.

Hinckley, Ted C. 1970. "The canoe rocks: We do not know what will become of us." The complete transcript of a meeting between Governor John Green Brady of Alaska and a group of Tlingit chiefs, Juneau, December 14, 1898. *Western Historical Quarterly* 1 (3): 265–289.

Hosley, Edward H. 1981. Intercultural relations and cultural change in the Alaska plateau. *Handbook of North American Indians* 6 (Subarctic): 546–555. Washington, DC: Smithsonian Institution.

Hunt, William R. 1993. *Whiskey Peddler, Johnny Healy, North Frontier Trader.* Missoula, MT: Mountain Press Publishing Company.

Illingworth, Kevin M. n.d. "Timeline of important laws and events impacting tribal governments in Alaska." University of Alaska Fairbanks Tribal Management Program. Fairbanks, AK.

Jackson, Sheldon. 1897. *Introduction of domestic reindeer into Alaska.* Washington, DC: Government Printing Office.

Jones, Eliza, and Jules Jetté. 2000. *Koyukon Athabascan Dictionary.* Alaska Native Language Center. University of Alaska Fairbanks.

Jones, Richard. 1981. *Alaska Native Claims Settlement Act of 1971 (Public Law 92-203): History and analysis together with subsequent amendments.* Report No. 81-127 GOV. Previously published by Congressional Research Service (1972). Library of Congress.

Kari, James, ed. and trans. 1985. *Tatl'ahwt'aenn Nenn', The Headwaters People's Country: Narratives of the Upper Ahtna Athabaskans.* Fairbanks, AK: Alaska Native Language Center.

Katie John et al. v. the United States of America. 2013. Ninth Circuit upholds District Court ruling, *Katie John v. United States,* 720F, 3d 1214 (2013).

Kennedy, Roger G. 2003. *Mr. Jefferson's lost cause: Land, farmers, slavery, and the Louisiana Purchase.* New York: Oxford University Press.

Ketzler, Alfred R., Sr., Alaska Native Land Claims Settlement Collection, 1961–1977. "The Tanana Chiefs Conference, Tanana, Alaska, June 24–26, 1962." Dena' Nena' Henash (Our Land Speaks). Box 1. Alaska and Polar Regions Collections. University of Alaska Fairbanks Archives.

Ketzler, Alfred R., Sr., Alaska Native Land Claims Settlement Collection, March 11, 1962. Box 6, folder title "Nenana meeting of chiefs, 11 March, 1962." Alaska and Polar Regions Collections. University of Alaska Fairbanks Archives.

Ketzler, Alfred R., Sr., William Paul Collection. "Statement of Alfred R. Ketzler, Spokesman from Nenana, Alaska, February 8, 1968." Box 7, page 3. Alfred R. Ketzler Collection. Alaska and Polar Regions Collections. University of Alaska Fairbanks Archives.

Ketzler, Bear, Collection. Pamphlet. Chiefs Conference, Tanana, Alaska, June 24–26, 1962. Box 1. Alaska and Polar Regions Collections. University of Alaska Fairbanks Archives.

Knapp, Lyman. 1891. A study upon the legal and political status of the Natives of Alaska. *American Law Register* (May): 325–339.

LeFebre, Charlene. Kantishna Oral History Project Records, 1910–1984. Box
     1, folder 54. Collection assembled by Dianne Holmes. Consortium Library.
     Archives and Special Collections Department. University of Alaska Anchorage.
Leslie's Illustrated Weekly: 1891, vol. 72:339 and vol. 73.
Library of Congress. 1905. *Indian chiefs headed by Geronimo, passing in review before
     President Roosevelt, Inauguration Day, 1905, Washington, D.C., U.S.A.* Accessed at
     http://www.loc.gov/pictures/resource/cph.3b03887/.
Library of Congress. 1950. *Russian administration of Alaska and the Status of the
     Alaskan Natives.* Prepared by the Chief of the Foreign Law section, Law Library
     of the Library of Congress. Prepared by Dr. Vladimir Gsovsky. 81st Cong., 2nd
     sess., Senate document 152.
Mangusso, Mary. 1999. Interview on Judge Wickersham and the Wickersham
     House. Oral History Program. Oral History tape number 99-29-01. University
     of Alaska Fairbanks.
Mayo, Will. "Tom Alton, Will Mayo, and Bill Schneider on April 22, 2015,
     in Fairbanks, Alaska, about the historic Tanana Chiefs Meeting with James
     Wickersham in 1915." Recording 2015-10, Parts 1 and 2. Oral History
     Collection, Alaska and Polar Regions Collections and Archives.
Mayo, Will. 2017. Personal communication, February 20, 2017.
McClanahan, A. J. *A Reference in time, Alaska Native history day by day*. Anchorage.
     CIRI Foundation. 2001.
McDowell v. State of Alaska. 785 P.2d (1989).
McKennan, Robert A.1959. *The Upper Tanana Indians.* Yale University Publications
     in Anthropology 55. New Haven: Yale University Press.
———. 1965. Athapaskan groupings and social organization in Central Alaska. In
     *Contributions to Anthropology of Band Societies: Proceedings of the Conference on
     Band Organization*, 93–115. National Museums of Canada. Ottawa. Bulletin
     228. Anthropological Series 84.
———. 1981. Tanana. In *Handbook of North American Indians*. Vol. 6, *Subarctic*,
     562–576. Ed. June Helm. Washington. Smithsonian Institution.
Mendenhall, Walter C. 1900. A reconnaissance from Resurrection Bay to the
     Tanana River, Alaska, in 1898. In *Twentieth annual report, United States
     Geological Survey, 1898–99, part VII: Explorations in Alaska in 1898*, 265–340.
Mertie Baggen Papers. 1964-1967. Alaska and Polar Regions Collections and
     Archives, Archival Collections, University of Alaska Fairbanks.
Metcalfe, Peter. 2014. *A dangerous idea: The Alaska Native Brotherhood and the
     struggle for Indigenous rights.* Fairbanks: University of Alaska Press.
Mishler, Craig W. 1986. Report of Investigations 86-14. In *Born with the river:
     An ethnographic history of Alaska's Goodpaster and Big Delta Indians.* Juneau:
     State of Alaska, Department of Natural Resources, Division of Geological and
     Geophysical Surveys.
Mitchell, William. Collection. Manuscript. Alaska Microfilm 3637, box 20.
     University of Alaska Fairbanks Archives.

Mitchell, William L. 1988. *The Opening of Alaska, 1901–1903*. 2nd ed. Ed. Lyman Woodman. Missoula, MT: Pictorial Histories Publishing Company and Anchorage, AK: Cook Inlet Historical Society.

Natasha Singh, Kevin Illingworth, and Will Mayo are interviewed by William Schneider in Fairbanks, Alaska, on December 20, 2016, on the 150th Anniversary of the Alaska Purchase. Recording 2016-20-01, Parts 1 and 2. Oral History Collection, Alaska and Polar Regions Collections and Archives.

O'Neill, Daniel. 2007. *The firecracker boys: H-bombs, Inupiat Eskimos, and the roots of the environmental movement*. New York: Basic Books.

Patty, Stanton H. 1971. A conference with the Tanana Chiefs. *Alaska Journal* 1 (Spring): 2–18.

Paul, David, and Audrey Loftus. 1957. *According to Papa*. Fairbanks, AK: St. Matthew's Episcopal Guild.

Pratt, Richard Henry. 1964. *Battlefield and classroom: Four decades with the American Indian, 1867–1904*. Introduction and editing by Robert M. Utley. New Haven. Yale University Press.

Price, Robert. 1990. *The Great Father in Alaska: The case of the Tlingit and Haida salmon fishery*. Douglas, AK: First Street Press.

Prucha, Francis Paul. 1984. *The Great Father: the United States Government and the American Indians*. Vols. 1 and 2. Lincoln: University of Nebraska Press.

Quirk, William. 1974. *Historical aspects of the building of the Washington–Alaska Military Cable and Telegraph System with special emphasis on the Eagle–Valdez and Goodpaster telegraph lines, 1902–1903*. Anchorage, AK: United States Department of the Interior, Bureau of Land Management.

Raibmon, Paige. 2005. *Authentic Indians: Episodes of encounter from the late-nineteenth-century Northwest Coast*. Durham, NC: Duke University Press.

Ray, Patrick H. 1900a. Relief of the Destitute in the Gold Fields, 1897. In *Compilation of Narratives of Explorations in Alaska*, 495–504. Washington, DC: Government Printing Office.

———. 1900b. Relief of the Destitute in the Yukon Region, 1898. In *Compilation of Narratives of Explorations in Alaska*, 519–560 (inclusive of further correspondence). Washington, DC: Government Printing Office.

Raymond, Charles. 1900. Reconnaissance of the Yukon River, 1869. In *Compilation of Narratives of Explorations in Alaska*, 19–41. Washington, DC: Government Printing Office.

Richards, W. A. 1906. Rights of Natives under the public land laws. In *Extending certain rights to the Natives of Alaska*. Committee on Public Lands. Senate document 101, 59th Cong., 1st sess.

Robert McKennan Collection. University of Alaska Fairbanks. Alaska and Polar Regions Collections and Archives.

Roberts, Cecil. 1970. Economic, administrative, and environmental consequences of the Alaska Land Freeze. MA Practicum. Natural Resources Administration. Ann Arbor: University of Michigan.

Roosevelt, Theodore. 1901. Address to both houses of Congress, December 3, 1901.

Rowe, Peter. 1908. Peter Trimble Rowe to James Wickersham, November 22, 1908; Wickersham to Rowe, December 18, 1908. Rowe to Wickersham June 5, 1909. Episcopal Church Records, Correspondence, Bishop Rowe, box 102, Alaska and Polar Regions Archives, Rasmuson Library, University of Alaska Fairbanks.

Rowe, Peter. 1910. Rowe to John Wood, July 22, 1910. Episcopal Church Records, Correspondence, Bishop Rowe, box 102, Alaska and Polar Regions Archives, Rasmuson Library, University of Alaska Fairbanks.

Saylor, Lee. 2000. Interview by Constance Friend, December 9, 2000. Oral History Program. Oral History tape number 2000-105-07. University of Alaska Fairbanks. Online at https://jukebox.uaf.edu/site7/interviews/2016.

Saylor, Lee. 2013. Interview by Karen Brewster. June 5, 2013, on Wrangell-St. Elias Project Jukebox. Oral History Program. Oral History tape number 2013-14-01, part 1, pp. 5, 7–8. University of Alaska Fairbanks.

Schieffelin, Edward. 1882–1883. Photographs of Edward Schieffelin's Prospecting Trip in Alaska. PhotCL264(12). The Huntington Library, San Marino California.

Schneider, William. 1985. Chief Sesui and Lieutenant Herron: A story of who controls the bacon. *Alaska History* 1 (Fall/Winter): 1–18.

———. 1986. On the back slough. In *Interior Alaska: A journey through time*, 147–194. Ed. Jean Aigner et al. Anchorage. Alaska Geographical Society.

———. Elders' voices echo links to land. *Heartland* magazine, *Fairbanks Daily News-Miner.* February 11, 1990, H-5.

Seward, William H. 1869. Speech of William H. Seward at Sitka. Washington, DC: Philip and Solomons. Referenced from Alaska State Library Collection. ASL F907.S38-1869.htm (16 pages).

Sherwood, Morgan. 1992. *Exploration of Alaska, 1865–1900.* Fairbanks: University of Alaska Press.

Simeone, William. 2007. The Arrival: Native and missionary relations on the Upper Tanana River, 1914. *Alaska Journal of Anthropology* 5 (1): 83–94.

Simeone, William, and James Kari. 2002. *Traditional knowledge and fishing practices of the Ahtna of Copper River, Alaska.* Technical Paper number 270. In collaboration with Copper River Native Association, Chee sh Na' Tribal Council, and Chitina Tribal Council. Prepared for the U.S. Fish and Wildlife Service. Agreement No. 7018101296. Project No. FIS 00-40. Juneau: Alaska Department of Fish and Game, Division of Subsistence.

Snapp, Tom. 1962. Interior Indian chiefs meet in Nenana: Plan session. *Fairbanks Daily News-Miner.* March 14, p. 8.

Sniffen, Matthew, and D. Thos. Spees Carrington. 1914. *The Indians of the Yukon and Tanana Valleys, Alaska.* Philadelphia: Indian Rights Association. No. 98. Second Series. 300.

Starr, Alfred. 1984 (February 28). Testimony to the Alaska Native Review Commission. Anchorage. Oral History Collection: 86-33-11.

———. 1972 (June 9). Oral History Collection: 00-00-178-06 P4. H95-47, Pt 1&2. Alaska and Polar Regions Collections, University of Alaska Fairbanks.

Stuck, Hudson. Hudson Stuck to John Wood, June 19, 1909. Episcopal Church Records, Correspondence, box 105, Alaska and Polar Regions Archives, Rasmuson Library, University of Alaska Fairbanks.

Thomas, Kenny, Sr., and Craig Mishler, eds. 2005. *Crow is my Boss, Taatsa'a' Shaa K' exalthet: The oral life history of a Tanacross Athabaskan elder.* Norman: University of Oklahoma Press.

Tlingit and Haida Indians of Alaska v. United States, 177F. Supp.452 (Ct Cl, 1959) United States Court of Claims.

Toghotthele Corporation. 1983. Nenana Denayee. Nenana, AK: Toghotthele Corporation.

Treaty of Cession. 1867. By the president of the United States of America: A proclamation, 15 Stat. 539.

U.S. Census Records for 1910.

U.S. Congress. 1862. *Homestead Act.* Public Law 37-64. 12 Stat. 392. May 20, 1862.

U.S. Congress. 1870. Letter of the Secretary of the Treasury communicating report of Captain Charles Bryant. Senate document 32, 41st Cong., 2nd sess., p. 14.

U.S. Congress. 1884. *Alaska Organic Act.* 23 Stat. 24. May 17, 1884.

U.S. Congress. 1887. *Dawes Act.* Feb. 8, 1887, Pub. Law 49-119 24 Stat. 387.

U.S. Congress. 1898. *Alaska Homestead Act.* 30 Stat. 409. May 14, 1898.

U.S. Congress. 1904. Senate Subcommittee of Committee on Territories. *Conditions in Alaska. Report of Subcommittee of Committee on Territories appointed to investigate conditions in Alaska. Hearings Report of Subcommittee of Committee on Territories appointed to investigate conditions in Alaska.* 58th Cong., 2nd sess. Senate report 282, part 2.

U.S. Congress. 1906. *Alaska Native Allotment Act.* 34 Stat. 197.

U.S. Congress. 1912. House of Representatives. Hearings before the Committee on the Territories on Conditions in Alaska. 62nd Cong., 2nd sess., January 16, 1912.

U.S. Congress. 1913. House of Representatives. Committee on the Territories Report No. 92, 63rd Cong., 1st sess., November 26, 1913.

U.S. Congress. 1914. House of Representatives. Alaska Railway Bill, Speech of Hon. James Wickersham, 6. 63rd Cong., 2nd sess., January 14 and 28, 1914.

U.S. Congress. 1914. House of Representatives. Hearings before the Committee on the Territories on H.R. 15763. 63rd Cong., 2nd sess., June 3 and 5, 1914.

U.S. Congress. 1926. Alaska Native Townsite Act of May 25, 1926, 44 Stat. 629.

U.S. Congress. 1934. *Indian Reorganization Act.*

U.S. Congress. 1958. *Alaska Statehood Act.* 72 Stat. 339. Public Law 85-508, 85th Cong, H.R. 7999, July 7, 1958. Amended June 25, 1959, Public Law 86-70, § 2(a), 73 Stat. 141.

U.S. Congress. 1971. *Alaska Native Claims Settlement Act.*

U.S. Congress. 1975. *Indian Self-Determination and Education Assistance Act.*

U.S. Congress. 1993. *Tribal Recognition Act.*

U.S. Congress. 1994. *Federally Recognized Tribe List Act.*

U.S. Department of the Treasury. 1870. Letter of the Secretary of the Treasury, communicating, in compliance with a resolution of the Senate of December 20, 1869, the reports of Captain Charles Bryant, late special agent of the Treasury Department for Alaska, and H. A. McIntyre, special agent for the Treasury Department. Senate Document 32, 41st Cong., 2nd sess., p. 14.

U.S. Department of the Treasury. 1899. *Report of the cruise of the U.S. revenue cutter Bear and the overland expedition for the relief of the whalers in the Arctic Ocean from Nov. 27, 1897, to Sept. 13, 1898.* Washington, DC: Government Printing Office.

United States Court of Appeals, District of Columbia Circuit Akiachak Native Community et al., Apellees v United States Department of the Interior and Sally Jewell, Secretary of the Interior, Appellee State of Alaska Appellant no. 13-5310 July 1, 2016.

United States Court of Claims. 1959. Tlingit and Haida Indians of Alaska v. United States 177F. Supp.452. Ct. Cl.

Webb, Melody. 1985. *The last frontier: A history of the Yukon Basin of Canada and Alaska.* Albuquerque. University of New Mexico Press.

Wells, E. Hazard. 1891. Exploring Alaska, Frank Leslie's expedition: Prefatory statements of its purposes and plans, how it was organized and what it discovered—changing the map of Alaska and revealing its hidden sources of wealth. *Frank Leslie's Illustrated Newspaper.* Vols. 72 and 73.

———. 1898. E. Hazard Wells's report: Rich gold deposits in United States Territory—said to rival those across the line. *New York Times.* February 11, 1898.

———. 1900. Up and Down the Yukon, 1897. In *Compilation of Narratives of Explorations in Alaska*, 511–516. Washington, DC: Government Printing Office.

Wickersham, James. 1884–1970s. Family Papers. Phyllis J. DeMuth Movius (archivist). Alaska Digital Archives. Accessed. http://library.alaska.gov/hist/fulltext/ASL-F909.W52-2000.htm.

Wickersham, James. 1900–1939. Diaries. Alaska State Library. http://library.alaska.gov/hist//hist_docs/wickersham/ASL-MS0107-diaries1900-1941.pdf.

Wickersham, James. 1915. "An Address Delivered at the Laying of the Cornerstone [July 4, 1915]." Rasmuson Library, University of Alaska Fairbanks.

Wickersham, James. 1915. James Wickersham to Franklin K. Lane, July 22, 1915. Alaska State Library. library.alaska.gov.

Wickersham, James. 2009. *Old Yukon: Tales, Trails, and Trials.* Edited and abridged by Terrence Cole. Fairbanks: University of Alaska Press.

Wickersham, James, editor, arranger, digester. 1906. Alaska Reports. Vol. 2. *Containing the Decisions of the District Judges of Alaska Territory from January 1, 1903, to January 1, 1906.* St. Paul, MN: West Publishing Company.

Wickersham, James, editor, arranger, digester. 1906. Naturalization of John Minook. In Alaska Reports. Vol. 2, *Containing the Decisions of the District Judges of Alaska Territory From January1, 1903, to January 1, 1906*, 200–224. St. Paul, MN: West Publishing.

Wickersham State Historic Site. Manuscripts, 1884–1970s. Proceedings of a Council, Held in the Library Room at Fairbanks, Alaska, on July 5, 1915, between the chiefs and headmen of the bands of Indians living along the Tanana River and Delegate James Wickersham, 1–33. ASL-MS-107. Alaska State Library. Historical Collections. Juneau. http://library.alaska.gov/hist/fulltext/ASL-MS-0107-38-001.htm.

Williams, Catherine M., and Peter M. Bowers. 2004. Illinois/Barnette Street Project historic resources update and re-evaluation, final report. Prepared for USKH, Inc., and the Alaska Department of Transportation and Public Facilities. Prepared by Northern Land Use Research, Inc. Fairbanks. Vols. 1 and 2.

Wilson, Woodrow. State of the Union Address. December 2, 1913. teachingamericanhistory.org./library/document/state-of-the-union-address-102/.pdf

Witten, Jas. W. 1903. Natives of Alaska. In Exhibit H of *Report of the Secretary of the Interior for the Fiscal Year 1903*, 275–279.

Index

Abercrombie, W. R., 22
aboriginal rights. See also Native rights
    aboriginal title, 1, 136
    Alaska Native Claims Settlement Act
      and, 139
    Berrigan case, 143n21, 150n94
    Congress's definition of, 62
    Minook case, 143n19
    Tanana chiefs meeting of 1915 and,
      70–71
    Tanana chiefs meeting of 1962 and, 62
    Treaty of Cession and, 115–118
    tribal control and, 64–66
Administrative Order 186, 140
agriculture, 25, 26, 40–41, 91, 146n45
Ahtna, 9–10, 133
Akiachak v. Salazar, 140, 154n129
Alaska
    ban of alcohol in, 134
    ban of breech-loading firearms, 134
    civil law/government of, 135, 136, 137
    declared Indian country, 134
    Department era, 134
    "discovery" of, 133
    Interior. See Interior Alaska
    purchase of, ix, xiii, xxvi, 23, 67, 71,
      84, 113–131, 134. See also Treaty
      of Cession
    reservation system in, debate on, 37–48,
      91, 135, 138
    reservation system in, established
      reservations, 135, 136, 138,
      145n39, 154n128
    statehood, 61–64, 138

    timeline of legislation and events,
      133–140
    transfer of departmental administration,
      135
    transfer of hunting and fishing regulation
      to state government, 139
    trust land in, 55, 127–128, 140,
      152n111, 154n129
Alaska Agricultural College and School of
    Mines, 47
Alaska and Polar Regions Collections and
    Archives, 113, 114
Alaska Anti-Discrimination Act, 138
Alaska Constitution, 65, 137, 142n110
Alaska District Organic Act, 135
Alaska Engineering Commission, xv
Alaska Federation of Natives, 64
Alaska Game Act/Law, 136, 137
Alaska Historical Society, 154n127,
    154n128
Alaska Homestead Act of 1898, 26, 136
Alaska Interior. See Interior Alaska
Alaska Journal, 68
Alaska National Interest Lands
    Conservation Act, 140
Alaska Native Allotment Act of 1906, 30,
    137, 139
Alaska Native Brotherhood (ANB), 57,
    58–59, 61, 136, 137, 150n90
Alaska Native Citizenship Act of
    1915, 31
Alaska Native Claims Settlement Act
    aboriginal land claims and, 139
    amendment of, 50, 150n88

Alaska Native Claims Settlement Act
(*continued*)
  land conveyance provisions, 155n134,
    155n135
  passage of, 50, 64, 68
  Tanana chiefs meeting of 1915 and,
    70–71, 142n6
  tribal sovereignty and, 125–126, 128
Alaska Native Health Care system, 125
Alaska Native Land Claims Settlement bill,
  139
Alaska Native Review Claims Commission,
  151n95
Alaska Native Rights Association, 61
Alaska Native Sisterhood (ANS), 150n90
Alaska Native Townsite Act, 138, 139
Alaska Natives
  aid to military expeditions/prospectors,
    xiii, 9–14, 23
  Alaska Purchase and, 113–131, 134
  citizenship of. See citizenship
  culture of, 41, 51–52, 70, 83, 91–92,
    95, 141n4, 147n59–148n59,
    152n109, 154n128. See also
    subsistence lifestyle; tribal lifeways
  English names and, 19
  federal investigations of impact
    of development on, 27–32,
    107n151–108n151
  federally recognized tribes, 122, 126,
    128, 140, 152n111, 154n130
  impact of Western culture on, xxiii,
    21–22, 38–39, 42, 46, 47–48,
    51–52, 53–54, 73–74, 94, 118,
    130, 136
  legislation and events affecting, timeline
    of, 133–140
  mineral claims, 142n11
  missions and. See missions/missionaries
  of mixed ancestry, 143n17, 146n43
  Organic Act and, 142n8
  productive life, conception of, 25–27
  Russian–American Treaty and, 134
  settlement/land use patterns, xxii–xxiii,
    7–9, 19–20
  sovereignty. See tribal sovereignty

subsistence lifestyle. See subsistence
  lifestyle
timeline of legislation and events
  affecting, 133–140
tribal identity, 30, 137, 147n58,
  148n59
tribal status of, ix, 31, 121–122,
  123–124, 129
"uncivilized tribes" classification, 1, 24,
  117, 126, 142n9, 146, 153n123
"use and occupancy" protection, 135
voting rights, 137, 139
Alaska Purchase, ix, xiii, xxvi, 23, 67, 71,
  84, 113–131, 134. See also Treaty of
  Cession
Alaska Railroad, 43
Alaska Railway Bill, xv, 44, 47
Alaska Range, 118
Alaska Statehood Act, 64, 138
Alaska Supreme Court, 140
Alaska Syndicate, 44
Alaska Townsite Act of 1891, 26, 135
Alaska Voter Literacy Act, 137
Alaskan Engineering Commission, 43, 44
Albert (of Tanana/Ft. Gibbon), xxi, 79
alcohol, 39, 40, 130, 134, 150n90
Aleutian Chain, 138
Aleuts, 133, 134, 136, 138
Alexander, Chief (of Tolovana)
  on allotments/reservations, 45, 89
  as delegate to Tanana chiefs meeting of
    1915, xix, xx
  on education, 104, 153n116, 153n116
  experience with U.S. government prior
    to 1915 meeting, 70, 153n116
  on medical care, 153n116, 153n116
  selection of Tanana chief representatives
    for 1915 meeting, xix
  Wickersham's meeting with, 38, 47–48,
    50–51, 80–82
Alexander, Titus (of Manley Hot Springs),
  xx, 50, 79, 90
Allakaket mission, xxiii
"All-American route," xiii
Allen, Henry, 9–11
Allman, Ruth, 68

allotments. *See also* reservations/
  reservation system
  Alaska Native Allotment Act, 30, 137,
    139
  Chief Alexander (of Tolovana) on, 45,
    89
  Chief Ivan/Evan on, 45, 86
  federal Indian policy, 30
  General Allotment Act, 30, 135
  Homestead Act, 26
  impact on tribal culture, 70
  Madara on, 42, 46, 51–52, 83,
    91–92
  procedure for, 84–85, 92–93
  Richie on, 42–43, 81, 82, 84–85,
    92–93, 96–98
  Riggs on, 43, 51–52, 85, 93
  role of federal government in
    establishing, xxv
  Rowe on, 38–41
  Tanana chiefs on, 41–42, 45–46, 47,
    51–52, 75–76, 86–88, 91, 92, 96,
    122, 149n83
  Wickersham on, 38–41, 46, 51–52, 70,
    74–76, 80, 81–82, 83–85, 93–94,
    95, 96, 97
  Williams on, 42, 45–46, 83–85, 90–91,
    96–98
Alton, Thomas, xxvi, 37, 50, 68, 73
Alutiiq, 133
American Agriculture in the Twentieth
  Century (Gardner), 26
American Fur Seal Company, 134
ANB (Alaska Native Brotherhood), 57,
  58–59, 61, 136, 137, 150n90
Andrews, Elizabeth, 145n32
Angoon, 135
animals. *See* game; hunting
ANS (Alaska Native Sisterhood), 150n90
Apache, 55
architecture, xvii–xviii, xix
Arctic Village, 119
Army Corps of Engineers, 62
artifacts, cultural, 28, 147n59–148n59
assimilation
  education and, xxiii

federal Indian policy and, xxv, 41, 135,
    154n128
  of Western culture, citizenship and,
    xxiii, 3, 4–7, 24–25, 31, 34–35,
    59, 70, 95, 110, 136, 141n5,
    147n58, 147n59–148n59
Athabascans. *See also* Tanana chiefs
  concept of ownership rights, 146n47
  concept of productive life, 25–27
  delegates to Tanana chiefs meeting,
    xviii–xxi, xxvii, 50, 79, 118
  impact of gold prospecting on, 22. *See
    also* prospectors/prospecting
  impact of railroads on, 37–48. *See also*
    railroads
  languages of, 39, 53, 75–76
  turn-of-the-century era, 7–9
atomic weapons, 62, 138
Atwell, H. J., xxv, 79, 87
Austen, Karen, xv

Baggen, Mertie, 144n24
bands
  concept of, 7
  as economic unit, 33
  marriage customs, 7–8, 144n24
  role of chiefs in, 7–8
Barnabasses, Bessie, 144n24
Barrow, 145n38
Barrow Duck-in, 139
Battle of Sitka-Kiks.ádi, 133
Beardslee, Captain, 13
Bearpaw mountain settlement, 52
Beaver, 61
Beinecke Library, 67–68
Bering, Vitus, 133
Bering Sea, 13
Berrigan case, 4–7, 25, 117–118, 123,
    136, 142n8, 143n21, 150n94
Big Delta, 5
Birch Creek, 2, 6, 10
Blix, R., 27
Board of Indian Affairs, 24
Brady, John, 58, 143n17, 146n43, 148n65
Broad Pass, 44

Brooks, Alfred Hulse, 14–15
Brown, Michael, 10, 29
Bryant, Charles, 58
Bureau of Education, 28, 103, 104, 138
Bureau of Indian Affairs, 124, 128, 138

Canada, 16, 154n126
canneries, 22, 27–28, 31, 116, 135,
    154n127
Cape Thompson, 62
caribou, 7, 18–19, 25, 29, 33, 54
Carlisle Indian School, xxiii, 59, 135,
    147n59
Carrington, Thos., 107n151–108n151
Case, David, 24
Castner, Joseph, 13–14
Catherine, Tsarina, 133
Charlie/Charley, Chief (of Tolovana/
    Minto), xx, 38, 45, 50, 79, 80,
    88, 105
Chena, xix, xxii, 41, 52, 75, 118
Chena mission, 33, 100
Chena River, 14, 41
Cherokee Nation v. Georgia, 153n124
Cherosky, Sergai, 2, 3, 6
Chief Andrew Isaac Health Center, xv
Chilkat Tlingit, 58
Chinook fishing moratorium, 53–54
Chisana River, 137
Chit'ai Theeg, 7–8
Chitina trail, 43
Christianity, xxiii, 26, 70
Circle, xiv, 10
citizenship
    Alaska Native Brotherhood and, 58
    Alaska Native Citizenship Act and, 31
    applicant requirements, 147n58
    assimilation of Western culture and,
        xxiii, 3, 4–7, 24–25, 31, 34–35,
        59, 70, 95, 110, 136, 141n5,
        147n58, 147n59–148n59
    Berrigan case, 4–7, 25, 117–118, 123,
        136, 142n8, 143n21, 150n94
    Emmons's view on, 31
    Minook case, 4–7, 25, 142n8, 143n19

permanent settlement issue, 5–7, 42,
    83, 93, 95
Tanana chiefs on, 63–64
Treaty of Cession and, 1–2, 24–25
civil law/government, 135, 136, 137
civilization, concept of
    as assimilation of Western culture,
        xxiii, 3, 4–7, 24–25, 31, 34–35,
        59, 70, 95, 110, 136, 141n5,
        147n58, 147n59–148n59. See
        also citizenship
    mixed ancestry and, 143n17,
        146n43
    tribal ties and, 24–25
    "uncivilized" classification status, 1–2,
        24, 117, 126, 142n9, 146n42,
        153n123
Clevenger, Reverend, 32
clothing, traditional, xv, xviii–xix, 81,
    86, 91
Coast and Geodetic Survey, 11
Coen, Ross, 67
colonialism, 130–131
Commissioner of Indian Affairs, 29
Conditions and Needs of the Natives of
    Alaska, 28–29, 136
Congress. See also U.S. government
    aboriginal rights definition, 62
    Alaska Game Law, 136
    Alaska Native Claims Settlement Act,
        50, 68, 150n88
    Alaska Natives' representation in, 53,
        63–64, 148n65
    Carter Code, 136
    Dillingham report to, 21–22
    economic opportunities for Alaska
        Natives, 55
    Emmons's report to, 28, 136
    Federally Recognized List Act, 122
    medical care for Alaska Natives, 55
    Native fishing rights, 135
    railroad authorization, 43, 47
    Roosevelt's address to, 30
    subsistence protection, 140
    Tlingit-Haida settlement, 60
    tribal sovereignty and, 128

Wickersham as Alaska's delegate, xiii, 37, 39–40, 44, 59, 73–74
continuous (permanent) occupancy, 4–7, 30, 42, 83, 93, 95
Cook Inlet, 13
Copper Center, 10, 32–33, 61
Copper River, xiii, 9, 22, 115, 118, 136, 137
Copper River Mining, Trading, and Development Company, 27
Copper River Valley, 10, 21, 22, 27–29, 31–32, 33, 58, 68, 70, 133
corporations, 44, 126–128, 129, 139, 155n134
Cosjacket (Crossjacket), xix, 22, 39, 52, 95–98, 99, 102, 118
Cosna River, xix
Cramer, G. Fenton, 38, 41–42, 43, 79
Cree, 54
crime, 130
cultural relativism, 32
Curtis, Natalie, 147n59–148n59

Dall sheep, 137
Davis, Jefferson, 134
Dawes Act of 1887, 40–41
Dawson, 7, 10–11, 16, 19, 42
Dawson City, 154n126
democracy, development and, 47
Democratic Party, 44
Department of Interior, 154n129
Department of Justice, 138
Department of Treasury, 135
Department of War, 135
development. See also economic development; prospectors/ prospecting; railroads
    1950s–1960s era, 61–64
    democracy and, 47
    impact on Interior Alaska, 73–74, 116–117, 148n65
    impact on subsistence lifestyle, 151n95
    impact on Tlingit, 148n65
    impact on tribal leadership/sovereignty, 120–122, 125–126

land claims/Native rights background and, 57–61
    Tanana chiefs on, 148n65
dialects, 39, 89
Dillingham, William P., 21–22, 31
discrimination, 140, 154n129
disease, 91, 120–121, 133
dominion, 153n123
Donnelly district, 15
Douglas City, 139
Douglas Indian Village, 139
Drane, Frederick, 41, 45
due process, 119

Eagle, 7, 10, 17, 19, 21, 145n38
Eagle trail, 136
economic development. See also employment opportunities
    Alaska Natives' contribution to, 55
    Fairbanks, xiv–xv
    hunting and fishing regulation and, 54–55
    as inevitable, 74
    railroads and, xiv, xv, 43–44, 47, 61–64
    Tanana chiefs' views on, 33, 122
    unit of production, 33
education
    aboriginal rights and tribal control, 64–66
    Alaska District Organic Act, 135
    assimilation and, xxiii
    Bureau of Education, 28, 103, 104, 138
    Carlisle Indian School, xxiii, 59, 135, 147n59
    Chief Alexander (of Tolovana) on, 104, 153n116, 153n116
    Chief Ivan/Evan on, 105, 153n116, 153n116
    Chief Jacob Starr on, 104
    Chief Thomas on, 55, 80
    colonialism and, 130–131
    industrial training schools, 29, 46, 98–106
    Madara on, 99–106
    missions and, 33, 89, 90, 98–106

education (*continued*)
  Rowe on, 40
  segregation and the Nelson Act, 136,
    143n17, 146n43
  Tanana chiefs' views on, xxv, 34, 46, 55,
    65, 69–70, 76, 80, 98–106, 108,
    109
  U.S. government control of, 136
  Wickersham on, 98–106
  Williams on, 46, 55, 98–106
elk, 55
Emmons, George Thornton, 28–32, 68
Emmons Family Papers, 67–68
employment opportunities
  government contracts, 33, 55, 107–
    108, 122, 124, 154n132
  modern-day status, 55
  river pilots, 33, 148n61
  Tanana chiefs on, 33, 46, 55, 65,
    69–70, 76
English language. See also language
  assimilation and, 4
  English names of chiefs, 19
  government consultation with tribal
    leadership, 53
  missions and, 9, 20
  Natives' knowledge of, 19, 20, 25, 39,
    75–76, 120
  Tanana chiefs' call for written
    explanations, 53, 60, 86, 87–88,
    89, 90, 119–120
epidemics, 133, 136, 137
Episcopal Church/Episcopal missions,
    xviii, xix, xxii–xxiii, 19, 33, 39, 41–
    42, 69, 98–106. See also missions/
    missionaries
Ewan, Markle, 62
Excelsior, 27

Fairbanks
  development of, xiv–xv, 41, 43, 44, 52
  map of, xx–xxi
  prospecting in, xiv–xv, 17, 22
  reservation system and, 75
  as supply center, 33

  trading posts, 32–33
  trails to/from, xix, 22, 33
Fairbanks Commercial Club, 43
Fairbanks Public Library, xviii, xix
famine, 40, 136, 137
farming, 25, 26, 40–41, 91, 146n45
Farnsworth, Charles, 15–17, 145n32
Farnsworth, Robert, 16
Farnsworth collection, 15–16
federal Indian policy
  agrarian model and, 26
  in Alaska, 134
  allotments/reservations, 30, 91, 141n5
  assimilation and, xxv, 41, 135,
    154n128
  colonialism and, 130–131
  Dawes Act, 40–41, 135
  "domestic dependent nations," 153n124
  extension to "uncivilized" tribes,
    146n42
  federally recognized tribes, 122, 126,
    128, 140, 152n111, 154n130
  General Allotment Act, 30
  Indian Self-Determination Act, 124
  legislation and timeline of events,
    133–140
  manifest destiny and, 114–116,
    153n125–154n125
  recognition of tribal status, 123–124
  tribal identity and, 30, 147n58, 148n59
Federal Land Planning and Management
    Act, 139
Federal Subsistence Management Program,
    140
Federal Trust relationship, 55
Federally Recognized Indian Tribe List Act,
    122, 152n111, 154n130
financial assistance/resources
  Emmons's call for, 29
  Tanana chiefs' views on, 34, 98
firearms ban, 134
Fish Creek/Fish Lake, 54
Fish, Oscar, 29
fishing
  access to/protection of, 8–9, 26–27, 34,
    135, 138

commercial/canneries, 22, 27–28, 31, 116, 135, 136, 137, 154n127
employment opportunities and, 46
fish traps, 135, 137, 139
fish wheels, 33, 85
fishing camps, 144n27
impact of development on, 136, 148n65
Karluk Reservation, 138
land in trust and, 127–128
Middle Tanana, 7
modern-day issues, 53–55
preferences, 142n110
prospectors' impact on, 22, 23, 33, 85
regulation of, 53, 54–55, 64–66, 135, 139
seasonal rounds, 25, 83, 144n27
subsistence lifestyle, 26–27, 136, 137
Tanana chiefs on, 34, 64, 91, 95, 107–108, 148n65
Upper Tanana, 12
Folger, John, 49
Folger, Johnnie (of Tanana), xx, 50
Fort Egbert, 15, 17
Fort Gibbon, xix, 13, 15, 38, 42
Fort Yukon, 10, 13, 142n10
Forty Mile, 7, 9, 10, 15–18
Forty Mile Country, 144n29
Fortymile River, 11, 17, 145n33
fossil-fuel industry, 129
Frank, Richard, 151n95
Frank v. State, 140
Franklin Gulch, 11, 12
free exercise of religion, 140
Freiburger, Annette, 49
Funston, Frederick, 27
Fur Seal Act, 137
fur trapping/trading
    early traders, 2–3
    prospectors' impact on, 29, 33–34
    protection of, 138
    Russian, 125, 133
    seasonal rounds, 25, 83
    subsistence lifestyle, 26–27
    tribal sovereignty and, 125

game. See also hunting
    access to, xxii–xxiii, xxv, 26–27, 34, 92
    Alaska Game Act, 136, 137
    impact of prospecting/development, 22, 23, 29, 85, 137
    modern-day status, 54–55
    respect for animals and, 25–26, 152n109
    Tanana chiefs' views on, 34
Game Commission, 137
Gardner, Bruce, 26
Gates, Merrill, 147n57
General Allotment Act of 1887, 30, 135
George C. Thomas Memorial Library, xvii–xviii, 37
Geronimo, xxiii, xxiv
Glacier Bay National Monument, 60
Goforth, Penelope, 154n127
gold prospecting/gold rush. See prospectors/prospecting
Goldschmidt, Walter, 146n47
Goodlataw, Chief, 137
Goodpaster, 14–15, 17–18, 144n24
Goodpaster River, 12, 13–14, 17, 19, 144n29, 145n33
Goodpasture, 5
Goodrich, Harold, 2
government contracts, 33, 55, 107–108, 122, 124, 154n132
government-to-government relationships
    establishment of, 154n130
    federal recognition of, 152n111
    Tanana chiefs on, 52–53, 60, 76, 80, 87–88, 89–90, 119–120, 124
Great Britain, 135
"Great Sickness," 136
Grimes Packing case, 138
Gsovski, Vladimir, 142n9
Guggenheim family, 44, 45

Hadjukovich, John, 20, 145n39
Harper, Arthur, 2
Harrison, William Henry, 135

health care. *See* medical services/
    health care
Healy, Chief, 7–8, 19, 20, 143n23,
    144n27, 145n33, 145n36,
    145n37
Healy, Jeany, 16–17, 145n33
Healy, Johnny, 10–11, 19, 143n23
Healy, Stella, 143n23
Healy Lake, 7, 67
Healy River, 33, 143n23, 144n27
Henry, 4–6
Herron, Joseph, 13
history, oral vs. written, 51
Hog River, 125
Hoggatt, Wilford, 45
Homestead Act of 1862, 26
homesteads. *See* allotments
House Committee on the Territories, 1912
    meeting, 40
Hudson's Bay Company, 2, 142n10
Hudson's Bay route, 13
hunting
    access to/protection of, 8–9, 92,
        135, 138
    Alaska Game Act, 136, 137
    commercial, impact of, 136
    communal, 9, 33
    federal Indian policy push toward
        agriculture and, 40–41, 91
    hunting camps, 16–17
    land in trust and, 127–128
    Middle Tanana, 7
    Migratory Bird Treaty, 137, 139
    modern-day issues, 54–55
    preferences and, 142n110
    prospectors' impact on, 33, 85
    railroads' impact on, 37–38
    regulation of, 54–55, 62, 64–66,
        137, 139
    respect for animals, 25–26, 152n109
    seasonal rounds, 25, 83
    subsistence lifestyle, 26–27, 136, 137
    Tanana chiefs on, 34, 91–92, 95,
        107–108
    telegraph lines and, 18–19
    Tlingit chiefs on, 148n65

hunting-and-gathering lifestyle, 40–41, 42
Huntington Library, 154n133–155n133

Illingworth, Kevin, xxvii, 67, 71, 113–
    131, 133, 141, 152, n110
Indian Citizenship Act, 137
Indian country, 155n135, 155n136
Indian Health Services, 124
Indian Reorganization Act of 1934, 138,
    154n128
Indian Rights Association, 107n151–
    108n151
Indian Self-Determination Act, 124,
    154n132
Indian Self-Determination and Education
    Assistance Act of 1975, 154n132
industrial training schools, 29, 46,
    98–106
industrialization, 26. *See also* development
infrastructure, development and, xiv
Inouye, Ron, 67, 68
Interior Alaska
    early land-use cases, 6–7
    early traders in, 2–4
    federal investigations of conditions in,
        27–32, 107n151–108n151
    impact of development, 73–74,
        116–117, 148n65
    impact of prospecting, 9–14, 22–24,
        117, 136
    post–prospector arrival, 21–35
    pre-20th century routes to, 13, 19
    pre–Alaska Purchase, 114–117,
        129–130
    pre–prospector arrival, xiii, 1–20
    Southeast vs., land claims issues, 58, 60,
        61–64
    telegraph stations, xix, xxii, 15–19, 23,
        33, 46, 107, 134, 145n33
    timeline of legislation and events
        affecting, 133–140
Interior Department, 44
Interior Natives. *See* Alaska Natives
internment camps, 138
Inupiaq Eskimos, 125

Ivan/Evan, Chief (of Cosjacket)
    age and health of, xiii, 1, 80, 84, 109
    on allotments/reservations, 45, 86
    as delegate to Tanana chiefs meeting of
        1915, xiii, xx, xxviii, 79
    on education, 105, 153n116, 153n116
    experience with U.S. government prior
        to 1915 meeting, 23, 70, 137,
        153n116
    on land protection, 95
    on medical care, 109, 153n116,
        153n116
    photographs of, xx, 50
    on wish to be left alone, 45, 86

Jackson, Senator, 139
Jarvis, Chief, 4–6, 17, 19, 20, 117,
        144n29
Jarvis, David, 19, 21, 145n38
Jeany Healy Collection, 17
Jefferson, Thomas, 146n45
Jesson, John, 5
Joe, Chief (of Salchaket)
    as delegate to Tanana chiefs meeting
        of 1915, xxi, 79
    family of, 144n24, 145n33,
        145n36
    language of, 39, 89
    Mitchell and, 17–19, 20, 68, 69
    photographs of, xxi, 8, 50
    on wish to be left alone, 60, 89
John, Chief (of Chena), xxi, 11–12, 50,
        79, 89–90
John, Katie, 10, 140
John v. Baker, 140, 155n136
Johnson, Albert, xv–xviii
Jones, Dixon, xxvii
Joseph, Chief, 68, 69, 145n32
Joseph Creek, 145n33
Joseph village, 17, 145n32, 145n33

Kake, 134
Kantishna country, xix
Karluk Reservation, 138

Kataba, 8
Katie John case, 140
Ketchumstuck, 8, 9, 29, 144n27
Ketzler, Al, 61, 62
Klawock, 116
Klawock Cannery, 154n127
Klondike, 10, 21, 116, 136, 154n126
Knapp, Lyman, 24, 58
Knowles, Governor, 140
Kodiak Island, 133
Kokrine, Effie, 49
Koyukon, 39, 142n12
Koyukuk River, 9, 22, 54, 125
Kuskokwim fisheries, 136

labor. See employment opportunities
Lakota, 135
land claims
    aboriginal rights. See aboriginal rights
    Akiachak v. Salazar case, 140,
        154n129
    Alaska Native Allotment Act, 30
    Alaska Native Claims Settlement
        Act. See Alaska Native Claims
        Settlement Act
    Alaska statehood and, 61–64
    areas without a settlement, 52, 61–64,
        117
    background/history, 57–66
    Berrigan case, 4–7, 25, 117–118, 123,
        136, 142n8, 143n21, 150n94
    citizenship and. See citizenship
    continental United States, 30
    corporations, 126–128, 129, 139,
        155n134
    Emmons's views on, 30
    Interior vs. Southeast, 58, 60, 61–64
    lack of due process, 119–120
    lack of treaties and negotiations, 119
    Land Claims Act, 50
    for "landless" Natives, 154n128
    Minook case, 4–7, 25, 142n8,
        143n19
    Nenana, 61–64, 75
    oil and, 116

land claims (*continued*)
  as ongoing issue, 49–52
  Organic Act and, 62, 142n8
  permanence issue, 4–7, 30, 42, 83,
    93, 95
  prospecting and, 2–3
  Southeast Alaska, 57, 58–61, 70–71,
    115, 117, 133, 136, 138,
    148n65
  sovereignty and. See tribal sovereignty
  state land selections/conveyances, 64,
    139
  Tanana chiefs meeting of 1915 and,
    broader focus of, xxv, 122–123,
    142n6
  Tlingit-Haida, 57, 58–61, 70–71, 136,
    138, 139, 150n94
  Treaty of Cession, 115–118, 142n8. See
    also Treaty of Cession
  tribal control, 64–66, 125–126,
    128–129, 140
  tribal recognition, 152n111
  trust lands, 55, 127–128, 140,
    152n111, 154n129
  Venetie tax case, 119, 128–129, 140,
    155n135
land in trust, 55, 127–128, 140, 152n111,
  154n129
land ownership
  clan ownership, 59–60
  current, land claims and, 127–128
  dominion and, 153n123
  mechanisms for acquisition and disposal
    of, 59–60
  Natives' conception of vs. Western
    concepts, 6–7, 23, 26–27,
    114–115, 146n47
  ownership marks, 14, 144n29
  turn-of-the-century patterns, 7–9
Lane, Franklin K., xiv, 44, 46, 47, 74, 76,
  80, 81, 82, 85
language. See also English language
  in Alaska Native Claims Settlement Act,
    126
  on sovereignty, 128–129
  on termination of tribal status, 129

translation/interpretation, 39, 75–76,
  80, 89, 119, 120
"uncivilized" classification status, 1,
  24, 117, 126, 142n9, 146n42,
  153n123
LaSalle University, 59
law enforcement, lack of, 40
LeFebre, Charlene, 13
legal cases
  Akiachak v. Salazar, 140, 154n129
  Alaska Native Brotherhood (ANB), 136
  Berrigan, 4–7, 25, 117–118, 123, 136,
    142n8, 143n21, 150n94
  Cherokee Nation v. Georgia, 153n124
  Frank v. State, 140
  Grimes Packing, 138
  John v. Baker, 140, 155n136
  Katie John, 140
  McDowell, 142n110
  Minook, 4–7, 25, 142n8, 143n19
  Tlingit-Haida settlement, 57, 58–61,
    70–71, 136, 138, 139, 150n94
  Venetie, 119, 128–129, 140,
    155n135
legal system
  Carter Code and civil law, 136
  influence of Western culture norms,
    xxvii, 3, 4–7, 23, 31, 69–70, 85,
    146n43
  precedence, importance of, 123
  right to sue U.S. government over
    land claims, 57, 59, 123, 136,
    143n21
  Territorial legislature, 59, 137, 138
legislation, timeline of, 133–140
Leslie's Illustrated Weekly, 11, 12
Leupp, Francis Ellington, 147n59
literacy tests, 137, 139
Little Delta River, 4–5, 144n29
Lower Tanana, 22, 33, 39

Mackenzie River, 2, 13
Madara, Guy
  on allotments/reservations, 42, 46,
    51–52, 83, 91–92

background of, 41–42
as delegate to Tanana chiefs meeting of
    1915, xix, xxii–xxiii, xxv, 34, 79
disposition of, 41
on education, 99–106
on medical care, 111
on tribal lifeways, 51, 83, 91–92
manifest destiny, 114–116, 153n125–
    154n125
Mansfield, 29
Mansfield Lake, 11
marriage customs, 7–8, 144n24
Marshall, John, 153n124
material culture, 28, 147n59–148n59
Mayo, Al, 2
Mayo, Arthur, 49
Mayo, Will, xxvi–xxvii, 67, 68–69, 71, 75,
    113–131, 142n7
McCartney, Leslie, 114
McDowell case, 142n110
McKennan, Robert, 17, 145n32
McQuesten, Leroy Jack, 2
medical services/health care
    aboriginal rights and tribal control,
        64–66
    Alaska Native Health Care system, 125
    Emmons's call for, 29
    lack of, 39–40
    Madara on, 111
    missions and, 33
    Rowe's views on, 40
    Tanana Chiefs Conference and, 142n7
    Tanana chiefs on, xxv, xvi, 34, 46, 55,
        69–70, 76, 88, 108–109
    tribal management of, 55
    tribal status and, 123–124
medicine men, 17
Mentasta, 29
Mentasta Pass, 10
Merriam, General, 11
Middle Fork, 17, 145n33
Middle Tanana, 7, 9, 19–20, 31, 33, 67,
    143n23, 144n24
Middle Yukon, 13
Migratory Bird Treaty, 137, 139
military expeditions, 9–14, 23, 27, 134

military posts/forts, 15–19, 27, 33, 42,
    46, 121
Millennium Agreement, 140
Minchumina, 52
mineral prospecting. See prospectors/
    prospecting
Mining Act of 1884, 25
Minook, John, 3, 4–7, 142n12
Minook case, 4–7, 25, 142n8, 143n19
Minto, xix, 61, 151n95
Minto Flats, 37–38, 47, 54, 139, 151n95
Mishler, Craig, 19
Mission Creek, 49
missions
    Allakaket, xxiii
    Chena, 33, 100
    Christian, xxiii
    Copper Center, 10, 32–33, 61
    education and, 33, 89, 90, 98–106
    Episcopal, xviii, xix, xxii–xxiii, 19, 33,
        39, 41–42, 69, 98–106
    goal of "civilizing" Alaska Natives,
        147n59
    medical care and, 33
    Nenana, 99–101
    Presbyterian, 150n90
    Salcha, 144n29
    Salchaket, 99–100
    St. James Mission, 42
    St. Luke's Mission, 41
    St. Mark's Mission, 41, 42
    Tanacross, xxiii, 33
    Tanana, xix, xxii–xxiii, 102–103
    Tanana chiefs on, 88
Mistassini, 54
Mitchell, Billy, 17–19, 31, 68, 69,
    145n33
Modoc, 135
Moffit, Eva, 19, 52
Moore, Agnes Mathew Mayo, 49
moose, 25, 29, 54, 140
Morgan, J. P., 44
Mount Hayes, 47
multilingualism, 39
municipalities, 155 n134
Murkowski, Governor, 140

National Native American Forums, 52
Native artifacts, 28, 147n59–148n59
Native Citizenship Act, 137
Native Priority, 140
Native rights
    aboriginal. See aboriginal rights
    Alaska Purchase and, 113–131
    enforcement of, 125
    Indian Citizenship Act, 137
    land claim background/history, 57–66
    Organic Act, 142n8
    Southeast Alaska, 57, 58–61, 70–71
    sovereignty. See tribal sovereignty
    U.S. government role in protection of,
        6–7, 23–24, 45, 47–48, 60–61,
        74, 81–82, 84, 88, 94, 117, 140,
        150n94
Native tribes, continental United States,
    xxiii, xxv, 30, 91, 125–126, 153n124
naturalization, 24
Nelson Act, 136, 143n17, 146n43
Nenana, xix, 22, 33, 39, 41, 42, 44, 61, 75
Nenana mission, 99–101
Nenana River, xix
Nenana Valley, 101
New York Times, 12, 26
Nez Perce, 135
Nome, 16, 27, 136, 145n38
Noochu Loghoyet, 63
North American Trading and
    Transportation Company, 10
Northern Quebec, 54
Northway, 61, 146n47
Northwest Alaska, 62
Northwest Coast, 28
Novi, 54, 118
Nulato, 125

Obama, Barack, 124
oil/oil industry, 64, 116, 139
Old Minto, xix, 22
Old Sam, 16–17, 145n32, 145n33
oral tradition, 51
Oregon, 136

Organic Act of 1884, 62, 142n8
Osprey Affair, 135
Overland Telegraph Route, 134

Pacific Coast, 74
Pacific Northwest, 116
Pacific Ocean, 43
Papal Bull, 133
paternalism, xxiii–xxv, 153n125–154n125
Patty, Stan, 68
Paul, William, 58–59, 138
Pavaloff, Ivan, 142n12
Pavaloff, Pitka, 2, 3, 6
permanence issue, 4–7, 30, 42, 83, 93, 95
Peters, Guy, 49
Pilot, Julius (of Nenana), xxi, 50, 90, 105,
    108
pilots, river, 33, 148n61
Pioneer Park, 141n2
Point Hope, 138
Porcupine River, 2, 13
potlaches, 8, 20, 45, 140, 145n39
Pratt, Richard Henry, xxiii
Presbyterian missionaries, 150n90
Prince William Sound, 13
Progressive philosophy, 44
Project Chariot, 62, 138
prospectors/prospecting
    aid from Alaska Natives, xiii, 9–14, 23
    development and, 43
    Fairbanks, xiv–xv, 17, 22
    federal government's investigations
        of and response to impact on
        Alaska Natives, 27–32, 107n151–
        108n151
    impact on fishing, 22, 23, 33, 85
    impact on game, 22, 23, 29, 85, 137
    impact on hunting, 35, 85
    impact on Interior Alaska, 9–14,
        22–24, 117, 136
    impact on Tanana Valley, 7, 17–19, 21,
        22, 32–35, 58, 60
    impact on trapping, 33–34
    Klondike, 10, 15, 21, 116, 136,
        154n126

land claims and, 2–3
military expeditions and, 9–14
mineral claims, Alaska Natives and,
    142n11
Yukon, xiii, 10, 12–13, 22, 136,
    154n126
Prudhoe Bay, 64, 139
Public Purpose Executive Order Reserve,
    138
Puyallup, 93
Puyallup Reservation, 70

Quit Claim, 134

Raibmon, Paige, 147n59
railroads
    Alaska Railroad, 43
    Alaska Railway Bill, xv, 44, 47
    development and, xiv, xv, 43–44, 47,
        61–64
    employment opportunities and, 46,
        107, 110
    government-authorized, xxv, 43–45, 47
    impact on hunting, 37–38
    impact on Interior Alaska, 61–64, 94,
        142n6, 148n65
    impact on Tanana Valley, 37–48
    Riggs and, xxv, 43, 46, 51–52, 53–54,
        81, 85, 110, 151n99
    Tanana chiefs on, 148n65
    Tanana Valley Railroad, 41
    White Pass Railroad, 61
    Wickersham on, 44–45, 47
Rampart, 2–3, 10, 49, 62
Rampart Canyon Dam and Reservoir, 62,
    139
Rat River, 13
Ray, Patrick Henry, 10–11, 12–13, 19
Ray Mountains, 118
Raymond, Charles P., 142n10
reciprocity, 59
Red Shirt, Chief, 125, 154n133–
    155n133
Refuge Rocks, 133

regalia, xv, xviii–xix
reindeer, 136
religion, free exercise of, 140
Report to Congress on Conditions and
    Needs of Alaska Natives, 28–29, 136
Republican Party, 44
reservations/reservation system
    in Alaska, debate on, 37–48, 91, 135,
        138
    in Alaska, established reservations, 135,
        136, 138, 145n39, 154n128
    Atwell on, 95
    Chief Alexander on, 45, 89
    Chief Ivan/Evan on, 45, 86
    in continental United States, 30, 91,
        141n5
    Emmons's views on, 29–30
    federal Indian policy, 30, 91,
        141n5
    impact on subsistence lifestyle, 30,
        149n83
    Madara on, 42, 46, 51–52, 83,
        91–92
    Mao on, 52
    Richie on, 42–43, 81, 82, 84–85,
        92–93, 96–98
    Riggs on, 43, 51–52, 85, 93
    role of federal government in
        establishing, xxv
    Rowe on, 38–41
    submissiveness and, 40
    Tanana chiefs on, 41–42, 45–46, 47,
        51–52, 75–76, 86–88, 91, 92, 96,
        122, 149n83
    Wickersham on, 38–41, 46, 51–52, 70,
        74–76, 80, 81–82, 83–85, 93–94,
        95, 96, 97
    Williams on, 42, 45–46, 83–85, 90–91,
        96–98
resource development, 44, 116–117.
    See also development; economic
    development
Richardson Highway, xxii
Richie, C. W.
    on allotments/reservations, 42–43, 81,
        82, 84–85, 92–93, 96–98

Richie, C. W. (*continued*)
    as delegate to Tanana chiefs meeting of
        1915, 74, 79
    photograph of, 50
Riggs, Thomas
    on allotments/reservations, 43, 51–52,
        85, 93
    background of, 44–45
    as delegate to Tanana chiefs meeting of
        1915, xxv, 74, 79
    as delegate to Tanana chiefs meeting of
        1962, 61–62
    on employment opportunities, 110
    photograph of, 50
    railroad construction and, xxv, 43,
        46, 51–52, 53–54, 81, 85, 110,
        151n99
river pilots, 33, 148n61
Roosevelt, Theodore, xxiii, xxiv, 28–29,
    30, 32, 68, 70, 147n57, 147n59
Rowe, Peter Trimble, xxiii, 39–41, 42
Rule of Discovery, 133
Rural Priority, 140
Russia, 23, 58, 114–116, 125, 133, 134,
    142n9
Russian American Fur Company, 133,
    142n12
Russian–American Treaty, 134

Salcha, 52, 69, 144n24
Salcha mission, 33, 144n29
Salcha River, xxii
Salchaket (Salchakat), xix, xxii, 5, 38, 39,
    41, 52, 144n24
Salchaket land claims, 117–118, 123
Salchaket mission, 99–100
salmon, 5, 12, 27–28, 53, 135
Sam, 145n32
Sam, Belle, 8, 16–17, 145n32, 145n33
Saylor, Lee, 17, 67, 69, 143n23, 144n24,
    144n27, 145n30, 145n32
Schieffelin, Edward, 154n133–155n133
Schneider, William, xxvi, xxvii, 1, 21, 57,
    67, 113–131
sea otter, 137

seasonal rounds, 25, 83, 95, 144n27
Seattle Post, 29
segregation, 136, 138, 143n17, 146n43
Sesui, Chief, 13
Seward, xv, 38, 44
Seward, William, 1–2, 116, 134
Seward Peninsula, 28
Shaw Creek, 5
Sheldon Jackson, 59
Shelikov, 133
Sherwood, Morgan, 9
Simeone, William, 144n25
Simpson, Peter, 59
Singh, Natasha, xxvii, 71, 113–131,
    150n88, 152n109
Sitka, 2, 133, 134, 135, 143n17, 146n43,
    147n59
Sitka-Kiks.ádi, Battle of, 133
Sitka Society, 150n90
Skagway, 11, 61
slavery, 134
Sniffen, Matthew, 107n151–108n151
social services, 123–124, 142n7
Solomon, Silas, 145n32
Southeast Alaska, 28, 57, 58–61, 115,
    117, 133, 138, 148n65
Southwest Alaska, 136
St. Barnabas, 41
St. George Island, 134
St. James Mission, 42
St. Lawrence Island, 136
St. Luke's Mission, 41
St. Mark's Mission, 41, 42
St. Michael, 9, 11, 145n38
Starr, Alfred, 75, 76, 151n95, 151n106
Starr, Chief Jacob (of Tanana/Ft. Gibbon)
    as delegate to Tanana chiefs meeting of
        1915, xxi, 79
    descendants of, 49, 75
    on education, 104
    on employment, 110
    photographs of, xxi, 50
    on representation in Congress, 53, 88
    on Wickersham and Chief Alexander's
        talk, 38, 80
steamboats, xiv, 2, 13, 22, 33, 61, 142n10

Stevens Village, 139
storytelling, 51
Strong, John F. S., 45
Stuck, Hudson, xxiii, 42
subsistence lifestyle
    aboriginal rights and tribal control,
        64–66
    Alaska National Interest Lands
        Conservation Act, 140
    federal takeover of on federal lands, 140
    fishing and, 26–27, 136, 137
    hunting and, 26–27, 136, 137
    impact of development on, 151n95
    Native lifeways and, 26–27, 33–34, 64
    preference and, 65
    protection of, 58, 135, 152n109
    reservations and, 30, 149n83
    Tanana Chiefs Conference, 142n7
    U.S. government view of, 34–35
supply routes/centers, xxii, xv, 10, 29, 33,
        46, 61

Taft, William Howard, 44
Tanacross, 61, 146n47
Tanacross mission, xxiii, 33
Tanana chiefs
    on allotments/reservations, 41–42,
        45–46, 47, 51–52, 75–76, 86–88,
        91, 92, 96, 122, 149n83
    on citizenship, 63–64
    clothing of, xv–xvi, xviii–xix, 81,
        86, 91
    delegates to Tanana chiefs meeting of
        1915, xviii–xxi, xxvii, 50, 79, 118
    descendants of, 49, 52, 65
    on desire to be left alone, 89, 121
    on desired protection of U.S.
        government, 45, 84, 88, 89–90
    on education, 34, 46, 55, 65, 69–70,
        76, 80, 98–106, 108, 109
    on employment opportunities, xxv,
        46, 55, 65, 69–70, 76, 107–108,
        109–110, 121
    on financial assistance, 34, 98

    on fishing access/protection, 34, 64, 91,
        95, 107–108, 148n65
    on government-to-government
        consultation, 52–53, 60, 76, 80,
        87–88, 89–90, 119–120, 124
    on hunting access/protection, 34,
        91–92, 95, 107–108
    on impact of development, 148n65
    on impact of railroads, 148n65
    on land protection, 64
    on medical care, xvi, 34, 46, 55, 69–70,
        76, 88, 108–109
    meetings prior to 1915 meeting, 148n65
    on missions/missionaries, 88
    on representation in Congress/
        Washington, 53, 63–64, 148n65
    as representatives of Alaska Natives,
        122–123
    role in bands, 7
    on tribal lifeways, 91–92, 95
    on written explanations, 53, 60, 86,
        87–88, 89, 90, 119–120
Tanana Chiefs Conference, 49, 62–63, 65,
    142n7
Tanana chiefs meeting of 1915
    Alaska Purchase and background to,
        113–131
    as benchmark, 35
    issues of, xxv, 122–123, 142n6. See
        also education; employment
        opportunities; land claims;
        medical services/health care
    lack of knowledgeable negotiator, 118
    language and translation, 39, 75–76,
        89, 120
    media coverage, xiv
    overview of, ix, xiii–xxvii, 73–76
    painting of, xv–xvi
    photographic record of, xiv, xv–xvi,
        xviii–xix, xx–xxi, xxvii, 50, 86
    prelude to, 37–48
    progress since, 49–56
    sources of information on, 67–71
    stenographer's role in, xiv, 39, 75, 76
    Tanana chief participants, xviii–xxi,
        xxvii, 50, 79, 118

Tanana chiefs meeting of 1915 (*continued*)
transcript of (actual), 77–111
transcript of (comments on), xiv, xxv–
xxvi, 46–47, 68
U.S. government participants, xxv,
74, 79
Tanana chiefs meetings of 1962 and 1963,
61–64
Tanana Crossing, 103
Tanana mission, 102–103
Tanana River, xiii, xix, xxii, 2, 4, 9, 11,
17, 33, 37, 41, 42, 46, 61, 63
Tanana Valley
impact of railroads, 37–47. See also
railroads
land settlements and, 52, 61–64
Lower Tanana, 22, 33, 39
map of, xx–xxi
Middle Tanana, 7, 9, 19–20, 31, 33,
67, 143n23, 144n24
mineral wealth of, 12
missions, xix, xxii–xxiii
photographic record of, xv,
143n23
prospecting impact, 7, 17–19, 21,
32–35, 58, 60, 69
prospectors' arrival in, xiv, 7, 21, 58
settlements of, xix–xxii
shift in trade to, 32–33, 69
sources of information on, 143n23
telegraph lines, 17, 22
trading shift to, 32–33, 69
Upper Tanana, 9, 12, 19–20, 29, 31,
118, 143n23
Wickersham's view of, 47–48
Tanana Valley Railroad, 41
Tanana-Yukon Historical Society, xxvi,
67, 68, 141n2
telegraph lines/stations, xix, xxii, 15–19,
23, 33, 46, 107, 134, 145n33
Territorial Act, 137
Territorial legislature, 59, 137, 138
Tetlin, 29, 146n47
Tetlin Indian Reserve, 138, 145n39
Thomas, Chief (of Nenana and Wood
River)

on allotments/reservations, 45, 87
as delegate to Tanana chiefs meeting of
1915, xxi, 79
on education, 55, 80
Nenana settlement and, 61–62
photographs of, xxi, 50
on what to expect from U.S.
government, 1, 53, 87
Thomas, George, xviii
Three Day Slough, 54
Three Saints Bay, 133
Tlingit, 28, 115, 117, 133, 134, 135,
147n59, 148n65
Tlingit-Haida settlement, 57, 58–61,
70–71, 136, 138, 139, 150n94
Tolovana, xix, 22, 45, 52, 118
Tolovana River, xix, 38, 47
Tongass National Forest, 60, 136
tourism, 147n59
trade/trading
alcohol and, 39
cash economy and, 27
early traders, 2–3, 21
English language and, 9, 20, 25
Russian–American Treaty, 134
shift from Yukon to Tanana, 32–33,
69
steamboats and, 2, 22, 142n10
supply routes/centers, xxii, xv, 10, 29,
33, 46, 61
trading posts, 7, 9, 10, 13, 20, 32–33,
125, 142n10
Trans-Alaska oil pipeline, 57
trapping. See fur trapping/trading
Treasury Department, 58
Treaty Clause, 124, 154n131
Treaty of Cession
aboriginal claims and, 115–118
Berrigan case and, 143n21
citizenship status of Alaska Natives and,
1–2, 24–25
impact on Alaska Natives, 67
land claims, 142n8
overview of, ix
timeline of events, 134
Tlingit and, 58

"uncivilized tribes" classification, 1, 24,
117, 126, 142n9, 153n123
tribal courts, 155n136
tribal leadership/relations
aboriginal rights and control, 64–66,
70–71. See also aboriginal rights
Alaska Native Claims Settlement Act
and, 125–126, 128
citizenship and. See citizenship
current status, 121–122, 130
government-to-government
consultation, 52–53, 60, 76, 80,
87–88, 89–90, 119–120, 124
Indian Reorganization Act and,
154n128
jurisdictional authority, 152n111,
154n129
medical care system, 55
pre–Alaska Purchase, 129–130
self-determination and, 130–131
Tanana Chiefs Conference and, 142n7
timeline of events and legislation,
133–140
treaty making, 154n131
tribal courts, 155n136
tribal identity, 30, 137, 147n58,
148n59
tribal sovereignty. See tribal sovereignty
tribal status, ix, 31, 121–122, 123–124,
129
U.S. Constitution and, 115
tribal lifeways
Madara on, 51, 83, 91–92
seasonal rounds, 25, 83, 95, 144n27
subsistence activities, 26–27, 33–34,
64. See also subsistence lifestyle
Tanana chiefs on, 91–92, 95
Tribal Recognition Act, 154n130
tribal sovereignty
Alaska Purchase and, 113, 114–115,
117
government-to-government
consultation and, 119, 120–122
federal recognition and, 124, 125–126,
128–129
powers of, 124, 125, 128–129

without territory, 128–129, 140
treaty-making and, 154n131
tribes
concept of, 7
federally recognized, 122, 126, 128,
140, 152n111, 154n130
language in Alaska Native Claims
Settlement Act, 126, 128–129
"uncivilized tribes" concept, 1, 24,
117, 126, 142n9, 146n42,
153n123
trust lands, 55, 127–128, 140, 152n111,
154n129
Tundra Times, 139

U.S. Army
military expeditions, 9–14, 23, 27, 134
military posts/forts, 15–19, 27, 33, 42,
46, 121
trail building, 136
Wounded Knee Massacre, 135
U.S. Civil War, 116, 134
U.S. Constitution, 115, 121, 124, 140,
154n131
U.S. government. See also Congress
control of Native education, 136
delegates to Tanana chiefs meeting of
1915, 74, 79
federal authority on "reserved waters,"
140
federal Indian policy. See federal Indian
policy
federally recognized tribes, 122, 126,
128, 140, 152n111, 154n130
government contracts, 33, 55, 107–
108, 122, 124, 154n132
investigations and response to impact
of prospecting on Alaska Natives,
27–32, 107n151–108n151
as protector of Natives' rights, 6–7,
23–24, 45, 47–48, 60–61, 74,
81–82, 84, 88, 94, 117, 140,
150n94
right to sue over land claims, 57, 59,
123, 136, 143n21

U.S. government (*continued*)
   Tanana chiefs' desire for government-to-government relationship, 52–53, 60, 76, 80, 87–88, 89–90, 119–120, 124
   transfer of hunting and fishing regulation to Alaska state government, 139
   Treaty of Cession and. See Treaty of Cession
   tribal status and, ix, 31, 121–122, 123–124, 129, 140, 152n111
   trust lands, 55, 127–128, 140, 152n111, 154n129
U.S. Navy, 13, 134, 135
U.S. Supreme Court, 140
Udall, Stewart, 64, 139, 151n103
Unalakleet–Kaltag trail, 125
"uncivilized tribes" classification, 1, 24, 117, 126, 142n9, 146n42, 153n123
United States. See also Western culture
   American identity, 26
   continental land rights, 30
   continental Native tribes, xxiii, xxv, 30, 91, 125–126, 153n124
   continental reservation system, 30, 91, 141n5
   military power of, xxiii
   paternalism of, xxiii–xxv, 153n125–154n125
   Russian–American Treaty, 134
   telegraph communications, 16
United States Geological Survey, 2
University of Alaska Fairbanks, 15, 17, 47, 143n23
Unungan, 133, 138
Upper Copper River, 10, 19–20, 31
Upper Kuskokwim, xix, 13
Upper Tanana, 9, 12, 19–20, 29, 31, 118, 143n23
Upper Yukon, xiii, 13

Valdez News, 29
Valdez, xiv, xxii, 16, 17, 19, 22, 27, 64
Valdez trail, 19, 22, 33, 43, 136

Vancouver Barracks, 11
Venetie Reservation, 138
Venetie tax case, 119, 128–129, 140, 155n135
Victor Joseph, Chief, 49
Volkmar River, 15
Voluck, David, 24
voting rights, 137, 139
Voting Rights Act, 139

wage labor. See employment opportunities
Walker, Governor, 140
Walton, Rudolph, 143n17, 146n43
WAMCATS (Washington–Alaska Military Cable and Telegraph System), xxii, 16, 22, 33
War Department, 29
Washington, D.C., 37, 40
Washington State, 70
Washington–Alaska Military Cable and Telegraph System (WAMCATS), xxii, 16, 22, 33
Webb, Melody, 142n12
Wells, E. Hazard, 10–11
Western culture
   American identity and, 26
   assimilation of, civilization/citizenship and, xxiii, 3, 4–7, 24–25, 31, 34–35, 59, 70, 81, 95, 110, 136, 141n5, 147n58, 147n59–148n59. See also citizenship
   concept of productive life, 25–27
   federal government's investigations of and response to impact on Alaska Natives, 27–32, 107n151–108n151
   impact on Alaska Natives, xxiii, 21–22, 38–39, 42, 46, 47–48, 51–52, 53–54, 73–74, 94, 118, 130, 136
   impact on tribal leadership/sovereignty, 120–122
   influence on legal system, xxvii, 3, 4–7, 23, 31, 59, 69–70, 146n43
   manifest destiny, 114–116, 153n125–154n125

paternalism, xxiii–xxv, 153n125–
154n125
Wickersham on assimilation of, xvii,
34–35, 59, 81, 110
westward expansion, 26, 74, 114–116, 135
White Act, 137
White Pass Railroad, 61
White River, 2
white society/culture. See Western culture
Whitworth University, 59
Wickersham, Deborah, xvi, xvii
Wickersham, James
on "America's destiny," 74
assimilation of Western culture and,
xvii, 34–35, 59, 81, 110
Berrigan case, 3, 117, 136, 150n94. See
also Berrigan case
Chief Alexander and, 38–39, 50–51,
80, 81–82, 153n116
as congressional delegate, 37–38,
110–111
as delegate to Tanana chiefs meeting of
1915, ix, xiv, 74, 79
disposition of, xiv, xv, xvii, xxv, 70
as district court judge, xiv
on education, 98–106
on Funston report, 27, 31
on government's role in protecting
Natives, 150n94
home of, xvi–xvii, 141n2
on impact of development and Western
culture on Natives, 38–39, 47,
51–52, 81–82, 118
Minook case, 3. See also Minook case
photographs of, xvii, xviii, 50
political affiliation, 44
on railroads, 44–45, 47
on reservations/allotments, 38–41, 46,
51–52, 70, 74–76
on reservations/allotments (Tanana chiefs
meeting of 1915 transcript), 80,
81–82, 83–85, 93–94, 95, 96, 97
Riggs and, 44–45
Southeast Alaska land settlement and,
58–61, 70–71, 150n94
on tribal status, 123

William, Chief (of Tanana), xx, 23, 49, 50,
53, 79, 87–88, 137
William/Williams, Chief Alexander (of
Tanana/Ft. Gibbon), xx, 87, 90, 92,
104, 106, 108–109
Williams, Chief Alexander (of Fort
Gibbon), 79, 87
Williams, Paul (of Tanana)
on allotment/reservations, 42, 45–46,
83–85, 90–91, 96–98
background of, 39, 83, 120
as delegate to Tanana chiefs meeting of
1915, xx
on education, 46, 55, 98–106
on employment opportunities, 107–108
as interpreter at Tanana chiefs meeting
of 1915, 39, 75–76, 80, 119, 120
opening comments at Tanana chiefs
meeting of 1915, 79
photographs of, xx, 50
Williams, Silas, 45
Wilson, Woodrow, xv, 43–44, 74
Witten, Jas, 27
women's suffrage, 137
Wood-Tikchik, 139
World War I, 137
World War II, 138
Wounded Knee Massacre, 135
Wrangell, 28, 134
Wright, Arthur, 99

Yukon
Donnelly district, 15
fisheries, 136
prospecting, xiii, 10, 12–13, 22, 136,
154n126
shift in trade to Tanana, 32–33, 69
trading posts, 7, 9, 10, 13, 32–33,
142n10
trails to/from, xix, 13
Yukon Flats, 10, 62
Yukon River, xiv, xix, 2, 7, 9, 10, 13, 22,
27, 33, 38, 42, 61, 62, 63, 139,
142n10
Yukon/Kuskokwim Delta, 53–54